GILLES MUNIER

THE BLACK GOLD SPIES

Translated by **James A. Pollard**

GILLES MUNIER

Originally published in French under the title

Les espions de l'or noir

Translated by James A. Pollard

The Black Gold Spies

Published by

OMNIA VERITAS LTD

www.omnia-veritas.com

© Omnia Veritas Ltd – Gilles Munier – 2018

By the same author:

Les Yézidis: ceux que l'on appelait les Adorateurs du Diable, with
Joachim Menant, 2014, Erick Bonnier, Paris

Iraq: An Illustrated History and Guide, 2004, Interlink Publishing,
Massachussets (originally published in French under the title *Guide de
l'Irak, 10 000 ans d'histoire en Mésopotamie*, 2000, Picollec, Paris)

Acknowledgements:

Without the common sense and painstaking work of Maryvonne Munier-Goarin, and the expert advice of Xavière Jardez, this book would not have been possible.

To the countless victims of Western imperialism and the unquenchable thirst for oil in the Middle East and the Caucasus.

"*Spying would perhaps be tolerable if it could be exercised by honest people ...*" (Montesquieu)

They say money has no smell: oil is here to prove it does.
(Pierre Mac Orlan)

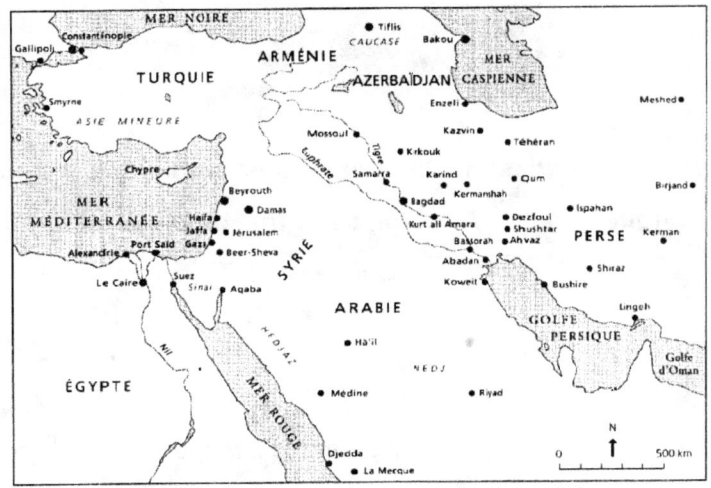

Le Moyen-Orient durant la Première Guerre mondiale.

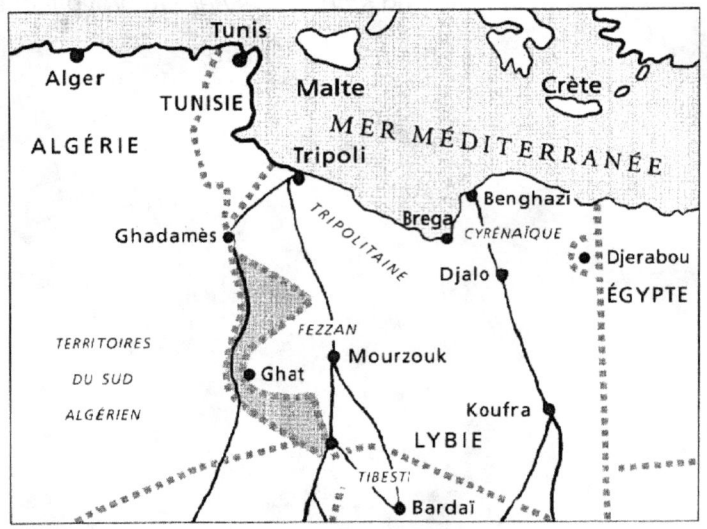

L'accord franco-italien de 1919.

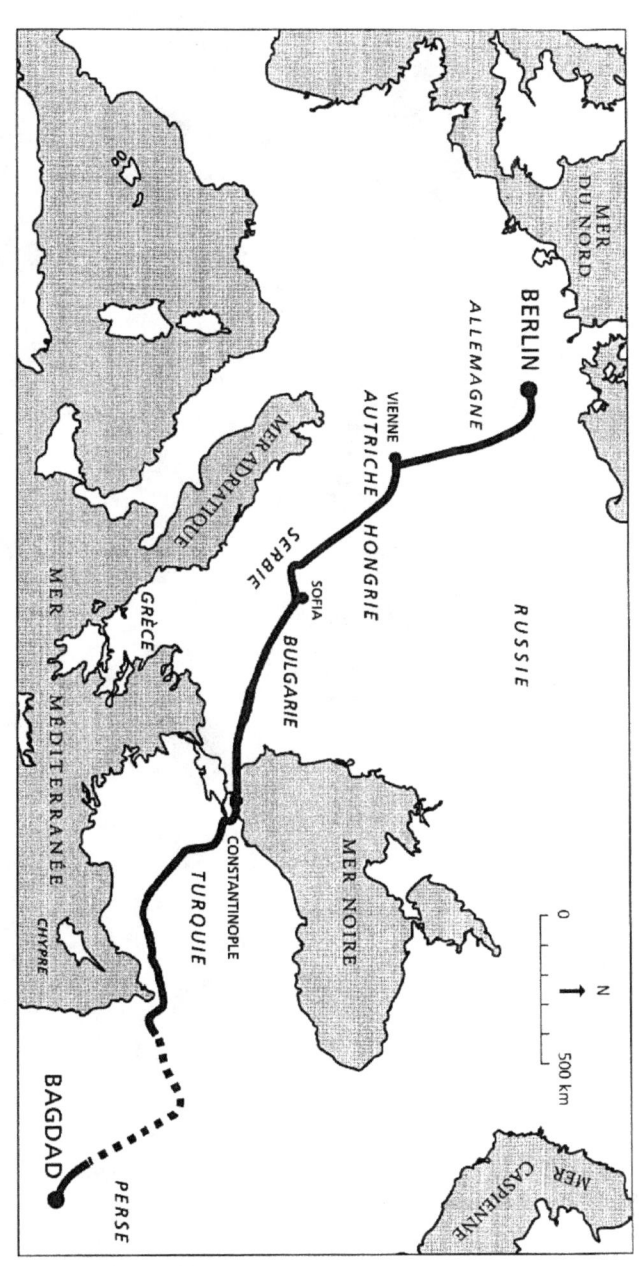

Le tracé de la ligne de chemin de fer Berlin-Bagdad.

WHO'S WHO?

(principal protagonists)

Of course, historical figures such as Napoleon I, Kaiser Wilhelm II, Winston Churchill or Adolph Hitler need no introduction. For the sake of easy reference, however, we thought it necessary to provide a few cursory details on some of the key players of the great oil saga.

Abdullah I of Jordan

King of Jordan and son of Hussein bin Ali, Sharif of Mecca. Assassinated on 20 July 1951 by a Palestinian nationalist.

Marguerite d'Andurain

Nicknamed "the spy from Palmyra" by the French press, she was frequently accused of murder, but never convicted for want of proof. Strangled to death in Tangier in 1948.

Bertrand Bareilles

Author and preceptor to the son of Abdul Hamid II, the Sultan of the Ottoman Empire. The sultan granted him a concession for the oilfields in the vilayet of Mosul, but France failed to lend him the support necessary for their exploitation. Died in 1933.

Gertrude Bell

Backed by Winston Churchill, she made Faisal I the King of Iraq, and enabled Britain to seize control of virtually all of Mesopotamia's oil fields. Died in 1926.

Vincent-Yves Boutin

Spy in the service of Napoleon I. Dispatched to the Near East to prepare for a French invasion of India. Died in 1815.

Johann Ludwig Burckhardt

Swiss orientalist recruited by the British secret service. Author of a number of travelogues recounting his adventures in the Arab world. Died in 1817.

Gilbert Clayton

Chief of the British secret service in Egypt and the Arab Bureau. Died in 1929.

Arthur Conolly

British spy who coined the term *The Great Game*. He was decapitated in 1842 in Bukhara, together with his fellow agent Charles Stoddart, who had failed to negotiate his release from prison.

Percy Cox

Secretary to the British Government of India and Chief Political Officer in the Gulf. Appointed British High Commissioner of Iraq in 1920. Died in 1937.

Henri Deterding

One of the founders of *Shell*. Nicknamed the "Napoleon of Oil." He financed the White Russian movement and the Nazi Party. Died in 1939.

Charles Doughty

British writer and explorer whose account of his voyage in Arabia - *Travels in Arabia Deserta* (1888) - influenced British spies sent to the Near East in the early 20th century. Died in 1926.

John Eppler

An Egyptian of German origin, Eppler was recruited by the *Abwehr*, the Wehrmacht's secret service. He carried out several missions on behalf of Rommel in preparation for a German invasion of Iraq, Iran, Afghanistan and Egypt.

Faisal I

Son of Hussein bin Ali, Sharif of Mecca. King of Syria and then Iraq. Died in mysterious circumstances in Geneva in 1933. According to Iraqi nationalists, he was poisoned by a British intelligence agent.

Ian Fleming

British spy before and during the Second World War. To create James Bond, he drew his inspiration from the life of Sidney Reilly and Fitzroy Maclean, two British secret agents engaged in the fight against Communism and the defence of British oil interests in the Caucasus and Iran. Died in 1964.

John Glubb

British agent who created the Arab Legion. He was the most powerful foreigner in the Kingdom of Jordan until the day he was dismissed by King Hussein. Died in 1986.

Fritz Grobba

The Third Reich's ambassador to Iraq and Saudi Arabia. He generated a wave of sympathy for Germany among Arabs. During the Second World War in Iraq, he supported an anti-British revolt, rapidly crushed by British troops dispatched from Jordan. Died in 1973.

Calouste Gulbenkian

Businessman of Armenian origin. During the early 20th century, he participated in the distribution of Near Eastern oil wealth. Nicknamed "Mr 5%". Died in 1955.

Werner Otto von Hentig

Together with Oskar von Niedermayer, von Henting was dispatched by Kaiser Wilhelm II to Afghanistan. His mission was to secure the Afghan king's support for a German invasion of India. He continued his activities as an agent in the Near East following Hitler's rise to power. Died in 1984.

Hussein bin Ali, Sharif of Mecca

Appointed Sharif of Mecca by the Ottoman sultan. Became the King of Hejaz, and then went into exile to escape the Wahhabis. Died in 1931 in Amman.

Hajj Amin al-Husseini

Grand Mufti of Jerusalem and Palestinian nationalist. He supported Nazi Germany in a bid to thwart British plans for the creation of a Jewish homeland in Palestine. Died in Beirut in 1974.

David Hogarth

British archaeologist and spy, who had recruited a number of agents on behalf of the Arab Bureau. Died in 1927.

Conrad Kilian

French geologist and spy who was assassinated in 1950 after having discovered the vast oil fields of the Sahara.

William Knox d'Arcy

Discovered the oil fields of Arabistan, in south-west Persia. Died in 1917.

Théodore de Lascaris

Napoleonic spy who became famous thanks to the French writer and poet Alphonse de Lamartine. Napoleon confided him a mission to persuade the Arab tribes of Syria and Mesopotamia to support his *Grande Armée*, in case he decided to conquer India. Died in 1817.

Thomas Edward Lawrence - Lawrence of Arabia

The most famous of all British spies who operated in the Near East. The media hero of the Arab revolt. Died in 1935.

Bruce Lockhart

Moscow-based British diplomat. Together with Sidney Reilly, he participated in various operations aiming to overthrow the Bolshevik regime and assassinate Lenin. Died in 1971.

Fitzroy Hew Royle Maclean

British diplomat and member of the SAS. During the Second World War, he carried out a mission in Iran to thwart the Shah's pro-German partisans who planned to seize control of the oil fields. He lent his support to Tito during the liberation of Yugoslavia. Died in 1996.

Louis Massignon

French orientalist. He was arrested for espionage by the Ottoman authorities in Mesopotamia. During the Arab Revolt, his activities meant he was a rival to T.E. Lawrence. Died in 1962.

Aloïs Musil

Czech orientalist who worked as a spy in Arabia on behalf of the Austo-Hunarian Empire. Author of a number of works on Arab archaeological sites and Bedouin customs. Died in 1944.

Oskar von Niedermayer

German spy sent on a mission to Afghanistan to win the king's support for Germany. Died in a Soviet prison camp in 1948.

Nobel

The Swedish Nobel brothers – Ludwig, Alfred and Robert – established a refinery in Baku, together with a pipeline to export the oil. They joined forces with the Rothschilds (*Caspian and Black Sea Petroleum Company*) in order to compete with Rockefeller's *Standard Oil*.

Max von Oppenheim

Archaeologist and German agent. He influenced both the Kaiser's and Hitler's policy vis-à-vis the Arab world. Died in 1946.

William Palgrave

British spy in the service of Napoleon III. His mission was to secure Wahhabi support for France which, at the time, was engaged in the construction of the Suez Canal. Died in 1888.

St John Philby

British spy and rival to T.E. Lawrence. He participated in the creation of Saudi Arabia, and was considered a traitor by the establishment for having given away Britain's share of the Saudi oil market to the Americans. Died in 1960.

Rashid Ali

Iraqi nationalist who turned to the Nazis in a bid to free his country from British control. Died in 1965.

Ibn Rashid

Emir of Ha'il, an oasis in the north of the Najd region. His family were the enemies of the Wahhabi tribes, and were backed by the Ottoman sultans. Died in 1920.

Sidney Reilly

Adventuer and British agent, dubbed the "Ace of Spies." Disguised as a priest, he was said to have duped Knox d'Arcy into handing over his south Persian oil concession. He attempted to overthrow the Bolsheviks and assassinate Lenin. In a bid to regain control of the Baku oilfields, he carried out a number of operations in the Caucasus. It is rumoured that he was executed by the *Cheka* in 1925.

John D. Rockefeller

An American oil tycoon, who once famously claimed that *"the way to make money is to buy when blood is running in the streets."* He attempted to ruin France's economy during the First World War by refusing to supply oil to the French government. In 1911, his *Standard Oil* giant was divided into thirty four separate companies, in accordance with the Sherman Antitrust Act. Died in 1937.

Kermit Roosevelt

CIA agent. He staged a coup to overthrow the Iranian prime minister, Mossadegh, who made the mistake of nationalising the Iranian oil industry. Died in 2000.

Alphonse de Rothschild

Alphonse de Rothschild, who died in 1905, was very active in the Caucasian oil business during the late 19th century. He later sold his companies to *Royal Dutch-Shell*. His brother Edmond, who died in 1934, was one of the main financers of the Zionist movement and the *Palestine Jewish Colonization Association*.

Ibn Saud

Emir of Nadj. King of Saudi Arabia. Died in 1953.

Captain William Shakespear

British spy who was reluctant to see the exploitation of the Arabian oilfields, believing that drilling rigs would disfigure the desert. He was killed on January 1915 when fighting alongside the Wahhabis. Succeeded by St John Philby.

Yitzhak Shamir

An influential member of the Zionist terrorist group *Lehi* (also known as the *Stern Gang*). He was responsible for the assassination of Lord Moyne, Britain's Resident Minister in Cairo. Later became a Mossad agent and then Prime Minister of Israel.

Lady Hester Stanhope

British spy in Syria, nicknamed "the chatelaine of Lebanon". Her uncle was a former British prime minister. She became infatuated with Vincent-Yves Boutin, one of Napoleon's agents. Died in 1839.

Freya Stark

British travel writer, famous for her adventures in the Near East. Died in 1993.

Abraham Stern

Leader of *Lehi*, the Zionist terrorist organisation. He liaised with Nazi Germany hoping that Hitler would help him create a Jewish homeland in Palestine. Following his arrest, he was assassinated in February 1942 by British intelligence.

Charles Stoddart

British spy engaged in *The Great Game*. Decapitated in Bukhara in 1842.

Mark Sykes

His name will forever be associated with the *Sykes-Picot Agreement*, signed with his French counterpart Georges Picot. He was behind the creation of the Arab Bureau and designed the flag of the Arab Revolt. Died of Spanish flu in 1919.

Percy Sykes

British Consul-General to Arabistan (Persia). He created the *South Persia Rifles* to combat German operations in the region. Died in 1955.

Sayid Talib

Iraqi nationalist leader, whose loyalties wavered between the Ottomans and the British. Gertrude Bell disliked him and stopped his rise to power.

David Urquhart

British diplomat and politician who worked to destabilise the Caucasus during the late 19th century. Ardent advocate of the Circassian cause.

Died in 1877.

Wilhelm Wassmuss

Wilhelm II's spy in Persia. His mission was to organise a tribal revolt in the south and snatch the oilfields from the *Anglo-Persian Oil Company*. Nicknamed the "German Lawarence". Died in 1931.

Preface

OIL... THE LATEST WESTERN CRUSADE

Pierre Mac Orlan once wrote that *"they say money has no smell, but oil is here to prove it does"*. Indeed, oil smells of blood. Since the discovery of the Baku oilfields in the 19th century, together with those in Persia and Mesopotamia in the early 20th century, the great powers have not ceased to vie for their control. The Caucasus, Iran and Iraq were - and remain - among the world's most troubled zones.

This book tells the story of the series of secret agents who, since Napoleon I and the *Great Game*, precipitated the collapse of the Ottoman Empire and then obtained control of the world's oil supplies - for the West in general, and for the Anglo-Saxon world in particular - at the price of two world wars and countless regional conflicts. Though this saga is akin to an adventure story, the immense misfortunes which have fallen upon the oil-possessing nations for over a century are far from the stuff of dreams.

In reaction to the 2005 London bus bombings, Ken Livingstone, the capital's mayor at the time, declared:

"If at the end of the First World War we had done what we promised the Arabs, which was to let them be free and have their own governments,

*and kept out of Arab affairs, and just bought their oil, rather than feeling
we had to control the flow of oil, I suspect this wouldn't have arisen."*[1]

He added:

*"We've propped up unsavoury governments, we've overthrown ones we
didn't consider sympathetic."*

Current events confirm that the black gold spies have a great future
ahead of them. But they also remind us that the spy business is well
on the way to being privatised, meaning that, to paraphrase
Montesquieu, the days when espionage might have been tolerated
when exercised by honest people are gone for good. Given that the
Western powers are not about to drop their double standards when it
comes to the protection of their oil interests, the future does not look
too bright.

---

[1] *Mayor blames Middle East policy*, BBC, 25 July 2005,
http://news.bbc.co.uk/1/hi/uk_politics/4698963.stm

Chapter I

JAMES BOND 007, A BLACK GOLD SPY...

J ames Bond did not just spring from Ian Fleming's fertile imagination. The author in fact drew inspiration from the people he met while on His Majesty's secret service at *Camp X*, where he was trained in the techniques of espionage. *Camp X* (MI6's *Special Training School 103*) was set up in Canada on the banks of Lake Ontario by William Stephenson (code name *Intrepid*) who led British efforts against the Nazis and ensured a secret liaison between Churchill and Roosevelt by means of a special telephone system.

Recruited in 1939 by the *Special Operations Executive* (SOE), Fleming learnt at *Camp X* what every perfect spy needs to know: the use of various weapons and explosives, sabotage, message encryption, the formation of resistance networks, and the art of assassination. At the end of his training, Fleming had to put into practice what he had learned. To test his nerve, the instructor asked him to assassinate a German spy, spotted in a Toronto hotel. In the lobby, he was handed a gun and the target's room number. Fleming went upstairs to the room, but he lacked the courage to go any further. It was just a test: the gun was loaded with blanks. *Intrepid* gave the final verdict: failed! Thus Britain lost a secret agent but gained a great spy novelist.

Fleming spent the war in Britain's *Naval Intelligence Division* (NID), decrypting messages sent using *Enigma*, Germany's electro-mechanical cipher machine. He was promoted to commander, the same rank as his fictional hero James Bond. In collaboration with the American general Wild Bill Donovan, he proposed a plan to restructure the *Office of Strategic Services* (OSS)[2], the American army's intelligence service which came to form the base of the CIA[3].

James Bond is essentially the spy that Fleming had always wanted to be. But he is also a combination of real-life 20th century British secret agents, most notably Sidney Reilly and Fitzroy Maclean, whose names are synonymous with the war for oil as well as the fight against Communism and Fascism.

Not a very Catholic Priest

Salomon Rosenblum – better known as Sidney Reilly - was a polyglot of a thousand faces. He is widely considered to be the *Ace of Spies*[4]. Gambler, serial bigamist and incorrigible womaniser, it was said he had a wife for each of his eleven passports. His career in British intelligence began with a masterstroke when he took possession of the vast oilfield in Arabistan and handed it over to the British government. This reservoir

---

[2] The *Office of Strategic Services* (OSS), overseen by "Wild Bill" Donovan, was created in 1942 after America joined the war against Germany.

[3] Ben Macintyre, *The Times*: *www.thetimes.co.uk/article/he-dreamt-up-bond-but-did-fleming-also-create-the-cia-l3nkg9blnmn*.

[4] Bruce Lockhart recounted his Russian exploits with Sidney Reilly in *Memoirs of a British Agent* (Putnam, London, 1932). For more information on the "Ace of Spies", see Richard B. Spence's excellent biography *Trust No One: The Secret World of Sidney Reilly* (Feral House, Los Angeles, 2002)

of black gold had in fact been discovered in 1908 by William Knox d'Arcy, to whom the Shah of Persia had granted a concession.

Several accounts of this operation circulated at the time. During the 1930s in France, the most well- known version was that of the Austrian author Anton Zishka, who published a work revealing the secret history of oil[5].

D'Arcy, having made his fortune, had only one goal in mind: convert the Persians to Christianity before returning home to die in peace. Making his way back home from Cairo, he was hounded by hordes of spies and businessmen, either threatening him or offering him astronomical sums for the drilling rights. He refused to be intimidated and rejected all offers, and even thought about destroying the document signed by the Shah. The British, fearing that his concession would fall into the wrong hands – i.e. Russian, French or, worse still, those of Kaiser Wilhelm II! - wanted to convince the eccentric millionaire to sell them his rights.

On the boat from Egypt, D'Arcy spent his time praying and reading missionary narratives. He spoke to nobody. Also on board was a priest, who was very reserved. He had been working as a missionary in Africa. D'Arcy confided in him. In what appeared to be an absent-minded fashion, the priest listened to all the problems he had encountered ever since he had taken possession of the oil field. A few days later, the priest proposed a solution: donate the Shah's *firman*[6] to the Catholic Church. Before they had even arrived in Manhattan, the deal was

---

[5] Anton Zischka, *La guerre secrète pour le pétrole*, Payot, Paris, 1934.

[6] A *firman* was an edict or a permit issued by the Shah of Persia or the Ottoman Sultan.

concluded. The priest, of course, was none other than Sidney Reilly. He handed the concession over to William Melville, alias "*M*", chief of British intelligence. Melville had recruited Reilly as an informer in 1896 when he was chief of *Special Branch* at Scotland Yard. News soon broke of the creation of the *Anglo-Persian Oil Compan*[7], 56% of which was held by the British admiralty. By way of consolation, D'Arcy was appointed to the board. He abandoned his hopes of converting the Persians to Christianity and remained a board member until his death in 1917.

Meanwhile, there were rumours that Reilly, just in case, had also offered the same concession to the chief of *Standard Oil*, Rockefeller, who was not interested! This version of events, redolent of a soap opera, is said to have been fed to Anton Zischka by the *Quai d'Orsay* in an attempt to scupper Anglo- Iranian oil negotiations.

Robin Bruce Lockhart, author of Sidney Reilly's biography[8], gives another version. According to Lockhart, *"M"* had sent Reilly to the South of France. His mission was to prevent D'Arcy from granting his concession to Baron Alphonse de Rothschild. Disguised as a priest, the British agent boarded the billionaire's yacht under the pretext of collecting donations for an orphanage. He took D'Arcy aside and whispered to him that the British government would double any offer made by the baron. Within days, d'Arcy was in London, signing the contract.

---

[7] Predecessor of *British Petroleum* (BP)

[8] Robin Bruce Lockhart wrote *Reilly – Ace of Spies*. The author is the son of Bruce Lockhart, who was a British diplomat in the Soviet Union.

Agent ST-1

Sidney Reilly was born in Odessa to a Tsarist family. When his mother died, he discovered that he was the son of her Jewish doctor. Disowned by his family, he stowed aboard a ship for South America. In Brazil, he took various odd jobs to earn a living before setting himself up as a guide for explorers deep in the Amazon. One day, a group he was leading was attacked by natives. Reilly saved the life of one of the explorers who, by way of thanks, provided him with a British passport and a ticket to England. So, at the age of 22, Reilly came to London where the explorer, impressed by his bravery and his sharp analytical skills, found him a post in British intelligence. In 1912, Agent ST-1 officially became a British subject: his successful grab of Persian oil deserved no less.

At the beginning of the First World War, Reilly made another master stroke. After having killed a German staff officer, he donned his uniform and attended a German high command meeting in the presence of Wilhelm II!

Among the missions Reilly was assigned, one in particular was to prove fateful for both his career and his life: the infiltration of Russian anti-Tsarist groups. Following the October Revolution, Mansfield Cumming (alias "C"), head of Britain's secret service, had him transferred to work for Denikin, a White Russian general, with the aim of creating an intelligence service. Reilly's mission was to overthrow the Bolshevik regime. Bruce Lockhart, the diplomat appointed by the Foreign Office to negotiate with Lenin, controlled the finance of British intelligence operations and subversive activities.

In 1917, just as the Communist government was preparing to sign a separate peace deal with the Kaiser, France and Britain secretly agreed to carve up between them what remained of the former Tsarist Empire. London chose the oilfields in the Caucus, while France plumped for the Donetsk coal and iron reserves. On 4 August 1918, the British seized control of Baku.

Plot to assassinate Lenin

Reilly worked tirelessly behind the scenes in St Petersburg. In late August, during a meeting at the American embassy[9] (chosen because the British and French embassies were under much closer surveillance), he announced that everything was in place for the arrest of Lenin, Trotsky and the Bolshevik Central Committee's chief. It was agreed that the operation would take place during the 28th congress, on the 28th day of the month. Before putting them on trial, Reilly planned to have them parade in Moscow wearing only their underwear.

An agent from the *2nd Bureau* (French military intelligence) was among the conspirators and he was accompanied by a certain René Marchand, correspondent for the French daily *Le Figaro*. The journalist, married to a Russian, immediately informed Captain Jacques Sadoul, who was a

---

[9] Xenophon Dmitrievich de Blumenthal Kalamatiano managed American intelligence in Moscow. A business man working in Russia, his network comprised thirty agents. Arrested in 1918 following the discovery of the *Lockhart Plot*, he was sentenced to death. But the sentence was not carried out, and he was released in 1921. Two years after having returned to the US, he died in mysterious circumstances.

member of both the French military mission in Russia and the *French Communist Group*, which had been created by the Bolsheviks. The *2nd Bureau's* agent requested Marchand to write a letter to the French president, Raymond Poincaré, asking him to condemn the plot and inform Trotsky[10]. His letter was published in the Russian broadsheet *Izvestia*.

Bruce Lockhart, Colonel Eduard Berzin – the commander of a Latvian battalion in the Kremlin Guard

– together with several members of the network were arrested[11]. Eight beautiful young women, all claiming to be Reilly's wife, were detained by the police, and a brawl broke out when they were all placed in the same cell! Reilly narrowly escaped the police raid thanks to a *laissez-passer* given to him by a Tsarist undercover agent in the Cheka. But the Bolsheviks had not heard the last of the *Ace of Spies*. On 20 August 1918, Fanny Kaplan, a member of Boris Savinkov's[12] *Socialist Revolutionary Party*, shot Lenin. Though Lenin managed to survive, he never completely recovered from his injuries. It was Reilly who had

---

[10] Marcel Body, *Les groupes communistes français de Russie, 1918-1921*, Éditions Allia, Paris, 1988. René Marchand was later employed by the Russian Commissariat for Foreign Affairs. In 1919, while in London, he wrote *Why I Support Bolshevism*, and joined the Communist Party when he returned to France.

[11] Bruce Lockhart, it was claimed, had masterminded the plot. He was sentenced to death but was saved in exchange for the release of Maxime Litvinof, his Russian counterpart in London.

[12] Boris Viktorovich Savinkov led an armed resistance movement against the ruling Bolsheviks following the October Revolution.

given her the pistol...

The War for Oil in the Caucus

When Reilly returned to London, "*C*" awarded him the Military Cross[13], and then sent him to Odessa on a reconnaissance mission. In December 1918, the region was occupied by the French. The Ukrainian and White Russian warlords were engaged in an internecine conflict. Rockefeller's *Standard Oil* benefited from the chaos, importing as much oil as possible, and paying in cash. But this situation did not last long. The *French Communist Group* dispatched agitators from Moscow to harass the soldiers. There was mutiny in the navy. Among the mutineers were André Marty and Charles Tillon, future leaders of the French Communist Party. They were arrested and sent to a labour camp. But the French government, fearing the spread of chaos, immediately withdrew its troops. Reilly left Odessa on a French cruiser. The Bolsheviks had won again.

Some years later, a certain Drebkov, who had participated in the failed coup of 1918, paid Reilly a visit while he was in London. He informed him that a new putsch was being prepared in Russia. A counter-revolutionary group called *Trust[14]* was awaiting the green light from the West to go ahead. According to him, the group needed a leader to unite the opposition. Reilly suggested his friend Boris Savinkov, former Deputy War Minister to Alexander Kerensky, renowned author and anti-

---

[13] It was only in 1920 that this was officially awarded.

[14] *Moscow Municipal Credit Association*, or *Trust*, was a front organisation, devised to deceive the *Cheka*.

Bolshevik terrorist. Savinkov had the advantage of being backed by both the France's *2nd Bureau* and British intelligence, as well as being on good terms with Churchill. The conspirators would thus easily obtain the approval of both Poincaré and Mussolini. The Foreign Office was banking on an uprising in the Caucasus. Noah Zhordania[15], leader of a short-lived separatist Georgian state, was confident he could return the oilfields to their rightful owners.

Savinkov made it across the border, but he was immediately arrested by the *OGPU*, the secret police which had replaced the *Cheka*[16]. In the end, the much-hoped for counter revolution in the Caucasus fizzled out in a series of skirmishes during which just one town was captured. The Red Army regained control. On 13 September 1924, the *New York Times* acknowledged that the uprising had been financed by former oil tycoons in Paris. Savinkov was given the death penalty, a sentence commuted to ten-year's imprisonment thanks to the *Trust*. But his confession sparked a scandal in London and Paris. According to the official version, he had committed suicide by throwing himself out of a window at *Cheka* headquarters in Lubyanka. Sidney Reilly moved to the US, where he waited for the media storm to clear.

---

[15] Commissioner of the executive committee of the *Tbilisi Soviet* in 1917. In 1918, he had led the new independent state of Georgia, until February 1921, when the Red Army invaded and toppled the government, forcing him to seek exile in France, where he died in 1953.

[16] Felix Dzerzhinsky, head of the *Cheka*, directed the *GPU* until July 1926, when he died very suddenly. He was said to have been poisoned after having discovered a document proving that Stalin was a member of *Okhrana*, the Tsarist secret police.

In the clutches of the OGPU

When Lenin died on 21 January 1924, Sidney Reilly believed that the moment to overthrow the Bolshevik regime had finally arrived. With this in mind, he had created *Torgprom*, a group which united former Tsarist millionaires together with their French and British associates. In addition, he had Henri Deterding, head of *Royal Dutch Shell*, acquire the largest oil fields in the Caucasus.

In the spring of 1925, Reilly received a coded message from one of his Finnish anti-Communist connections. Georgii Schultz and his wife, two delegates from the *Trust*, had important news for him. During his meeting with them in Paris, they painted an encouraging picture of the new Russian opposition. Since Stalin had come to power, the *Trust* had expanded. Trotsky's defection had to be exploited, they told him, in order to overthrow the regime. Following Savinkov's arrest, Reilly ought to have been on his guard. Indeed, this so-called Mrs Shultz was in fact Maria Zakharchenko-Radkevitch, a Soviet agent, known to her colleagues as the "*witch*"! British intelligence began to wonder whether the *Trust* really existed or whether it was merely a plot hatched by the *OGPU*. Regardless, Reilly left for Helsinki. He covertly crossed the border in order to meet members of the new Russian opposition. He was never seen again. The *Trust* had indeed been created to trap Communist opposition members living abroad.

The *OGPU* issued a photo of Reilly's corpse to the press and confirmed that he had been killed by the border guards. A few months after his death, however, his various bank accounts were mysteriously emptied...

A diplomat in the SAS

Fitzroy Maclean was a different breed. This Scottish nobleman was Secretary to the British embassy in Paris. Bored by social niceties, he requested a Moscow posting in 1937, shortly after Sidney Reilly's death. Needless to say, he was under tight surveillance. But he would often give his Soviet minders the slip to roam the Caucasus and Central Asia, regions officially forbidden to Westerners.

His diplomatic duties prevented him from joining the armed forces, so he resigned and joined the British Army. He was promoted to lance corporal in 1941, the year in which he was elected to parliament. When he was in Egypt, disguised as an officer of the *Afrika Korps* or as a Bedouin tribesman, he carried out several missions behind German lines with the SAS. In the Isfahan region of Persia, he kidnapped Fazlollah Zahedi, the pro-German Iranian general who controlled Arabistan (known today as Khuzestan), whose oilfields were vital for the Royal Navy. The general was held prisoner in Palestine until the war ended. In 1951, Reza Shah made Zahedi his internal affairs minister. Following the nationalisation of the *Anglo Iranian Oil Company* and concerned by the growing influence of the Iranian communist party (*Tudeh*), Zahedi helped CIA agent Kermit Roosevelt overthrow Mossadegh in 1953.

In 1943, Winston Churchill dispatched Maclean to Yugoslavia to find out more about Josef Tito, chief of the communist *Yugoslav Partisans*[17]. Parachuted into the Balkan wasteland, with the SS on his tail, Maclean

---

[17] Fitzroy Maclean's memoirs, *Eastern Approaches*, read like an adventure story.

became one of the principal advisers to the Yugoslavian leader. At the end of the war, he was awarded the *Order of the Partisan Star* for his active participation in the liberation of the country.

Fleming's Inspiration

Ian Fleming was perfectly *au fait* with the spy game in the USSR. He had been a *Reuters*[18] correspondent in Moscow from 1929 to 1933, and then worked as foreign manager for the *London Sunday Times*. Bruce Lockhart told him the story of Sidney Reilly. Greatly impressed by Reilly, he later admitted that James Bond fell far short of the man who had inspired his fictional hero. Fleming was friends with Fitzroy Maclean, who was in post in the Soviet capital during the Stalin show trials. Later, when he was a commander in the *Naval Intelligence Division*, Fleming helped Macelan with his operations in Yugoslavia.

---

[18] Baron von Reuter, founder of Reuters, was naturalised as a British subject in 1857. Before William Knox d'Arcy, he had obtained an oil concession from the Shah of Persia, together with permission to construct a railway between the Caspian Sea and the Gulf. He was forced to abandon his plans, however, when the Shah gave way to demands made by Tsarist Russia.

Chapter II

NAPOLEON'S SPIES, FORERUNNERS TO *THE GREAT GAME*

Before the discovery of the Atlantic route to India by the Portuguese explorer Vasco de Gama in 1498, caravels did not venture beyond the Cape of Good Hope. Spices, perfumes, hardwood, porcelain and rare fabrics were unloaded by Arab traders in the ports of the Gulf. Indian or Chinese goods destined for Europe were transported up the Tigris or the Euphrates Rivers, turning Muscat, Basra and Baghdad into prosperous cities. Goods were then transported on camel-back. Caravans crossed Kurdistan and part of Asia Minor, and would then descend the Orontes valley, in order to reach the various Venetian and Genoese trading posts on the Syrian coast. From here, the precious merchandise was shipped to European ports.

The Portuguese, highly accomplished navigators, were the first to understand the strategic importance of the Arabian - or Persian – Gulf, and decided to make a profit by controlling its access. In 1513, to stop the Muslims from using the Red Sea as a trade route, they constructed a fortress on Hormuz Island[19]. For over a century, all ships sailing for

---

[19] King Manuel of Portugal's letter to the Pope.

Mesopotamia had to pay the Portuguese a tithe. With the establishment of the *East India Company* in 1622, however, the British found allies in the Arab and Persian ports, and then drove the Portuguese out of their maritime stronghold.

The discovery of the Cape Route meant that shipping to and from India became cheaper[20] and more reliable, so the traditional Gulf route became unviable and gradually fell out of use. It wasn't until Napoleon's expedition to Egypt that that the Near East, asphyxiated, emerged from the depths of economic depression into which it had been plunged by the British. Indeed, Bonaparte's unaccomplished dream of conquering India is thought to mark the debut of *The Great Game*. During the second half of the 19th century, this game pitted Russia against Great Britain. Later, during the two world wars, the game was played between the Allies and Germany. Following the oil wars in Iraq and in the Caucasus, the game is yet again underway.

The Conquest of India

Napoleon Bonaparte quickly discovered the strategic importance of the ancient caravan routes. He had read *Memoirs on the Turks and the Tartars* written by Baron de Tott, a French military officer and Hungarian aristocrat who had restructured the navy of Sultan Abdul Hamidl. In 1778, after having secretly visited the Levant and Egypt, he submitted a plan for the invasion of Egypt to Louis XVI, presenting this as a means to destroy British trade with India. An avid reader, fascinated by the

---

[20] Pepper brought back to Lisbon by Vasco de Gama cost five times less than the Venetian price.

Near East and India, Bonaparte had devoured the works of Savary and Volnay[21]. Impressed by Islam and the Prophet Muhammad's military genius, he had written a short story entitled *The Mask of the Prophet* while completing his military studies at the *École de Brienne*. It was said that he had converted to Islam while in Egypt and that he had even changed his middle-name to Ali[22].

Bonaparte was fascinated by the idea of following Alexander the Great's footsteps. Much later, as *Empereur des Français*, he had confided to German officers that *"There is nothing more to be done in Europe. It is only in the Near East that we can accomplish great work. It is only there that great reputations and great fortunes are made."*[23] To this end, it was necessary to reduce Britain to its simplest expression by separating it from India, the jewel in the British colonial crown. During the Egyptian expedition, Bonaparte sent French officers to India on a mission to train Tipu Sultan's troops in order to support his rebellion against the British. But French inferiority in the domain of intelligence, coupled with Britain's naval supremacy, stopped Napoleon in his tracks. Following the death of Tipu Sultan, killed by the British in 1799, Bonaparte asked Charles Decaen, Governor General of Pondicherry, to make contact with the sultan's son, but this was to no avail.

When Napoleon returned to France, he took stock of his Arab and Indian adventures. He attributed the failure of his Syrian expedition to French ignorance of the Bedouin and the Arabian Desert, and came to

---

[21] Georges Spillmann, *Souvenir Napoléonien*, July 1970.

[22] Christian Cherfils, *Bonaparte et l'islam*, Alcazar Publishing Ltd., Studley, 2005.

[23] Quoted in Jacques Benoist-Méchin, *Ibn Séoud ou la naissance d'un royaume*, Albin Michel, Paris, 1955.

the following conclusion: France had to establish an effective intelligence service. This decision was made in 1792. Money from the Revolution, it was decided, should be used to fight its enemies. As the National Convention declared in less than diplomatic terms, if French secret agents can do no good for the nation, then they should destroy the enemy and burn his ports, his arsenals, his shipyards, and have his leaders slaughtered![24]

Bonaparte ordered a plan to be drawn up for the invasion of India. Syria and Mesopotamia were at the centre of this vast project. Secret reports were sent to him from Aleppo, Erbil (known as Arbela in the time of Alexander the Great) and Baghdad. Fearful, the British asked the Afghan chief Shujah to kill any French agents seen passing through his country, but this was in vain... In 1802, Colonel Sébastiani travelled the length and breadth of Syria to assess the strength of the British and Ottoman forces. In 1803, the Sheikh of Kuwait allowed the British to place one of their agents in Basra to infiltrate French support networks in Mesopotamia. Threatened with an economic blockade by the British, Badr bin Saif, the regent of Muscat, refused to welcome Jean-Baptiste de Cavignac[25], who had come to propose the establishment of diplomatic relations with France. Had he not been threatened by the British, he would have happily agreed to the proposal. After all, it was a French squadron which had once protected the Omani Sultanate from

---

[24] Aulard, *Mémoire sur l'organisation des agents secrets*. Quoted in Eric Denécé – *Renseignement et Opérations Spéciales* n° 4 – L'Harmattan, Paris, mars 2000.

[25] Jean-Baptiste de Cavaignac (1762-1829) was a member of the *Montagnards* during the French Revolution, and was accused of regicide by the royalists after having voted for the execution of Louis XVI during his trial.

Abdul Aziz's[26] Wahhabi warriors. Despite this initial refusal, a Franco-Omani treaty was finally signed in 1807, following the proclamation of the French Empire.

Napoleon I had a very clear idea of what he wanted. His *aide-de-camp* at the battle of Austerlitz, General Charles Gardanne, was appointed French ambassador plenipotentiary to the Shah of Persia (Fath-Ali Qajar). But this diplomatic mission was soon cut short, as the emperor preferred the support of Russia, considered to be more reliable from a military point of view. During his exile on the island of Saint Helena, Napoleon revealed to his Irish doctor, Barry O'Meara, that he had planned a joint expedition to India with Paul I of Russia. Had the Tsar not been strangled to death in 1801, this mission, involving some 100 000 men, would have set sail from a port in the Caspian Sea. He then proposed this project to the Tsar's successor, Alexander I, during the signing of the Treaty of Tilsit in 1807.

Boutin, a French spy in Sidi Ferruch

Vincent-Yves Boutin, promoted to colonel in Napoleon's *Grande Armée* at the age of 38, had scarcely recovered from an injury sustained during the battle of Wagram when, in 1810, the emperor confided him a mission to conquer India. General Clarck, Napoleon's war minister, was not keen to execute this sort of order. Napoleon wrote to him to stress the urgency of Boutin's departure. *"Boutin may conceal his mission in*

---

[26] Son of Emir Muhammad Ibn Saud and second ruler of the Saudi state. He was assassinated in 1803, probably by a Shiite looking to avenge the Wahhabi sack of Karbala in 1802.

any way he sees fit, but he must accomplish it..."[27] The minister had no choice. So, in agreement with the Napoleon, he dispatched Auguste Merciat[28] to assess the situation in Palestine and asked Bernardino Drovetti, France's consul in Cairo, to recruit somebody capable of infiltrating the Bedouin community, separating them from the Ottomans, and reconnoitring the desert as far as the border with India.[29] This epic operation was entrusted to Théodore-Jules Lascaris de Vintimille.

Vincent-Yves Boutin was not short of courage or intelligence. He had romped across Europe, following the Emperor's military campaigns, sometimes carrying out exploratory missions in preparation for the various battles. In 1808, he carried out a secret mission in Algeria, where he identified the ideal location for the landing of French expeditionary forces: the peninsula of Sidi Feruch. Napoleon's idea was to send his forces from Spain to occupy Algeria, which would serve as a departure point for the invasion of Egypt and British India. During the return voyage, Boutin was taken prisoner by the British, who had attacked his ship off the coast of Ajaccio. He managed to escape from prison in Malta by disguising himself as an Italian sailor. Travelling across Constantinople, he finally reached Paris, only to learn that fierce Spanish resistance had forced Napoleon to postpone his invasion

---

[27] Frédéric Meyer, *Boutin Vincent-Yves, Colonel d'Empire*, Éditions France-Empire, 1991.

[28] Auguste Merciat returned to Paris six months later in poor health. He failed to accomplish his mission because of the conflict between the Turks and Wahhabis.

[29] Gérard Arbois, *Le dernier rêve oriental de Napoléon*, Revue de l'Institut Napoléon, n° 163 (1994).

plans.[30]

In 1811, Boutin, who spoke fluent Arab and Turkish, arrived in Alexandria under cover. He had disguised himself as a merchant and claimed to be fascinated by the study of ancient civilisations. A few days later, Bernardino Drovetti, the French consul in Cairo, introduced him to the ruler of Egypt, Muhammad Ali Pasha[31], who had just tightened his grip on power in a murderous purge. Highly suspicious of the Mamluk[32] chiefs, Ali Pasha had practically every single one of them massacred. Only the former soldiers of Napoleon's army who had converted to Islam were spared. Boutin was under close surveillance. Major Misset, the British consul, suspected he was a spy.

Reconnaissance Mission in Arabia and Libya

With the support of Ali Pasha, Boutin explored Egypt, noting everywhere he went the ways in which the country had changed since Napoleon's departure. He made a short trip along the coast of Arabia to Yemen in

---

[30] In 1830, during the reign of Charles X, Colonel Boutin's report allowed France to conquer and colonise Algeria. The French expeditionary forces in Sidi Ferruch were commanded by former chief of the Les Chouans (a royalist counter-revolutionary movement), General Bourmont, who had defected just before the Battle of Waterloo.

[31] Muhammad Ali Pasha, chief of an Albanian contingent within the Ottoman army, seized power after Napoleon left Egypt.

[32] An Ottoman military caste, the Mamluks were slave soldiers who had converted to Islam. The majority were Circassians. In 1811, 450 Mamluk chiefs were massacred at the Cairo Citadel by Muhammad Ali Pasha's troops. Those who had escaped sought refuge in Upper Egypt but they were all killed the following year. This massacre put paid to their political influence.

order to buy a consignment of coffee at Mocha - or so he claimed. In truth, the purpose of his voyage was to meet Wahhabi imams. Tusson-Bey, Muhammad Ali Pasha's son, was at war with the Wahhabi sect from Najd. He did not fall for Boutin's ruse, and so stopped him from going any further, telling him that it was for his own safety. Boutin returned to Cairo by road, after having climbed Mount Sinai.

Muhammad Ali later granted him permission to explore the ruins of the *Temple of Amun*, located in the Siwa Oasis[33], where the oracle Amun had once confirmed that Alexander the Great was the legitimate pharaoh of Egypt. Boutin assessed whether the oasis and its lake could be used as stopping point by French expeditionary forces coming from Tunisia or via the Libyan coast. He had planned to map waterholes, evaluate various possible routes and secure the support of the tribal sheikhs. But not far from the oasis he was captured by a group of Berber warriors, who were members of a fundamentalist Islamic sect. Luckily, he was saved by his guide Saladin, a former French soldier who had converted to Islam. He warned them that *Sultan el-Kebir* (Napoleon) would avenge them should either of them come to any harm. A few months later in Syria, however, Boutin was less fortunate.

Lady Stanhope – "The Chatelaine of Lebanon"

Upon his return in Cairo, Boutin received an invitation from Major Misset, the British consul. Misset was eager to know whether Boutin was one of Napoleon's spies. At the insistence of Drovetti, Boutin

---

[33] Situated some 560km to the north of Cairo, the Siwa Oasis is located in Egypt.

accepted the invitation to a dinner in honour of William Pitt's[34] niece, Lady Hester Stanhope, later nicknamed "the chatelaine of Lebanon", for whom espionage was something of a hobby. She had him recount his adventures in Egypt and opined that, for a merchant, he travelled a great deal and in most peculiar locations. Jokingly, she told him that he looked like one of Bonaparte's spies.[35] Among the dinner guests, was a certain Sheikh Ibrahim - the alias of the Swiss explorer Johann Ludwig Burkhardt – who listend intensely to the conversation. He, too, took a particular interest in Libya, but did so on behalf of the British secret service which had recruited him[36]. He had had disguised himself as a Muslim so as to move about freely without arousing suspicions[37].

During the summer of 1814, Boutin travelled to Sidon (Lebanon) and then to Syria, where he visited the cities of Aleppo, Damascus and Hama. Everywhere he went he carefully examined the fortifications and took detailed notes. He moved into the disused Mar Elias monastery, where Lady Stanhope had taken residence. It was said they fell in love. Here Boutin was informed that Napoleon had been exiled on the island of Elba following his defeat by the alliance (Britain-Russia-Prussia-Austria). Despite this news, he continued his reconnaissance mission, and went as far as the Euphrates.

---

[34] William Pitt the Younger, Prime Minister of Great Britain (1783 – 1801) and then the United Kingdom (1804-1806), led various anti- French coalitions.

[35] Amaury Faivre d'Acier, *Les Agents de Napoléon en Égypte*, Mémoire, 1990.

[36] Burckhardt's travels were financed by the *African Association*, used as a cover by the British secret services. The association expanded the scope of its activities in response to the Napoleonic threat to British interests in the Near East.

[37] Danielle Masse, *Burckhardt, le Bédouin de Pétra*, Plein sud, Toulon, 1996.

When Napoleon triumphantly regained power on 1 March 1815, Boutin decided to return to France. But, before doing so, he decided to explore the Ansarieh Mountains, inhabited by Alawites[38]. This region also happened to be populated by the Hashashin[39], an Ismaili warrior sect which fiercely defended all access to the region. Only members of the tribe or invitees could enter and leave - alive. Undeterred, he set off for the mountains... His rotting corpse was later found in an unspecified location between Aleppo and Latakia. He was most likely killed at some time between June and August 1815, long before Napoleon's defeat at Waterloo.

Grief stricken, Lady Stanhope was determined to take her revenge. Since the French officials refused to assume their responsibilities, she led her own investigation and found the culprits. Dressed in oriental garb and accompanied by a retinue of almost regal proportions, she went to see her protector, Abdullah Pasha, the governor of Saint-Jean-d'Acre. Tossing two pistols at his feet, she demanded that he avenge Boutin. Fearing that she would turn the Sultan of Constantinople against him if he refused, he organised a punitive expedition. Over 300 people were killed and 52 villages were set ablaze.

---

[38] A Shiite sect present in Syria and Lebanon.

[39] The order of the *Hashishin* was founded by Hassan-i Sabbah who resided in Alamut castle, located in the Alborz mountain range, close to the Caspian Sea. He was born in Qom to a Yemeni father who had emigrated to Kufa in Iraq. *Hashishin*, meaning "users of hashish", is said to be at the origin of the word assassin. But according to the author Amin Maalouf, assassin is in fact the plural of the Arab noun *assas* which means protector. The order, then, was perhaps the Islamic equivalent of the Knights Templar.

Théodor-Jules Lascaris de Vintimille, mythomaniac and visionary

Bernadino Drovetti[40], France's consul in Cairo, gave the knight Théodore Lascaris de Vintimille the mission of winning over the Bedouin to the French cause, exactly as Napoelon had ordered. The emperor needed them to escort his *Grande Armée* across the Syrian and Arabian Deserts and to secure the Red Sea coast. Lascaris' adventures, recounted by his guide Fathallah al-Sayegh, have gone down in history thanks to the French poet Alphonse de Lamartine, who published them in the fourth volume of his *Voyages en Orient*. According to Fulgence Fresnel - orientalist, archaeologist and former French consul in Jeddah - the accounts given by Lascaris are somewhat fanciful. Auriant, in his biography of Lascaris, comes to the same conclusion.[41] According to Auriant, Lascaris' tales of adventure were a hoax, elaborated to squeeze money out of Lamartine.

Knight of the Maltese Order, Lascaris had followed Bonaparte across Egypt after the French invasion of the island in June 1798. According

---

[40] A veteran of Napoleon's Italian and Egyptian campaigns, Bernardino Dovetti (1776-1852) was the French consul general to Egypt (1803- 1829) and then French consul to Russia (1821-27). Having developed a penchant for antiquities, he organised illegal archaeological excavations. His agents shamelessly raided Pharaonic sites, and went as far as Sudan. Museums in Paris, Turin and Berlin are indebeted to him for part of their collection.

[41] Auriant, *La vie du Chevalier Théodore de Lascaris ou l'imposteur malgré lui*, Gallimard, Paris, 1940. 24. Henry Laurens, *Le Chevalier de Lascaris et les origines du Grand jeu*, Cahiers de l'Orient, N° 7, 1987.

to some, he was an eccentric dreamer and inveterate liar, who lived in a fantasy world. Others, however, considered him to be a visionary. Among his grand schemes was the construction of a dam to the south of the Nile Delta and the establishment of a new capital, *Menoupolis*, named after General Menou, who had converted to Islam and succeeded Jean-Baptiste Kléber following his assassination. He had even elaborated a scheme for the independence of Egypt, which would have been governed by "General" Yaq'ub, a Copt who had supported the French. But Yaq'ub had left Egypt in August 1801 with the expeditionary forces and died while sailing to Europe on a British vessel. His corpse was stored in a barrel of rum until the ship docked in Marseille, where he was buried. The Ottomans were said to have poisoned him.[42]

Lascaris of Arabia!

Fictitious or not, the adventures of Lascaris prefigured those of Palgrave and T. E. Lawrence, whose accounts are also of questionable veracity. Lady Stanhope welcomed Lascaris in Syria. At first, she was impressed by this flamboyant character. Later, however, she thought him to be deranged.

According to Fathallah al-Sayegh, whose version of events was translated and published by Lamartine, Lascaris is said to have negotiated a treaty in 1811 between Ibn Sha'lan, leader of the Ruwallah Bedouin, and the Wahhabis. Following the advice of Lascaris, Sha'lan

---

[42] Laurens, *Le Chevalier de Lascaris et les origines du Grand jeu*, Cahiers de l'Orient, N° 7, 1987.

had created a federation of over twelve different tribes in Mesopotamia, and was prepared to help Napoleon's troops cross the desert unhindered. 'Sheikh Ibrahim' is said to have informed London of the outcome of the mission. Following the fall of Napoleon, the report written by Lascaris was handed to a British consul and placed under seal. It has never been found since.

In 1817, Lascaris died impoverished in Cairo. The circumstances surrounding his death are suspicious. Joseph Roussel, French counsul in Egypt, reported his death to the Duke of Richelieu, president of Louis XVII's council and former Governor of Odessa[43]. According to Roussel, it was rumoured that Lascaris had been poisoned by Boghos Bey Yusufian, the secretary to Muhammad Ali of Egypt. Lascaris, it was said, had been accused of meddling in Egyptian affairs and influencing the viceroy's son, Ismail, to whom he taught French.

With the end of the Napoleonic era, Britain finally appeared to be out of danger. But it had been a close call, and the British would never forget their lesson. They realised that Mesopotamia, Egypt, Palestine, the Gulf, and Central Asia could provide a route via which ambitious conquerors might invade India. Accordingly, policing the ancient caravan routes became a priority for the British. Their renewed vigilance, however, failed to stop one or two characters, nostalgic for the Napoleonic age, from trying their luck. The most striking example is General Jean-François Allard, a former hussar in Napoleon's Old

---

[43] In 1803, the Duke of Richelieu, who had emigrated to Russia following the overthrow of Louis XVI, was appointed Governor of Odessa by Tsar Alexander I. He thus participated in the Russian campaigns in the Caucasus and in Circassia.

Guard, who, in 1832, helped Prince Ranjit Singh establish a Sikh state, comprising the Punjab and Kashmir. But this problem for the British solved itself in the end: the Maharaja[44] died, enabling them to annex the region with ease.

---

[44] Ranjit Singh, who died in 1839, had the *Sri Harmandir Sahib* in Amritsar covered with gilded plates. This Sikh shrine has been more commonly known as the *Golden Temple* ever since. Indira Gandhi was assassinated by her Sikh bodyguards partly because she had authorised the storming of the temple.

Chapter III

WILLIAM COHEN-PALGRAVE, THE JESUIT SPY WHO WANTED TO CONVERT THE WAHHABIS

In the series of spies who had operated in the Near East since the 19th century, William Gifford Cohen-Palgrave - "Palgrave of Arabia", as he was later nicknamed – stands out as the most singular. Palgrave had worked for both the French and the British. Though Jewish at birth, he converted to Catholicism, became a Jesuit, and then served Pope Pius IX. Operating in a region which - with good reason - was thought to be infested with spies, his mission in Arabia for Napoleon III was an extremely perilous one. His travelogue, *A Year's Journey through Central and Eastern Arabia*, became essential reading for all black gold spies.

His father, Francis Cohen, a renowned historian, converted to Anglican Christianity so that he could marry. William then changed his name to Palgrave, his mother-in-law's maiden name. Though of fragile health, he joined the British Army (8th Regiment of Foot) in 1846 at the age of 21, after completing his studies at Oxford, and was posted to India. In 1848, while in an Indian military hospital, a Jesuit priest converted him to Catholicism. He joined the Jesuits (Society of Jesus) in Madras and then travelled to Rome, where he learnt Arabic. After having been ordained to the priesthood, he was posted to Beirut, where he adopted the name of Father Michel Souhail, so as to blend in with the local population[45]. He took an interest in *Ismailism* (a branch of Shia Islam), preferred the company of Greek Melkite Christians to that of the Maronites, and was often seen in the Damascene souks, where he would discuss desert life with merchants and passing Bedouin tribesman.

Napoleon III and the Wahhabis

Palgrave completed his religious studies in the town of Liesse, where he submitted a dissertation to his superiors on the possibility and methods of converting Arabs to Christianity[46]. His idea was very simple: convert the Wahhabis in order to then use them as a tool for French expansionism in the Near East[47].

The Jesuits, having privileged access to government circles, succeeded in obtaining Palgrave an audience with Napoleon III, who was preoccupied by the need to secure the Suez Canal. The French had begun tunnelling works the year before, and Napoleon needed to obtain first-hand information on Arabia and Syria. The Wahhabis worried him, and many of his questions remained unanswered. Had they, at some point, threatened Damascus? They had endured the Ottoman

---

[45] Joseph Hajjar, *Napoléon III et ses visées orientales* (tome III), Éditions Tlass, Damas, 1988.

[46] The official title of Palgrave's thesis: *La possibilité de la conversion des Arabes de l'Asie et la manière de l'opérer.*

[47] Ibid.

crackdown in 1814-16, but they were said to have regrouped under the leadership of Emir Faisal. Were they capable of attacking the Suez Canal? And what of the Shammar princes, who had always opposed Wahhabi control of Arabia's Najd and Hejaz regions? For Napoleon, good relations with Arabia seemed to be a prerequisite for French control of the Mediterranean and Indian Ocean.

Napoleon III asked Father Cohen (the name under which he was ordained) to meet the Wahhabi imam in order to secure his support against the British. The priest accepted the mission, and was granted 10 000 francs to cover his expenses. His first stop was to be Egypt, where he would inform a certain Halim Pasha that France would lend him military support should he attempt to seize power. He was then to go to Riyadh and the Ha'il region in order to assess the balance of power between the different tribes. After having received Pope IX's blessing for the mission, he set off for Alexandria.

An Arab-French Confederation

In Damascus, his superiors insisted that he be accompanied by a priest. Palgrave, therefore, contacted Boutros Géraigiry[48], whom he had converted to Catholicism some years previously. Géraigiry, a former seminarist, was working as school teacher in Lebanon's Beqaa Valley[49] before Palgrave convinced him to take holy orders. In March 1862, he was ordained. Before setting off, Palgrave sent a letter to Napoleon III,

---

[48] Boutros Géraigiri (or Jaraijiry) later became Peter IV Barakat Géraigiry, patriarch of the Melkite Greek Catholic Church (1898 - 1902).

[49] During the Ottoman Empire, Lebanon was a Syrian province.

warning him of the activities of British agents within the Bedouin tribes of southern Syria. His letter paid particular attention to the Ruwallah tribe, which was the most powerful tribe. Up until this point, the various tribes had been sympathetic to the French cause[50].

The mission was then modified. Still supported by the Pope, it now included the creation of a new Arab Church, to be comprised mainly of former Wahhabis who had converted to Christianity. The ultimate objective was to create an Arab-French federation. On June 1862, Palgrave left Ma'an, Arabia Petraea's[51] largest city, and followed the pilgrim's trail to Ha'il and Mecca. He was disguised as a Syrian doctor and went by the name of *Salim Abu Mahmud al-Ays*, while his aide, Father Géraigiry, adopted the name of *Barakat ash-Shami* (Barakat the Syrian).[52]

Foreign visitors were rarely seen in Mecca. In 1814, Johann Ludwig Burckhardt, the Swiss explorer (and British agent) who had discovered the ancient city of Petra, disguised himself as an Egyptian, *Sheikh Ibrahim*, in order to gain access to the holy city. Similarly, in 1853, Richard F. Burton, British adventurer and orientalist, explored Mecca by claiming to be *Haji Abdullah*. In fact, very few foreigners had dared enter the walls of Riyadh since Carsten Niebuhr had reported the danger posed by the Wahabbi tribes. Member of an expedition team financed by Frederik V of Denmark, Niebuhr had traversed both the Hejaz and

---

[50] Joseph Hajjar, *Napoléon III et ses visées orientales* (tome III), Éditions Tlass, Damas, 1988.

[51] Modern-day Jordan.

[52] Zahra Freeth, *Explorers of Arabia from the Renaissance to the End of the Victorian Era*, Allen and Urwin, London, 1978.

the Nadj regions during the period 1762 to 1773. Only George Forster Sadleir, a British captain, had entered the Wahhabi capital, but he had done so in 1819, when this was Diriyah - or rather what remained of it. From the emirate of Ras al-Khaimah, the captain had set off in search of Ibrahim Pasha, the son of Muhammad Ali of Egypt, who had ordered the destruction of the city at the behest of the Ottomans.

Accused of espionage

A few days after leaving Ma'an, Palgrave entered the oasis at Djof. At Ha'il, he was warmly welcomed by Ibn Rashid Talal, the 37 year-old emir of the Shammar tribe, sworn enemies of the Wahhabis. This man, whose eagle-like gaze commanded respect, was a potential ally for France. Candidly, Palgrave revealed to him the true purpose of his mission. Though the prince said he could not grant his official consent, he assured Palgrave that when he returned his word would be as good as law in his land and that his wishes would be granted.[53] Charles Doughty, a British explorer who concealed neither his identity nor nationality (he was later accused of espionage at Ha'il) tells of the mortal fear which had gripped Palgrave when he met somebody who knew his true identity.[54]

When Palgrave finally arrived in Riyadh, the Emir Faisal - elderly, ailing and virtually blind - refused to meet him, terrified at the idea of breathing the same air as a foreigner said to be gifted with evil powers. He even fled his palace by a secret door, taking his retinue of advisers with him,

---

[53] William Gifford Palgrave, *Palgrave d'Arabie*, Éditions France-Empire, Paris, 1992.

[54] Charles Montagu Doughty, *Voyages dans l'Arabie déserte*, Karthala, Paris, 2002.

convinced that the holy city had been profaned. Palgrave was thus dispensed of the need to ask the emir or his son, crown prince Abdallah, whether they would support the French against the British.

In November 1862, Palgrave narrowly escaped death. Abdallah asked him to sell him some strychnine. Since Palgrave refused, making it clear to the prince that he suspected it would be used to poison his brother Saud, his main rival to the throne, Abdallah accused him of being a Christian agent on a mission to destroy Islam and the state. In great danger, Palgrave escaped by leaving the city during evening prayers.

Palgrave's moment of triumph came when he returned to Europe. After having briefed Napoleon and the Pope on the outcome of his voyage, he then travelled to London, where he gave a series of conferences attended by the political elite. In 1866, his account, written while in a German monastery, became a bestseller. But his stay in Arabia had profoundly marked him, and the harsh realities he had encountered there had shattered his dream of converting the Arabs to Christianity. He left the Jesuit order, publically renounced Catholicism, and then married. Though he had once been virulently anti- British, he went on to pursue a successful diplomatic career in the Foreign Office. He was appointed consul at Sukhumi in Abkahzia, and was then posted to the four corners of the world. But he would never see Arabia again. Before his death in Montevideo in 1888, at a time when had become fascinated by Shintoism, he returned to Roman Catholicism. He was buried in a Christian cemetery.[55]

---

[55] Kathryn Tidrik, *Heart Beguiling Araby: The English Romance with Arabia*, Tauris,

Chapter IV

DEADLY GAMES IN THE CAUCASUS AND CENTRAL ASIA

T*he Great Game*, a term popularised by Rudyard Kipling in his novel *Kim*, was coined by Arthur Conolly (alias *Khan Ali*). From 1829 to 1831, Connolly had carried out secret missions in the Caucasus and in Central Asia. In a report, he had alerted Britain to Russia's advance towards the Black Sea and the Persian Gulf, a potentially dangerous development for British India. At the time, Britain was still reeling from the shock of Napoleonic and Russian attempts to dominate the world and seize control of British colonies. In order to prevent the advance of Tsarist troops, British strategists decided to utilise certain nations located between the Russian and the British Empire as buffer zones.

In 1839, the British agent Colonel Charles Stoddart was given the task of turning Nasrullah Khan[56], the Emir of Bukhara, against the Russians by persuading him to form an alliance with Britain. Stoddart had participated in Major Eldred Pottinger's[57] defence of Herat, one of the

---

London, 1981.

[56] Nasrullah Khan came to power after having assassinated thirty of his relatives. On his deathbed, he had his mistress and her two daughters killed before him.

[57] Maud Diver, *Le défenseur d'Herat*, Payot, Paris, 1936.

gateways to India. Pottinger, making his journey through Afghanistan in disguise, had decided to reveal his true identity to Wazir Yar Muhammad Khan, when he discovered that the city was threatened by Prussian forces, led by a group of Russian officers. Pottinger introduced himself to the wazir as an officer of the "White Queen", as Queen Victoria was known in the region, and offered his services. In Kabul, Alexandre Burnes, a British agent famous for his travels in Central Asia[58], had failed to convince Dost Mohammad Khan (Emir of Afghanistan) to dismiss his Russian advisers and agree to British rule. So he came back to Kabul in 1839 with an expeditionary force and overthrew his regime.

Zindan, The Black Well

Arrogant, irascible, and not very well versed in the ways of diplomacy, Charles Stoddart did not go down very well in Bukhara. The Wazir of Herat had warned Nasrullah Khan to be wary of the British agent. What's more, Khan claimed to be humiliated by his proposal to form an alliance because it was not signed by Queen Victoria herself. He had the British agent arrested for not having shown him sufficient respect: when the emir had passed by, he had *"remained on horseback"* in the presence of the emir *"whereas he should have walked"* and *"he had walked whereas he should have crawled"*. He was imprisoned at the notorious *Zindan*, where was he thrown into a vermin infested well. Voracious ticks, specially bred at the prison, were poured onto his head. After enduring six months of this treatment, he was given the choice:

---

[58] Alexandre Burnes, *Voyages de l'embouchure de l'Indus à Lahore, Caboul, Balkh et à Boukhara ; et retour par la Perse*, Arthus Bertrand, Paris, 1835.

convert to Islam or face execution. Stoddart converted, and his sentence was immediately commuted to house arrest.

Arthur Conolly was sent to Bukhra to negotiate Stoddart's release. But he, too, was arrested, thrown into the *Black Well* and given the choice of Islamic conversion or death. Conolly, who dreamed of converting the whole of Asia to Christianity, refused to convert to Islam. Consequently, Stoddart was sent back to the well where both were unceremoniously informed that they were to be executed. The death of Alexandre Burnes in 1841, lapidated by anti-British protesters in Kabul, and the chaotic retreat of 16 500 Anglo-Indian soldiers and officers, followed by their massacre at the Kyhber Pass in January 1842, meant that Khan was on his guard. He was keen to do away with foreign agents who could conspire against him. On 24 June 1842, both Conolly and Stoddart were decapitated.

The flag of the Circassian revolt

In 1835, David Urquhart, a young Scottish propagandist, published a *Declaration of Circassian Independence* in his periodical, *Portfolio*. Read and approved by a handful of Circassian chiefs, the document stated that the Circassians *"are an honest people, and peaceable when let alone"*. Needless to say, the same could not be said of the Russians, who were directly targeted by this proclamation. Urquhart alerted the British to the invasion of the Caucasus by Tsarist troops. The Russian strategy was to proceed gradually by a series of minor encroachments, none of which were sufficiently grave to jeopardise their diplomatic relations with the *Great Powers*. He warned that if the Russians were to reach Herat, nothing would stop them from invading India.[59]

Urquhart is said to have been recruited to the Foreign Office by Jeremy Bentham[60], the head of its intelligence service. He carried out several secret missions abroad, including a covert exploration of the Caucasus. In 1835, he was appointed secretary at the British embassy at Constantinople, where he was better known as Daoud Bey. In this post, he led secret operations in Circassia. In November 1836, however, the British schooner, *Vixen*, transporting weapons and gunpowder to the Circassians, was seized by the Tsarist navy, triggering a serious diplomatic crisis. The two empires were on the verge of war. Terrified at this prospect, the British prime minister, Palmerston, climbed down, admitting that the Russian seizure of the vessel was legitimate. Accordingly, he had Urquhart recalled from the embassy at Constantinople.

Britain had abandoned the Circassian cause. But James Bell, owner of the *Vixen*, decided to remain in Circassia and refused to admit defeat. He was joined by *Times* journalist, John Longworth, and a Scottish officer by the name of Knight, who was said to be on a "private mission", a convenient catch- all for concealing a gamut of subversive activities. Longworth had arrived illegally on a ship, smuggling several tons of ammunition. Bell travelled the length and breadth of the country in order

---

[59] David Urquhart, *Progrès positions actuelles de la Russie en Orient*, Paris, 1836.

[60] British philosopher (1748-1832) who founded the school of thought known as "utilitarianism." In 1792, he was made an honorary French citizen for his services to the Revolution. He was a close friend of *Girondist* and National Convention member, Jacques Pierre Brissot, guillotined in 1793 by the Jacobins who accused him of being a British spy.

to win the support of the mountaineers. He urged them to join the resistance movement, reassuring them with the illusory hope of decisive British military intervention in their favour. Meanwhile, in London, demonstrators paraded behind the Circassian flag, designed by Urquhart.[61]

Edmond Spencer's *Travels in Circassia*, a best seller, called for the British to support the Circassian movement[62]. The independence of this country, he wrote, was extremely important because it would enable Britain to maintain its control of the various routes into India. But Palmerston refused to revise his policy. In 1847, Urquhart was elected to the House Commons. He relentlessly condemned Palmerston, claiming that he was incompetent. He even accused him of being a Russian double-agent! Karl Marx, who at the time was working as a journalist[63], concurred with Urquhart's accusations of treason made against the British prime minister.

Double standards

With the exception of the Armenians and the Georgians[64], the various

---

[61] The Republic of Adygea (population 500 000), a member of the Russian Federation, still uses this flag.

[62] Before the *Vixen* was seized, Edmond Spencer secretly travelled across Circassia in 1836, disguised as a commercial attaché and sometimes as a Genoese doctor.

[63] Karl Marx wrote for the *Free Press*, one of Urquhart's newspapers.

[64] The Armenian Apostolic Church rejects the conclusions of the Chalcedon council, held in AD 451. The majority of Georgians are Orthodox Christians, but their patriarch is independent. Georgia has a Muslim minority, located in Adjara. In recent years, this minority has faced pressure to convert to Christianity.

ethnic groups in the Caucasus have a common denominator which transcends their different origins, languages and customs[65]: Islam, as taught by the *Naqshbandi*[66] and the *Qadiriyya*[67], the two major spiritual orders of Sufism. Up until the 19th century, they lived in isolated and fiercely independent communities, some of which had never known foreign occupation. While Tsarist troops prevailed in Georgia and Baku, they struggled with Dagestan and Chechnya which, officially at any rate, had been conquered. The Russians faced a well- organised popular resistance movement, led by Imam Shamil[68], a genius of guerrilla warfare and a follower of *muridism*, a Caucasian variant of Sufism which professes asceticism and the spirit of sacrifice. He called for Caucasian Muslims to wage *Ghazawat* (Holy War), and he had created an Islamic state governed by sharia law.

The story of Shamil's exploits, glorified by the British and French press, was hugely popular. This was at a time when, in Paris, it was frowned upon to draw a parallel between the Caucasian resistance movement

---

[65] Eric Hoesli, *À la conquête du Caucase*, Éditions des Syrtes, Paris, 2006. Eric Hoesli is director of *La Tribune de Genève*.

[66] This Sufi order was founded by Baha-ud-Din Naqshband Bukhari (1318-1389), born in Bukhara (Uzbekistan). In contrast to other Sufi orders, the *Naqshbandi* trace their spiritual roots to the Prophet Muhammad via Abu Bakr, the first Caliph and the Prophet's companion. This order took root in the Caucasus under the influence of Khâlid-i Baghdâdî, born in the Sharizur region, close to Sulaymaniyah in Iraqi Kurdistan. Today, followers of this order can be found in the Kurdish region controlled by Masoud Barzani and in the Ba'athist resistance movement.

[67] The *Qadiriyya*, founded in Baghdad, is the best known of all the Sufi orders. It continues the teachings of Abdul Qadir Gilani (1077-1166), born in the Gilan province of Iran.

[68] Imam Shamil was an Avar, an ethnic group in Dagestan.

and Emir Abd el Kader's[69] armed struggle against the French in Algeria. Symptomatic of these double-standards was the opera programmed by a Parisian theatre, the *Théâtre de la Porte Saint-Martin*. The performance, entitled *Shamil*, was inspired by the exchange of two Russian princesses, taken hostage by the Chechens, for the *Lion of Dagestan's* eldest son, kidnapped at an early age by the Tsar. Hugely popular, tickets for the opera sold out every night. Books written in praise of Shamil flew off the shelves. A newspaper was even specially created to serialise Alexandre Dumas' story, written in honour of Shamil.[70]

The Crimean War

Britain's interest in the Caucasian resistance movement was renewed when Nicolas I made a bid to carve up the Ottoman Empire and occupy Constantinople. In 1853, the Tsar proclaimed himself the protector of the Slav and Orthodox Christian population in the region. He then demanded unfettered access to the Dardanelles and the Bosporus, in order to obtain an outlet to the Mediterranean. For France, ruled at the time by Napoleon III, this was out of the question: this move would have posed a clear threat to French interests in Egypt. As for the British, forever fearful of losing their control of India, they considered the Tsar's move to be beyond the pale. On 28 March 1854, both the British and the French declared war against Russia. This was a pivotal moment in

---

[69] The two Muslim leaders were in contact with each other.

[70] Alexandre Dumas, *Chamil et la résistance tchétchène contre les Russes*, Nautilus, Paris, 2001. This was serialised under the title *Le Caucase, journal de voyages et romans paraissant tous les jours*.

the Crimean War, which was to last three years.

The British and the Turkish invited Shamil to join them in an alliance against Russia. However, Muhammad (Asiyalo) Amin, his right-hand man and his representative before the Circassian community, was wary of this proposition. The Caucasian chiefs were in no hurry to replace a Russian occupying power with a Turkish one. What's more, they considered that Turkey deformed the Islamic faith. Of course, the support promised by Britain might have proved useful, but they were doubtful that it would have been sufficient to secure victory. Moreover, Shamil suspected that any peace deal concluded under such conditions would have been to the detriment of the Circassians.

Events were to prove that Shamil's misgivings were founded. Napoleon III, anxious not to favour the British, called off hostilities following the Siege of Sevastopol in 1855[71]. Since the treaty signed in Paris on March 1856 made no mention of the Caucasian communities, the Tsar was free to continue his programme of colonisation. Taking advantage of the presence in the region of 200 000 of his troops, mobilised for the Crimean War, he launched the final assault. Significantly outnumbered, Shamil and his supporters surrendered. Placed under house arrest, the *Lion of Dagestan* eventually agreed to pledge allegiance to the Tsar. In 1869, the Tsar granted him permission to make his pilgrimage to Mecca. He died in Medina two years later.

---

[71] This was a time when the French had plans to construct the Suez Canal, an idea which horrified the British.

Deadly Game

The Great Game, played to prevent the Tsar's colonisation of the Caucasus, had killed 400 000 Russian troops and hundreds and thousands of civilians. What's more, there had been countless atrocities and mass deportations in Turkey. The entire Circassian population was deported[72]. According to figures, over a million mountaineers were driven out of their villages.

Despite this horrific toll, this deadly game was set to continue. During the conflict, Western intelligence services had taken the opportunity to map much of the region, identify its ethnic groups along with their particularities, and assess the potential value of its mineral assets. Those who explored the region emphasised its potential oil wealth, which was already fuelling ambitions. Following Nicolas II's decision in 1870 to abolish the oil monopoly system in Baku, new players entered the arena, most notably the Nobel brothers, Alphonse de Rothschild and John D Rockfeller's *Standard Oil Company*. Another round of the game looked inevitable.

---

[72] A proportion of the Circassian population moved to Syria and Jordan. The majority of the troops in the Jordan Royal Guard are Circassians.

Chapter V

THE INVENTION OF THE "MIDDLE EAST"

The English expression *Middle East* only came into use in the late 19th century. Prior to this, the British spoke of the *East* or the *Far East* when referring to Palestine, Persia, India and China. In 1894, the expression Middle East appeared for the first time in the media, following Alfred Mahan's visit to London. Mahan was an American naval officer and author of several works on the situation in Persia. He advised the British government to protect the Gulf, in order to fulfil its obligations in India and secure its lines of communications into Asia. He congratulated the British for having taken control of the Suez Canal and Egypt, and urged them to rapidly occupy Persia[73].

The German railway invasion

In October 1902, *The Times* popularised the expression Middle East in a series of articles written by Ignatius Valentine Chirol[74], a highly influential British journalist who, like Mahan, believed that the definition of the Middle East should not be confined to Persia. Indeed, he considered there was a need to add Iraq, the Arabian coast, and the

---

[73] Roger Adelson, *London and the Invention of Middle East*, Yale University Press, New Haven, 1999.

[74] *Idem.*

regions close to India, including Tibet[75]. In 1896, he highlighted the growing importance of Baku and its oil, and warned of the German railway invasion of Turkey and Asia.[76]

The *Mashriq* was the name the Arabs gave to the Islamic territories to the east of Egypt, comprising Libya, Damascus and Baghdad. The French spoke of the *Levant,* a broad translation of *Mashriq,* when referring to Libya and Syria. Of course, the term *Orient* (East) was used, but its precise meaning was somewhat altered following the episode known as *La Question d'Orient* (The Eastern Question). This principally referred to the series of crises triggered during the 18th century when the Russians and the Austro-Hungarians joined the game in an attempt to carve up the Ottoman Empire, sparking the Crimean War (1853-56). Following this, the term *Orient* referred to the European provinces of the Ottoman Empire.

The Defence of Christians in the Near East

In France, the term *Proche-Orient* (Near East) was used to distinguish the eastern Arab provinces of the Ottoman Empire from those of North Africa. The French also used the expression *Échelles du Levant*[77], when referring to the Mediterranean ports where France had obtained a privileged status for its traders. The first series of concessions granted

---

[75] In China, Britain had participated in the suppression of the anti-colonial Boxer Rebellion (1899-1901) and was seeking – already - to destabilise Tibet.

[76] Roger Adelson, *London and the Invention of Middle East*, Yale University Press, New Haven, 1999.

[77] *Échelle* here is a transliteration of the Turkish word *Iskele*, meaning jetty or dock.

to the French by the Sultans – more precisely termed *capitulations* - date from the alliance concluded between François I and Suleiman the Magnificent in 1535. The sixth capitulation, which Louis XIV had wrenched from Mehmed IV after much negotiation, included further conditions, authorising France to defend the rights of Catholics in the Ottoman Empire. This privilege not only meant France could portray itself as being the guardian of all Christians in the Near East, even during the Revolution, but it also enabled Vatican missionaries to use French diplomatic cover to persuade the Nestorian and Jacobite communities to recognise papal primacy.

Chapter VI

CAPTAIN WILLIAM SHAKESPEAR, THE BELOVED SPY

O f all the British spies sent to the Near East, Captain William Shakespear was the only one whose death was met with genuine sadness. Paradoxically, however, he is also one of the least well- known, perhaps because his adventures were eclipsed by the tensions leading to the First World War, though it is more likely that he is less celebrated because his views clashed with those of the British establishment.

William Shakespear (his namesake, the playwright, spelt his surname with a final "e") was born in 1878 in Bombay, where his family had settled almost a century before. He was already bilingual at an early age. Intending to pursue a military career, he entered *Royal Military Academy Sandhurst* and, at the age of 20, achieved the rank of second lieutenant. He joined the *Bengal Lancers* and, thanks to his energy and spirit of initiative, rapidly achieved the rank of captain and then requested a transfer to the *Indian Political Department*.

Formidable efficiency

Shakespear's career in intelligence began in 1904 when, at the age of

25, he was appointed British Consul to Bandar Abbas, a Persian port strategically situated on the Strait of Hormuz. His ability to speak Farsi and Arabic, as well as Urdu and Pushtu, meant that he was appointed deputy to Major Percy Cox, the British Acting Political Resident in Bushehr. Shakespear always carried in his luggage certain items, which encapsulated his personality: an enormous Union Jack; his *Bengal Lancers* uniform; a camera; a sextant; bottles of whisky and Moselle wine. Later, he ordered a special tent, equipped with a darkroom and even a bathroom!

Before leaving India, Shakespear studied the official reports on Persia and Arabia, noting how London and Shimla (where British Indian government headquarters were located at the time) differed in their assessment of Arabia's future. The Arabia which enchanted Shakespear was, from London's point of view, a mere Ottoman province of no great interest. Indeed, the *East India Company*[78] had closed its Arabian trading posts. Shakespear feared that Germany and France, on the look-out for the slightest weakness in the Ottoman Empire, took a very different view on this matter. Intensely disliking all matters relating to Persia and finding Persians unbearable[79], Shakespear preferred to spend his time on the other side of the strait, in the souks of Oman, where he could perfect his Arabic.

Major Percy Cox, a shrewd judge of character, found Shakespear to be formidably efficient when it came to resolving disputes on the ground.

---

[78] Founded in the 17th century to conquer the Indian and Southeast Asian markets, the company successfully eliminated its French and Dutch rivals.

[79] H. V. F. Winstone, *Captain Shakespear*, Quarter Books Limited, London, 1978.

But he believed Shakespear would not make a career in the embassies, where diplomatic reserve was a prerequisite for success. At Bushehr, he took Shakespear under his wing, and they became friends.

The Bushehr-London rally

In 1907, having completed his mission in Persia, he returned to India (Hyderabad). He had only one idea in mind: buy a car and then drive from Bushehr to London. From north Persia, he planned to take the following route: the Black Sea, Turkey, Greece, the Adriatic Coast, Italy and then France. This had never been done before and, for the time, was a genuine exploit. He bought a Rover, obtained the necessary authorisations, secured the support of the British diplomatic services in the relevant countries, and drove off. Despite countless difficulties – the absence of roads and bridges, bandits, mechanical problems – he reached his final destination. The media duly praised his extraordinary achievement.

During his short stay in Britain, he met Dorothea Bird, the daughter of a British-Indian army colonel. She had devoured the books of Richard F. Burton and Charles Doughty on Arabia. Shakespear, besmitten by this beautiful 26 year-old, revealed to her his plans for the next adventure: trek cross the central Arabian Desert. At the end of summer, promising to write to her often, he left Britain to resume his duties in Hyderabad.

Two months later, Cox recalled him to Bushehr. The consul post in Kuwait was vacant, and Cox was convinced that Shakespear's profile matched the demands of the job. The post required somebody who could withstand the arduous and dangerous desert crossings, somebody with a sturdy character, capable of dealing unswervingly with hard-headed tribal chiefs. Shakespear spent a year studying Britain's chaotic relations with Arabia as well as the history of the great desert families, their disputes and their alliances. From London, Dorethea sent him some books she had found on Arabia, including Palgrave's famous *Narrative of a Year's Journey through Central and Eastern Arabia*, a copy of which he carried with him at all times.

Strangled Half-Brother

Kuwait was a strategic position. It was located close to the border with Arabia and, though enjoying a degree of *de facto* autonomy, it belonged to the Ottoman *vilayet* of Basra. It had become of paramount importance for the British following news of Germany's Berlin-Baghdad railway line, the terminus of which could well have been either Basra or Kuwait itself.

Sheikh Mubarak Al-Sabah became ruler of Kuwait in 1896, following his return from Bombay, where he had lived in grand style. Though origins of his fortune were unknown, the only possible source was The Indian Office. Aided by two slaves, he had strangled to death his half-brother, Muhammad, while he was in his bed. Three years later, London had signed a treaty with the emirate, making it a British protectorate. To calm the uproar in Istanbul following this intrusion into Ottoman affairs, the British promised to remain neutral in all Arabian conflicts and to temper Mubarak's military aspirations.

The Saud family, expelled from Riyadh by the Emir of Ha'il, went into exile in Kuwait, where Emir Muhammad Al-Sabah kept them under close surveillance on behalf of the Turks. He disliked them and made a point of making them feel unwelcome. But everything changed for them when Mubarak came to power. Their pension was reinstated, and Mubarak took charge of the young Abdulaziz's political education, as he considered he had great leadership potential. In retaliation, the Turks pushed the Rashidis to storm Kuwait.

Mubarak fought back, but his allies from the Iraqi tribal confederation, *Al-Muntafiq*, fled in disarray. The Wahhabi expedition - commanded by Abdul Rahman with his son, Abdulaziz, second in command - were within sight of Riyadh when they were forced to retreat and make their way back to Kuwait. Raishid was close to victory when a British naval vessel appeared in the bay. He was summoned to withdraw his troops from the province. Seething with anger, Rashidi reluctantly withdrew at the behest of the Turks.[80]

First Meeting with Ibn Saud

Shakespear's arrival in Kuwait caused a stir. His Rover was the first ever car seen in the emirate. He hoisted his enormous Union Jack above his residence and did so wearing full uniform, believing that dressing like the Arabs was akin to wearing a disguise. To earn respect, he preferred to show his true personality and give display to his marksmanship, his capacity to endure desert hardships, and his ability to ride a horse bareback.

Mubarak, 70 years old at the time, gave Shakespear a warm and

---

[80] Jacques Benois-Méchin, *Ibn Saoud ou la naissance d'un royaume*, Paris.

sincere welcome. The emir confirmed that Ibn Saud, who had succeeded in restoring his family's violated rights, had the support of the Bedouin from the Najd region. Since nobody could verify whether this was true, the British government was wary. The Turks had managed to achieve a delicate balance of power between the various Arab tribes. London, which had plans to poach the Sultan of Istanbul's closest allies, ordered Shakespear not to disrupt this political equilibrium.

The British were unaware that the young Ibn Saud would lay down arms only after having taken his revenge on the Rashidi dynasty of Ha'ail. Having seen Britain in action during Ibn Rashid's invasion of Kuwait, he believed that British support would be vital to fulfil what he considered to be his destiny. He had to convince the British that they could count on him. Shakespear met him and his brothers for the first time in February 1910, when they came to his residence for a British-style halal lunch in the company of Mubarak. Though the meal left the Emir of Najd somewhat perplexed (lamb with mint sauce!), he nonetheless invited him to Riyadh, pointing out that he would be the first Englishman to be officially received in the city. While Ibn Saud avoided all discussion of political issues, he did mention that Kuwait's friends were his friends and that the only Turks in the region were based in Ha'il, where his enemy Ibn Rashid resided. He was impressed by Shakespear's fluent command of the Najd dialect.

British duplicity

Lieutenant-Colonel Gerard Leachman, a British agent based in

Mesopotamia, informed Shakespear that he was being held in Ha'il, after a battle between the Shammar and the Anaiza[81], a tribe which had been helping him with his "research". He had met Ibn Rashid, still a teenager at the time, and his regent Ibn Subhan, who had recently seized power after having poisoned his cousin. Leachman's description of the situation was of great interest. But Shakespear sensed that he was hiding something. Shakespears suspicions were later confirmed when he learnt that the Leachman was in fact working for *MO2*, British military intelligence. Shakespear did not appreciate being faced with a *fait accompli*.

In September 1910, Mubarak warned Shakespear that Hussein bin Ali, the Sharif of Mecca, had spoken of his plans to attack Ibn Saud, in order to put an end to Wahabbi atrocities. Hussein was supported by both the Turks and Ibn Rashid. But the British raised no objections, given that a return to order in the desert would be to the benefit of Hussein, their secret Hashemite *protégé*. The newspaper *Al Ahram* (censured in Cairo) devoted many pages to the success of the battle, claiming that Hussein's war coalition numbered some 25 000 men (a clearly exaggerated figure) and that Ibn Saud surrendered to secure the release of his brother who had been taken prisoner. He had paid a ransom and sworn allegiance to Hussein, agreeing to pay him an annual rent. Was this true?

Mubarak gave another version of events. According to him, the

---

[81] Present in parts of Arabia, Iraq and the Syrian Desert (where Napoleon's secret service made contact wtih the Ruwallah), this large tribal confederation was frequently at war with the Shammar. Leading Anaiza families include the Saud family from Najd and the Al Sabah family from Kuwait.

operation was now finished: Hussein and Ibn Rashid had regained their respective territories, and Ibn Saud still reigned in his kingdom. For Shakespear, the only way to obtain reliable information on the situation in Najd was to go there in person. In early 1911, as nothing seemed to be changing in Arabia, the British government, curious to know the state of affairs between Hejaz and Najd, asked Shakespear to pay his friend Ibn Saud a visit.

A warning from Thaj

Shakespear fixed a meeting with Ibn Saud at his encampment close to Thaj, one of the wealthiest cities during the antiquity period and home to the remains of an ancient civilisation which fascinated Shakespear. It was here that he photographed a stela bearing mysterious inscriptions, probably written in Sabean[82].

Ibn Saud arrived in early March, and gave his version of events. Indeed, he had paid a ransom for the release of his brother (a standard practice in tribal conflicts, considered to be in no way dishonourable by either of the parties involved) and had promised to pay a rent to Hussein. But, since the capture of his brother was the result of treason, he had no intention of paying. As for the Turks, his opinion of them was far from nuanced: like all Wahhabis, he hated them, though slightly less than he hated the Persians, who, in his view, debased Islam with their infidel practices[83]. The emir declared he was ready to form an alliance with

---

[82] Trading with Palestine and Babylon, the Sabaean kingdom, located in Yemen (Hadhramaut), was one of the most prosperous ancient civilisations.

[83] H. V. F. Winstone, *Captain Shakespear*, Quarter Books Limited, London, 1978.

Britain, and hoped that Shakespear would be chosen to represent British interests in Riyadh. Before leaving, Ibn Saud warned him that he was in great danger and that, unfortunately, he could not always protect him.

In his report, Shakespear stressed Ibn Saud's lucidity and his conviction that the Turks would soon be history in Arabia. Indeed, they were so hated that the opposing factions were united against them. They could no longer divide and rule, and a general revolt was in the offing. The only thing that the Emir of Najd wanted to know was whether he could trust the British! But London refused to listen to what Shakespear had to say on the matter.

Shady dealings in the desert

Following his visit to London in May 1911 to watch the coronation of George V and to spend time with Dorothea, who found her consul much too in love with desert and in no hurry to marry, Shakespear returned to Bombay in his Rover to participate in the celebrations organised in honour of the new Emperor of India.

Upon his return to Kuwait in 1912, he was dismayed to learn that Mubarak was to be decorated by the Turks for having raised funds for the reconstruction of a part of Istanbul which had been destroyed in a fire. Sakespear surmised that Sayid Talib, the son of a wealthy merchant family in Basra, was likely to be behind this move. Talib, an opportunist politician, had handed over to the Turks the rebel Muntafiq sheik, Saadoun al-Mansur, widely believed to have been poisoned by the Ottoman authorities. Angered by this news, Shakespear berated the emir and never set a foot in his palace again, until the day he had to present his apologies for having accidentally killed a Kuwaiti man, crushed by the propeller of his boat. Smiling, the emir told him that if the only way to have the pleasure of seeing him was for one of his subjects to be killed, then he should kill one every day!

In December 1912, at a time when all British agents had been forbidden by the Foreign Office from crossing Ottoman Arabia, Shakespear discovered that Leachman, probably in disguise, had left Damascus and was heading for Najd. But what was his mission? A few days later, Dorothea, tired of waiting, told Shakespear that she was in love with a young army officer serving in the British Army in India. Though greatly saddened by this, he wished her good luck. He treasured his photo of her and kept it in his pocket until the day he died.

In March 1913, during one of his desert explorations, he learnt that Ibn Saud had set up camp just a few days walk from his. He decided to pay him a courtesy call, paying little heed to what London might have to say about this personal initiative. While it is known that he spent hours discussing with the emir, the exact details of the conversation remain a mystery to this day. Oddly, he had left no record of this meeting in his log book.

When he returned, his superiors, having got wind of his secret meeting, informed him that he was henceforth forbidden from meeting all tribal chiefs outside of officially approved missions. Asked what Ibn Saud had told him, Shakespear responded they had not discussed politics, and reiterated that he had merely made a courtesy call. Had he, as many believe, let the cat out of the bag and revealed to the emir what Britain really planned to do in the region? In August, the Foreign Office ordered Shakespear to remain within Kuwaiti borders. In December, with his mission in Kuwait drawing to a close, his superiors in India, after much prevarication, finally granted him permission to make a desert crossing from central Arabia to the Red Sea coast.

Five months in the heart of the desert

In January 1914, Shakespear introduced Mubarak to his successor, Colonel Grey, with whom he had no particular affinity. He said goodbye to his many friends and left the emirate. Two months later, after a long exploration in the desert, he camped close to Riyadh. On 11 March, Ibn Saud, accompanied by his family, came to bid him farewell. Moved, the emir reaffirmed his friendship and his conviction that Arabia's future lay in an alliance with Great Britain. Shakespear left the next day, travelling part of the way with Ibn Saud. Little did Shakespear know, they were to soon cross paths again.

After an arduous month in the desert - trekking from well to well, collecting insects and wildlife specimens, noting all he saw, and recording what tribal chiefs taught him of desert topography – he entered the territory occupied by the Shammar. Here he learnt that Ibn Rashid had his regent killed. Avoiding Ha'il, he followed a section of the Hejaz railway, between Sinai and north-east Aqaba (today part of Israel, a state created 34 years later) and, in late May, arrived at Port Said, in Egypt. In all, Shakespear took 111 days to cover over 1800 miles, two thirds of which was across territories unknown to Westerners. The British press heralded his achievement while the prestigious *Royal*

Geographical Society invited him to give a lecture when he was next in London. His surveys allowed the *War Office* to fill the blanks on its desert maps, which were classified "Top Secret" until the Arab Revolt during the First World War.

Anticlimax

In London, his superiors gave him an icy welcome. They acknowledged his expertise and were no doubt impressed by his achievement. But they feared that he would be liable to criticise Britain's role in Arabia. While in Cairo, he had written to Ibn Saud. Written in English, his letter gave Ibn Saud an account of his exploration and alerted him to the fact that the Turks were arming Ibn Rashid against him. He also reassured the emir, however, that during the course of his exploration he had not seen any Turkish soldiers or administrators. To avoid the system of postal censorship, Shakespear also sent him a letter written in French. To this day, the contents of this letter remain unknown.

Sir Arthur Hirtzel of the India Office sternly reminded him that Britain supported the Turkish presence in Arabia and that Britain would only envisage backing Ibn Saud if it were in keeping with Ottoman policy. Hirtzel forbade him from sending any information to the press without having first obtained both his and the Foreign Office's approval.

Shakespear's mission report did not please the British government at all. It pleaded Ibn Saud's cause, asserted that the Turks were headed for disaster, that their days in the region were numbered and that, sooner or later, Ibn Saud would rule Arabia, which was destined to become a confederation covering the whole country. By way of response, London sent Shakespear to an officer training centre...

Death on a dune

The tide turned with the outbreak of the First World War. The British government had finally understood that a German alliance with Turkey would enable Wilhelm II to gain access to India and Asia. Within a matter of a few hours, Shakespear's friendship with Ibn Saud and his relations with the tribes of central Arabia, hitherto considered with suspicion and contempt, became vital for Great Britain. In September 1914, he was urgently summoned to London and sent to Arabia as Political Officer on Special Duty. He was asked to persuade his Arab friends to support the British, promising them guns and fortune if they did so. One key condition was stipulated: they should attack the Turks only if they declared war against Britain.

He arrived in Kuwait on 7 December. *Force D*, one of the Anglo-Indian expeditionary forces, had already arrived in Iraq. Having discovered that Sayid Talib was in Riyadh on behalf of the Turks, he quickly went to see Ibn Saud. Did Shakespear sense that he would come to a sticky end? Before leaving the emirate, he handed Colonel Grey a letter which designated his brother as executor of his will.

On 31 December, he discovered that the Emir of Najd was furious with Britain. He couldn't understand why all of a sudden they wanted him to kill his worst enemy, whereas only six months ago they prevented him from doing so. Sayid Talib, on a military mission on behalf of the Turks, could see what was coming. He justified his position by claiming that he was obliged to take the Ottoman side because, otherwise, his family in Basra would have faced the consequences. The outcome of the fierce battles in the Iraqi port was uncertain, so he bided his time before choosing sides.

Ibn Saud raised an army of 6 000 men to fight Ibn Rashid, who was heading towards Riyadh. On 19 January 1915, Shakespear informed Major Cox that he planned to accompany the emir. In his British army uniform, he rode beside him to Jarrab, the area chosen for the battle. Ibn Saud asked him to follow his son, Turki, and leave the battlefield. But Shakespear refused to leave, explaining that it would be a blemish to his honour and that of his government. He had also refused to wear traditional Arab dress which meant he could easily be picked out. The morning after, on 24 January, protected by a Bedouin guard, he positioned himself high upon a dune with his revolver, binoculars and camera. He was observing the battle when the Shammar cavalry suddenly appeared before him. He took three bullets, one of which struck him in the head. He was thirty-six years old.

According to some, he had deliberately put himself in danger so as to die in battle: his honour could no longer stomach his government's deceitfulness. Ibn Saud wrote to Percy Cox to express his condolences and his grief, and asked him to dispatch an Arab-speaking delegate so that he may tell him the details of the deal concluded with Shakespear. London chose his rival, Gerard Leachman...

During Shakespear's posting in Kuwait, there was never any mention of oil – officially, at any rate. In Bushehr, Shakespear had diligently followed all events in the Gulf. On numerous occasions, he had warned the sheikhs of the German threat, as epitomised by the agent Wilhelm

Wassmuss, who was at large in the region. He had prevailed upon Emir Mubarak to not grant concessions to the *Anglo- Persian Company*, though this didn't stop passing visitors from ferreting around the dunes in search of the precious liquid. One such visitor was admiral Sir Edmond Slade, an exceptionally determined character. Accompanied by the emir's son, he came to find a source of bitumen in the very same place where, some thirty years later, the world's largest oil field was discovered. Shakespear, it was said, did not want drilling rigs disfiguring his beautiful desert.

Chapter VII

GERMANY: THE MARCH TO THE OILFIELDS OF THE EAST

Drang nach Osten
Act I: The Spies of Wilhelm II

Wilhelm II, King of Prussia and Emperor of the Germans, was a cultured man and, for the standards of the time, he could even be considered to be liberal. But he was also capricious and imperious, convinced that what he considered to be his divine right meant he was accountable to nobody. The accusation of warmongering, often repeated abroad, was chiefly due to his determination to transform Germany into a world economic power. In fact, he believed that going to war was counterproductive and heeded the advice of the *Alldeutscher Verband* (Pan-German League) only when it was in keeping with his own designs. Nonetheless, as a good Prussian aristocrat, and in honour of his grandfather Wilhelm I – the victor of the 1870 war which concluded with France's loss of Alsace-Lorraine – he strictly adhered to the Roman maxim *si vis pacem para bellum*[84].

---

[84] *If you want peace, prepare for war.*

The Kaiser on the Road to Damascus

Wilhelm II's overriding priority was to secure new markets for his industries and, in contrast to Chanellor Bismarck, find new territories to colonise. But neither colonialist France (suspicious and vengeful) nor Britain (triumphant and imperialist) were about to back down in the face of his ambitions.

In 1889, the Kaiser began touring. He travelled to Constantinople for a meeting with Sultan Abdul Hamid II and, in 1898, spent a month travelling the Ottoman Empire. In November of the same year, he made his mark in Damascus when he declared that the 300 million Muslims who recognised Abdul Hamid II as their caliph were his eternal friends. What's more, he went down on his knees before entering the Mausoleum of Saladin. He was even rumoured to have converted to Islam! The myth of *Hadji Wilhelm* was born...

In Jerusalem, he inaugurated the *Lutheran Church of the Redeemer*, built not far from the *Church of the Holy Sepulchre* on land donated by the sultan as a token of friendship. The Kaiser lent a sympathetic ear to the founder of the Zionist movement, Theodor Herzl, who was seeking to create a Jewish state either in Palestine or elsewhere. A year later, Germany obtained the first concession for its *Bagdadbahn*, the Berlin-Baghdad railway. According to article 22 of the concession, the Germans were entitled to exploit all resources discovered within a forty kilometre zone on either side of the line. Wilhelm II, it was claimed at the time, had reaped benefits comparable to those obtained by the French during the Crusades and three centuries of alliance with the

Turks.[85]

In 1901, Theodor Herzl succeeded in securing an audience with the sultan. Abdul Hamid had him decorated with great pomp, though he also told him that he would rather push a sword into his body than lose Palestine. Nonetheless, Hamid did promise him that he would give his project some thought, if the Jews agreed to reimburse the Ottoman foreign debt... Disappointed, Herzl turned to Britain.

The Bagdadbahn and the Sultan's Secret Oil Map

Britain was determined to maintain its control of the routes to India, so it was terrified by Germany's plans to construct a railway line into Baghdad and to equip itself with a fleet capable of taking on the Royal Navy. Wilhelm II, the favourite grandson of Queen Victoria, was well aware of this. His project to create German colonies between the Tigris and the Euphrates would have scuppered the British Indian government's plans to locate the families of its native auxiliaries in the same area.

Of course, oil was also an important consideration. A map of the oilfields, secretly drawn for the sultan, confirmed that Mesopotamia was saturated with the precious liquid. The Kaiser had taken the precaution of involving British and French banks in his *Bagdadbahn* project. But this did little to allay fears in London, especially since British intelligence had warned that the line would cross the regions possessing the

---

[85] Édouard Driault, *La question d'Orient*, Felix Alcan, Paris, 1921.

greatest potential wealth. The British Indian government's decision to seize Mesopotamia was only partly due to the strategic need to protect its oil wells in Arabistan from the Kaiser. What weighed far heavier in the balance was the need to undermine the construction of Germany's Berlin-Baghdad line, coupled with a craving for colonial expansion and oil wealth.

The Kaiser's men

While the British had T.E. Lawrence and its elite team at the Arab Bureau, the Kaiser had Wilhelm Wassmuss and the *Nachrichtenstelle für den Orient* (NfO) – Intelligence Office for the East – which covered the Near East, Persia and India, where the Germans lent their support to the *Ghadar*[86] independence movement and the Indian revolutionary activist Raja Mahendra Pratap[87]. The Kaiser's bureau was managed by Baron Max von Oppenheim, an archaeologist whose activities at Carchemish had been closely followed by Lawrence. Son of a Jewish

---

[86] Founded by Sikh immigrants in the US and Canada, *Ghadar* (meaning revolt in Urdu) was an Indian independence movement which took root in Punjab. The agents of W. C. Hopkinson, a former Calcutta police inspector, infiltrated the movement as early as 1909. Its newspaper, *Ghadar di Gunj*, had close to a million readers. With war obliging the British to reduce their military presence in India, the movement posed a serious threat to British rule. Accordingly, the crackdown was brutal.

[87] Raja Mahendra Pratap met Kaiser Wilhelm II in 1915. In 1918, he met both Lenin and Trotsky in Petrograd. After the war, he moved to Japan, in order to continue his fight against British colonialism. In 1946, he returned to India, where he immediately made contact with Ghandi. He was elected to the Indian parliament in 1957 and then in 1962.

banker, Oppenheimer, who had converted to Catholicism, was fascinated by the Near East and Islam. In 1908, when working as an attaché at the German consulate in Cairo, he met Hussein bin Ali, before he had been made Sharif of Mecca by the Turks, and, at his own expense, explored the Mesopotamian archaeological site of Tell Halaf[88]. In 1911, in Constantinople, he held talks with Faisal who had secretly made contact with Arab nationalists in favour of a revolt against the Turks in Syria. In 1915, while he was crossing the Sinai and the Hejaz disguised as a Bedouin, his cover was blown. Hussein had him deported to Syria.

Faisal manipulated the Germans, while his father made an alliance with the British. In February 1916, he met Dr Loytved-Hardegg, the Kaiser's consul in Damascus[89], and told him that he would have no quarrel with the Turks if they stopped supplying weapons to Emir Ibn Rashid. He had him believe that Sharif Hussein refused Britain's opportunistic offer of support, claiming that a descendant of the Prophet could not depend on a Christian government.

But the Baron von Oppenheim still had a few tricks up his sleeve. He persuaded the Kaiser to play the Pan-Islamic[90] card while, at the same

---

[88] Max von Oppenheim discovered Tell Halaf in 1899. This Syrian site, dating from the 5th BC, is located close to the source of the Khabur River, a tributary to the Euphrates.

[89] Loytved-Hardegg to Wolf-Metternich, 26 February 1916, NARA/ T-137/ 25/ 03030305. Quoted in Donald Mckale, German Policy toward the Sharif of Mecca, The Historian, 1993.

[90] The Kaiser also met the pro-German Swedish writer and explorer, Sven Hedin. He assured the German emperor that he had the support of Muslims in Russian

time, he manipulated Zionist leaders. He wrote a 136 page manual which explained to German spies how to recruit Muslim nationalists in India and Egypt. Furthermore, in collaboration with Franz Oppenheimer, he created the *Committee for the Liberation of Russian Jews*, which Wilhelm II hoped to use as a means to spy on Tsarist Russia[91]. Had the Kaiser's initiative suceeded, it is likely that a Jewish state linked to Germany would have been created.

Enver Pasha, who was the *Young Turks'* most influential leader, was suspicious of German calls for Holy War. But he did not resist German entreaties for very long. On 23 November 1914, he asked Sultan Mehmed V to declare Holy War. But this was in vain. The impact of this declaration fell far short of Oppenheim's expectations. Worn out by five centuries of power and destablised by the Pan-Turanianism movement[92], the Ottoman Empire was no longer feared or respected.

The Afghan mirage

One of Max von Oppenheim's most audacious operations aimed to incite a rebellion against British rule in Afghanistan and India. This mission was led by Werner Otto von Hetig and Oskar von Niedermayer. In April 1916, the two spies set off for Kabul with a letter from the Kaiser. It was addressed to the Emir Habibullah, King of Afghanistan, and

---

Turkestan, in the Caucasus and in British India. They were, he said, prepared to wage Holy War against the British.

[91] Kimche, Jon, *Le Second réveil arabe*, Robert Laffont, Paris, 1970.

[92] Pan-Turanianism is a nationalist doctrine which essentially aims to create an alliance of all people with Turkic origins.

proposed German military support against the British, together with territorial gains in India and Central Asia. The Germans were accompanied by the Indian nationalist leader R.M. Pratap and a group of agitators from the *Indian Independence Committee*, financed by the NfO. *The Hindu-German Conspiracy*, as British intelligence termed it, was underway...

Delayed by disputes between the different expedition members and numerous detours made to avoid British assault commandos in southern Persia and the Russians based in the north, they finally arrived in Kabul on 1 October. Von Hentig immediately understood that they were not welcome and that it was the British who held sway in Afghanistan. They were confined to a hotel, ostensibly for their own security, and were not authorised to leave unless accompanied by armed guards. Their requests for an audience with the emir were repeatedly postponed. Three weeks later, following threats made by Hentig and Niedermayer to go on a hunger strike, Emir Habibullah finally agreed to receive them. Feigning to doubt the authenticity of the Kaiser's letter, however, the emir treated them like merchants. He refused to join a jihad, had no wish to establish diplomatic relations with Germany, and certainly did not intend to attack India.

Meanwhile, the British government in Delhi sensed the stirrings of a revolt in the northern tribal zones. On 1 December, with the support of the powerful Islamic *Deobandi*[93] movement, R.M. Pratap established in

---

[93] *Deobandi* is said to follow the teachings of Abu Hanifa, who died in 767 while in a Baghdadi prison. It played an important role in the creation of the Afghan Taliban movement.

Kabul an Indian government in exile, known as the *Provisional Government of India*. The Afghan emir, keen to see the back of the German agents, made them some vague promises concerning a treaty of friendship and trade relations with Germany. Partially satisfied, Hentig and Niedermayer left Kabul on 21 May 1916. They both went their separate ways. Werner von Hentig, pursued by the British, took over a year to reach Germany. He had traversed China, the Gobi Desert and then headed to the United States where, taken prisoner, he was then transferred to Berlin in an exchange of diplomats. Niedermayer's journey, on the other hand, took him through Turkestan and Persia. The Emir Habibullah was assassinated on 20 February 1919 by his brother Nasrullah Khan, who in turn was killed by Amanullah Khan, his nephew. They had supported the idea of an alliance with Germany.

Koba extorts money from the oil tycoons

Nothing went as planned for the Germans in the Caucaus, either. Wilhelm II's *Drang nach Osten* – the march to the East – stumbled on an unforeseen obstacle in the form of a man named Joseph Vissarionovich Dzhugashvili, who was later better known as Stalin[94]. An avid reader of Russia's great novelists as well as the French authors Victor Hugo and Zola, Stalin wrote poems in his spare time. A former seminarist, he was once devoted to Christ, but then had decided to devote himself to Bolshevism instead. As a professional revolutionary, he adopted many pseudonyms. Before and during the First World War, his favourite alias was Koba (Turkish for invincible), taken from *The*

---

[94] Soviet propaganda called him the "father of nations" or the "broad chested Ossette."

Patricide, a popular novel at the time. The novel's protagonist, Koba, was an anti-Russian Caucasian bandit.

In 1901, Koba moved to Batumi, a Georgian oil port, where he took a job at Baron Edmond de Rothschild's[95] *Caspian and Black Sea Oil Company* (BNITO). Three months later, a fire destroyed the plant! In April, the *Okhrana*, the Tsar's secret police, already all too familiar with Koba and his activities, arrested him. But he continued to orchestrate the oil workers' revolt from his prison cell. Sent to Siberia, he escaped and resurfaced in Tiflis (modern day Tbilisi), in January 1904. Following yet another arrest later that year, he fled to Baku, where strikes and demonstrations became an almost a daily occurrence.

Koba went into hiding in the mountains and created the *Red Battle Squad*, a paramilitary unit comprising teenage delinquents and bandits. They ambushed Cossacks, murdered police informers, and ran an extortion racket, forcing the oil tycoons to pay a revolutionary tax. His squad also held up trains and coaches. In 1906, they carried out the first in a series of bank robberies, termed "revolutionary expropriations", in order to finance the Bolsheviks. Later that year, in London and in Berlin, he secretly met Lenin to discuss a new round of raids. The largest robbery was carried out in June 1907, in Tiflis. This action had in fact been vetoed by the *Russian Social Democratic Labour Party* (RSDLP)[96] congress in London. Despite several attempts by the

---

[95] Simon Sebag Montefiore, *Le jeune Staline*, Calmann-Levy, Paris, 2008.

[96] The Russian Social Democratic Labour Party (RSDLP) was divided into two camps: Julius Martov's Mensheviks, a minority in the party, and Lenin's Bolsheviks, which formed the majority. But the Mensheviks' influence was inversely proportional, as it corresponded to the result of a vote which had been held in 1903 in Belgium.

RSDLP's Menshevik majority to exclude Koba from the party, they never succeeded, as he was supported by Lenin behind the scenes.

In 1912, Lenin created the Bolshevik Party and made Koba a member of the *Central Committee*. Stalin then became his *nom de plume* for the articles he wrote in *Pravda*. Under police surveillance, he spent part of the First World War in a hamlet located in the Arctic Circle region, and returned to St Petersburg in March 1917, following the Tsar's abdication. He joined the Politburo where, working in the shadows, he contributed to the success of the October Revolution.

Dunsterforce, Dunster-farce!

Nicolas II's fall had created a power vacuum in the Caucasus. The anti-Tsarist opposition stepped into the breach, while the independence movements in Azerbaijan, Armenia and Georgia reared their heads. British intelligence had set up an office in Tiflis, so as to be prepared for any eventuality. The Turks rallied their supporters in the name of the Pan-Turanian ideal, formed *The Islamic Army of the Caucasus*, and set out to claim Azerbaijan for the Turks.

Although the Baku Commune – led by Armenian Bolsheviks – had nationalised the region's oil and the tankers necessary for its transportation[97], the new regime's supply was under threat. Worried by this, Lenin proposed the Kaiser a deal: he could take half of Baku's oil if he maintained order in the region. Stepan Shaumian, head of the Baku Commune, refused to supply the Germans upon the advice of

---

[97] The nationalisation of the Soviet oil industry was to take place two years later.

Major Aeneas Ranald MacDonell[98], a British diplomat and intelligence officer. But Shaumian also refused MacDonell's proposal to call in a special British regiment to protect the city.

The regiment in question was almost ready. In January 1918, the British in Mesopotamia had created *Dunsterforce*, named after its commander General Lionel Dunsterville[99]. Its purpose was to keep the Pan-Turanian forces at bay and occupy – or destroy, if necessary - the Baku oil wells. After having crossed the north of Persia, the unit arrived at the Caspian Sea port of Enzeli, where they prepared to set sail for Azerbaijan. To clear the way for the unit in Baku, MacDonell made an attempt to overthrow Shaumian, aided by the Socialist Revolutionaries, Armenians from the *Dashnak* party and the *Mensheviks*. The coup failed. With the police on his tail, MacDonell was forced to flee.

A few weeks later those who supported British intervention finally ousted Shaumian. General Dunsterville arrived on 4 August 1918. Lacking the means to defend the oil city, *Dunsterforce* – henceforth nicknamed *Dunster-farce* by its French opponents – returned to Iran on 15 September without telling anyone and without having destroyed a single oil well. A deserter from the *Army of Islam* had told Dunsterville that the final assault was scheduled for the following day! Meanwhile, twenty six Bolshevik commissars were arrested and then released by a commando led by the Armenian Anastas Mikoyan[100]. Captured again on 20

---

[98] Ranald MacDonell was the British Vice-Consul at Baku, where he had lived for a number of years prior to his appointment.

[99] Rudyard Kipling's character Stalky, in the book *Stalky and Co.*, is based on Lionel Dunsterville, a friend from his school days.

[100] Anastas Mikoyan was made Chairman of the Presidium of the Supreme Soviet

September, Shaumian and his comrades were executed under orders of the British, who were preparing to make a counter-attack. Following Baku's capture by the combined Ottoman-Azerbaijani forces, several thousand Armenians were massacred in retaliation for the pogrom which had killed 20 000 Muslims six months previously. The Turks declared Azerbaijan an independent state. The British feared that they might advance to Tiflis, and so relocated their secret services to Vladiskavkaz in the north. Their agents, arrested by the *Cheka* for their involvement in the *Lockhart Plot*, were imprisoned in Moscow[101].

Colonel Alfred Rawlinson[102], head of *Dunsterforce's* intelligence service, was transferred to Tiflis, where, between 1919 and 1920, he attempted to foment a regional revolt against the Bolsheviks and the Turks. With the world war at an end, he attempted to convince Kâzım Karabekir, chief commander of the Turkish armed forces, as well as Mustafa Kemal, to transform the Caucasus into an anti- Communist buffer zone, but this was to no avail[103].

Following the *Mudros Armistice*, General Thomspon arrived in Baku with 30 000 troops, accompanied by French and Cossack officers. Among

---

in 1964. He remained in the corridors of power until the day he died.

[101] The British had deported a number of Kemalist activists to Malta. In retaliation, the Turks arrested Alfred Rawlinson in November 1920 while he was in Anatolia. He was released a year later.

[102] Colonel Rawlinson was the son of Sir Henry Rawlinson, one of the archaeologist/spies of the *Great Game*.

[103] Bülent Gökay, *The Illicit Adventures of Rawlinson* – a revised version of the paper *"Spying in the Ottoman Empire"*, the Skilliter Centre for Ottoman Studies, Newnham College, Cambridge, 29 April, 1995.

other decisions, Thompson derailed a deal between the Azerbaijani government and Rockefeller's *Standard Oil* in an attempt to impose Deterding's *Royal Dutch Shell*. Thompson recognised Nogorno-Karabach as belonging to Azerbaijan, an opinion shared by Mikoyan (who had joined Lenin in Moscow) for whom the attachment of the region to Armenia would have robbed the inhabitants of their commercial and ancestral ties with Baku.

The Nobel brothers, who understood what was happening better than the other players, sold their shares to Rockefeller. In France, suffering from illness, Baron de Rothschild's morale was at its lowest ebb. In a bid to reassure him, his family created a false newspaper, reporting good news from the Baku front[104]. In the end, the British did not obtain a mandate at the 1920 *Paris Peace Conference*. They pulled out of Baku.

In Moscow, Lenin turned to Stalin for all matters related to Caucasian oil. In 1918, he entrusted Stalin with the reorganisation of the Tsaritsyn front, where Bolshevik forces had been pushed back by Tsarist troops. He reinstated north Russia's wheat supply, which had been blocked by Anton Denikin's Cossaks. The following year, the White Army made a renewed offensive in an attempt to control the North Caucasus, but Stalin drove them back. Denikin had been confined to this zone by the British, stopping him from moving his forces close to the oil wells. On 27 April 1920, the Red Army (the 11th Army) attacked Azerbaijan and overthrew the government. The next day, Grigory Ordzhonikidze, Stalin's comrade from his days in Baku, arrived in his armoured train,

---

[104] Eric Hoesli, *À la conquête du Caucase*, Éditions des Syrtes, Paris, 2006.

the *3rd International*. The town fell without a single shot being fired.

Amidst the euphoria of the October Revolution, Trotsky, in 1919, had threatened to reduce Britain to the status of an isolated and wretched island by conquering India and Afghanistan. According to him, Asia and Persia were the gateways to the control of London and Paris[105]. When Lenin died in 1924, Stalin seized power and put an end to Trotsky's outbursts.

---

[105] Quoted by Svetlana Gorshenina, *Explorateurs en Asie centrale*, Olizane, Paris, 2003.

Chapter VIII

WILHELM WASSMUSS, THE ELUSIVE GERMAN SPY

After the First World War, the British had disparagingly nicknamed Wilhelm Wassmuss, the Kaiser's spy in southern Persia, "The German Lawrence." But they ought to have named him "Wassmus of Persia"[106] or the "great *Germani*", as the Persians called him. His adventures became famous thanks to a book written in 1936 by Christopher Sykes who had made use of authoritative - albeit biased – sources[107]. Indeed, his father, Percy Sykes, former British consul in Kerman and Mashhad, was transferred to Bushehr in order to protect British oil interests, counteract German propaganda, and thwart Wassmuss.

Although Persia had declared its neutrality at the beginning of the war, Percy Sykes created the *South Persia Rifles*[108]. Commanded by British officers, the ranks of this 6000-strong militia comprised Sikhs, sepoys[109] and local mercenaries. Sykes' mission was far from easy, because

---

[106] Wassmuss' Persian adventures predate those of T.E. Lawrence in Arabia.

[107] Christopher Sykes, *Wassmuss, le Lawrence allemand*, Payot, Paris, 1936.

[108] Hated by the population, the *South Persia Rifles* were disbanded in 1921 by Reza Khan, the Persian minister of war and future Shah of Iran.

[109] Hindu soldiers serving in the British Indian Army.

Persia was profoundly pro-German. Moreover, the German intelligence networks he sought to uproot were efficient and well-established. They were either linked directly to the II Reich or had connections with the mercantile and shipping business *Robert Wönckhaus & Co*[110], which had been active in the Gulf region since 1897. The Persian gendarmerie, responsible for maintaining law and order in the provinces, were of no help: they were commanded by Swedish officers, who were notoriously pro- German.

Fight the British by any means necessary

British intelligence was all too familiar with Wassmuss. In 1909 and 1913, he had been the vice- consul to Bushehr. His official and unofficial activities left no doubt as to his true mission: fight the British presence in southern Persia by any means necessary. Respecting Persian laws, the British, at first, chose not to take decisive action. However, after having declared war against Germany on 5 August 1914 and invaded Iraq in November 1914, the British behaved like conquerors.

Wasmuss - cultivated, shrewd and charismatic - spoke Farsi fluently. He was on good terms with the leaders of the region's different ethnic groups. He also spent a great deal of his time talking to nomads in their tents and travelled to the remotest villages to meet peasants, explaining to them that Germany was a great nation which respected different religions and traditions. He claimed that Wilhelm II had converted to Islam in 1898, following his excursion to *al-Quds* (Jerusalem), and had

---

[110] *Robert Wönckhaus & Co.* specialised in the trade of nacre, pearls and... espionage.

secretly made his *Hajj* to Mecca.

Tribesmen were impressed by what he had to say, especially in Tangestan, whose dialect he spoke fluently. This coastal region, situated to the south-east of Bushehr, was in a state of financial ruin. The British, who laid down the law and ruled according to their own interests, accused the local fisherman of piracy and smuggling. Under the pretext that they were supplying weapons to the Afghan tribes, including the Pashtuns on the northwest border with India, the British confiscated their boats and sometimes even destroyed them. It was no coincidence, then, that Wasmuss took great interest in Tangestan, whose inhabitants had been harrassing the British since 1857.

Wassmuss: a threat to British interests

On 6 March 1915, when the British administration in Basra learnt that Wassmuss (aged 35 at the time) had returned to Persia and was leading a group of professional agitators, the order was given for his immediate arrest. Being at war, Britain considered it was now free from its diplomatic obligations. The British were determined to maintain their control of Abadan's oil wells, essential for the Royal Navy, especially as the British invasion force was making slow progress four months after having landed in Iraq. General Charles Townshend, commander of the expeditionary force, was making no headway at Qurna, some 70km north of Basra, at the confluence point of the Tigris and Euphrates rivers[111].

---

[111] The Garden of Eden was located where the two rivers meet. At this sight, locals

The Iraqis did not greet their "liberators" with flowers! Ajami al-Saadoun, the *Muntafiq*[112] sheikh, remained loyal to Abdul Hamid II, the Ottoman Sultan and caliph, and his stance influenced the chief of the Banu Lam in neighbouring Persian Arabistan. The Iraqi-Persian border was badly guarded. Turkish battalions would circumvent the Anglo-Indian positions with ease, crossing into Southern Persia in order to attack British forces from the rear, and the squadrons dispatched to pursue them were often ambushed by Arab resistance fighters.

In Persia, the *Bakhtiari*[113] were paid substantial royalties by the British for the oil they extracted from their land. But they could not be counted on, either. They declared themselves neutral, implying that they were liable to change their mind. Meanwhile, the need to arrest Wassmuss became increasingly urgent. After having intercepted and decoded a German diplomatic message, British intelligence learnt that Wassmuss planned to foment a tribal uprising, sabotage the *Anglo-Persian Company's*[114] pipeline and attack the British consulate in Bushehr.

---

once worshipped an ancient jujube tree, because it was thought to be the biblical Tree of Knowledge. The tree was destroyed during the American invasion in April 2003.

[112] The *Muntafiq* (*Al-Muntafiq*) is the main tribal confederation in southern Iraq. The majority of members are Shiites, but the group's leaders from the Al-Saadun branch are Sunni Muslims. Nouri al-Maliki, former Iraqi prime minister, belongs to one of its Shiite branches.

[113] The ethnic origins of the *Bakhtiari* are said to be either Median or Aryan.

[114] Samuel Spencer, *Decision for War, 1917: The Laconia sinking and the Zimmermann Telegram*, R. R. Smith, 1953.

Wasmuss escapes

After having made the journey through Turkey and Baghdad, the German mission arrived in Persia not far from Kut Al Amara, where Wasmuss had made contact with Haidar Khan, one of the local tribal chiefs. Unfortunately for Wassmusss, Khan was beholden to the British, who paid his family revenues so that their boats could access the Shatt al-Arab river. Percy Cox ordered Captain Noel, based in Bushehr, to arrest the Germans. Wassmuss was duly apprehended and news of his arrest was telegrammed to Basra. Very shortly afterwards, however, another telegram announced that Wasmuss had just escaped! The Kaiser's spy slipped away into the darkness of the night. His baggage, dumped while fleeing, was loaded with inflammatory tracts, written in several languages, calling for jihad against both the British in southern Persia and the Russians, who occupied the north of the country.

Christopher Sykes claims that Wassmuss was first arrested after having fallen into a trap. A member of Kahn's tribe had poisoned Wassmuss and then sold him to the British. He then escaped, but nobody knows how. Cavalrymen, commanded by Captain Noel, finally apprehended him. But the officer made the mistake of entrusting a Persian police officer to escort Wassmuss to Bushehr. He exploited this weakness and escaped a second time.

There are several versions of his escape. According to Sykes, Wassmuss, worried that his horse was ill, went to the stable every thirty minutes, accompanied by his guard. Exhausted, the guard finally let him see his horse unescorted. Wassmuss seized his opportunity, and fled at full gallop to Tangistan, where he could count on trusted friends. The alternative version is more mundane. Wassmuss had simply made a hole in his tent, crawled through, and disappeared into the night. But the locals believe that Haidar Khan had let him leave, in honour of their old friendship. Humiliated by Wassmuss' disappearance, the British fell back on Helmuth Listemann, the German consul in Bushehr. They arrested him because they feared he might conspire with the fugitive. The German consulate was stormed with ease and the consul was taken to India, where he was held prisoner[115].

The British seized the consulate's files, in which they found: instructions for Wassmuss and Niedermayer (the Kaiser's agent, tasked with sparking an Afghan revolt); a codebook for decrypting diplomatic messages; a list of Persians collaborating with the consulate; confirmation that Germany was behind the recent sabotage of the sub-sea cable linking London to India; and documents demonstrating the extent of German infiltration in Tangestan.

The secret code of *Willemstrasse*

Thanks to another code book found in Wassmuss' baggage, Admiral William Hall is said to have decrypted the famous telegram sent by Arthur Zimmerman, the German minister of foreign affairs, to his ambassador in Mexico. The publication of this message brought the United States into the war. In the telegram, the Kaiser proposed that Mexico form a military alliance with Germany against the US, should the Americans decide to abandon their neutrality. In exchange, he

---

[115] Victor Winstone, *The Illicit Adventure*, Cape, London, 1982.

promised that Germany would help Mexico reclaim Texas, New Mexico and Arizona. After America's entry into the war, Mexico declined the offer, as it considered that Germany was not militarily capable of honouring its promise.

Hall possessed several manuals of German code. One had been handed to the British in Belgium at the start of the war by an Austrian, who worked as a code breaker for the occupying army. Another had been found in the pocket of a German officer, who was killed when the *Magdeburg* sank[116]. It is not known why *Willemstrasse*, the German ministry of foreign affairs, did not change its codes, even though it knew the British were capable of reading the messages sent to its diplomats.

Calls for tribal revolt

Wherever he stayed, Wassmuss spread the good word of the Reich. In Kazerun, to the west of Shiraz, he told Nasir Diwan, the local sheikh, that the government in Tehran trembled with fear when an *Inglesi* spoke but that the *Germani* "sustained by law and culture" were stronger than them. He told him to await his signal, promising him that he would soon see the *Inglesi* "wailing in chains".

Wassmuss resurfaced in Shiraz, out of reach of the British who, all the same, clamoured for his deportation. The Persian gendarmerie, commanded by pro-German Swedish officers, gave him an enthusiastic welcome. Wassmuss encouraged the Bakhtiari chiefs to attack the

---

[116] Samuel Spencer, *Decision for War, 1917: The Laconia sinking and the Zimmermann Telegram*, R. R. Smith, 1953.

British, but this was futile, serving only to exacerbate their feeling of resentment. He had explained to them the increasing importance of oil and proposed royalties greater than those paid by the *Anglo-Persian Company*. But they felt cheated when, not long afterwards, their demands for the increase were rejected by the oil companies.

Wassmuss then made contact with Saulat al-Daula, the leader of the *Qashqai*, a Turkmen tribal confederation[117] with links to Enver Pasha and the *Mujahedeen*, a secret group frequently mentioned by Christopher Sykes. Saulat al-Daula was preparing a tribal rebellion in the south. The *Young Turks*, who had seized power in Istanbul, complicated matters for the Germans. Their project to create a Turanian Empire[118] – comprising Iraq, Azerbaijan, Persia, Afghanistan and Central Asia –conflicted directly with the aims of the Kaiser and his agents.

When Wassmuss arrived in Tangestan, he assured Zair Khidir, a leading local chief, that Turkey and Germany would win the war, invade India and put an end to British colonial rule. He asked him to follow the example of certain Shia mullahs, who had responded to the Sultan of Istanbul's call for Holy War. As he had done when talking to other tribal chiefs, he claimed that he had converted to Islam, just like the Kaiser,

---

[117] The Black Sheep Turkomans (*Kara Koyunlu*) and the White Sheep Turkomans (*Ak Koyunlu*) progressively settled in Iraq and Persia before the creation of the Ottoman Empire in the 13th century. It is said the *Qashqai* accompanied the Mongol conquerors Hulagu Khan and Amir Timur.

[118] The *Young Turks*, led by Enver Pasha, advocated the creation of a Turanian empire which would have unified all Turkic peoples from Eastern Europe, Central Asia, China, Persia and Iraq.

who was known as *Hajji Wilhelm*! Dressed as tribesman, with a Mauser pistol at his hip, Wassmuss then addressed the crowd: *"O Persians, now is the time to give yourselves to the Holy Cause. If you shrink from the sacrifice when the whole of Islam is threatened by the infidel enemy, what will your answer be to the Prophet on the Day of Judgement?"*

Wanted, dead or alive

Wassmuss had convinced them. On 12 July 1915, three days before Ramadan, armed Tangestani tribesmen attacked the British consulate in Bushehr. While crossing a desert region, some of the aggressors were intercepted by an Anglo-Indian platoon. The British captain, a major and several Indian soldiers were killed. But the consulate attack failed. The British then took their own particular form of revenge. A group of *Royal Marines*, accompanied by sepoys, cut down the date palms, the main source of food and revenue in Tangestan[119], further fuelling the enmity of the natives. The Indo- British forces killed Rais Ali Delvari, one of the tribal chiefs who had led the revolt, but they were forced to make a rapid retreat to Bushehr, leaving sixty or more dead behind them.

Increasingly worried, Percy Cox offered a reward of 5000 pounds for the capture of Wassmuss. Though wanted dead or alive, his death was considered preferable... Despite the significant sum offered, nobody turned him in. The reward was then tripled, but this only led to admonishment from the government in London, which demanded that

[119] Peter Hopkirk, *Like Hidden Fire: The Plot to bring down the British empire*, Kodansha Globe, 1997.

the sum be reduced. The British found this initiative abhorrent, and it only served to increase the popularity of Wassmuss.

Nonetheless, Wassmuss had not won the game. True, Persia glorified Rais Ali Delvari's sacrifice and the courage of the Tangestani rebels, and decried British imperialism. But the Shah had still not declared war against Britain. By prudence and weakness, the Shah had chosen to pay compensation to the families of the Anglo-Indian soldiers.

Tales of the Tangestani uprising inflamed the situation. On 10 October 1915, the Persian gendarmerie in Shiraz arrested the British consul Major Frederick O'Connor and the director of the *Imperial Bank of Persia*, along with forty other British subjects. Wassmuss had them imprisoned in the fortress at Ahram in Tangestan. Though the women were quickly released, the men were detained for up to a year. The British were against the ropes. A month later, General Townshend lost the Battle of Ctesiphon in Iraq. Accompanied by 12 000 men, he made a retreat to Kut, where his troops were then besieged by the Ottoman forces. An operation launched to liberate the prisoners in Ahram came to an abrupt end when Zaid Khidir lined them up against the fortress wall and threatened to execute them. One of them, petrified, collapsed with a heart attack. They were finally released following the fall of Kut, on 29 April 1916, in exchange for Tangestani prisoners and the payment of a ransom. Christopher Sykes believes that Wassmuss was partly responsible for the British defeat at Kut, in so far as the Anglo-Indian forces, tied down in Bushehr and Abadan, were not able to rescue General Townshend.

End Game

Enver Pasha's Turanian dream came to end following Turkey's failure to occupy the Persian regions with a large Turkmen population. The capture of Baghdad by General Maude, who had replaced Townshend (held prisoner in Baghdad), altered the course of the First World War in the Near East. The cancellation of Conrad Preusser's[120] Turkish-German offensive to reclaim Baghdad, followed by the death of Field Marshal von der Goltz, who had consummately commanded on the Iraqi front, spelt the end of German dreams to colonise the Near East.

In September 1917, after having created a special German intelligence group named *Muntafiq Mission* (or *Missmont*) in Aleppo, Conrad Preusser moved to the Iraqi town of Hit, on the western bank of the Euphrates. He kept a close eye on British activities in the region. Von der Goltz[121] had planned to make Ajami al-Saadoun, the *Muntafiq* chief, ruler of Iraq. But Turkey's *Yildrim Army Group*, which had been given the mission of reclaiming Baghdad, was then sent to Palestine. Al-Saadoun went into hiding, pursued by Gerard Leachman, one of Britain's most violent agents.

The funds at Wassmuss' disposal were rapidly dwindling. Lacking the means necessary to honour his commitments, the tribal chiefs deserted

---

[120] German archaeologist and spy, reputed to be a master of disguise.

[121] Wilhelm Leopold Colmar von der Goltz, highly respected by the Turks, was one the few who could make the Turanian extremists see sense. He died from typhus while in Baghdad, though some believe he had been poisoned. Not long after the death of von der Goltz, General Frederick Maude took up residence in the very same house. He died shortly afterwards...

him. Percy Sykes led a counterattack on all fronts and wrote to Wassmuss to inform him that he was finished: Saulat al-Dauleh had changed sides. But if he agreed to leave Tangestan, Sykes would ensure that he was repatriated.

Wassmuss then survived an assassination attempt. Stabbed deep in the thigh (the wound was bone- deep) and left for dead, he was found by friends, who then took care of him. His attacker, a member of the *Qashqai*, was arrested but, after having berated him, Wassmuss demanded that he be released.

Once he was back on his feet, Wassmuss made a tour of all the tribes in the region, but he excluded the leaders and spoke only to their members. His influence was so great that, six months later, Saulat al-Dauleh was forced to admit that his authority as chief had diminished. Wassmuss even went to see mercenaries engaged in the *South Persia Rifles*. He met them while they were on leave in their villages, and urged them to defect or desert. After having spent several months in India, Percy Sykes, returned to find his units on the verge of disintegration and the region in a state of unrest. Saulat had changed sides again and threw his lot in with Wassmuss: he declared war against the British! *Qashqai* riflemen staged a mutiny and killed their commanding officer. But the rebellion fizzled out. The British received reinforcements and, in Bushehr, soon counted 20 000 troops, a number sufficient for them to effortlessly restore order in the entire region.

On 20 November 1918, the British administration in Bushehr informed Wassmuss that the war was over and gave him the choice of either being interned as a prisoner of war or being repatriated. Wassmuss replied that only the German government gave him orders. He then fled to Turkey, accompanied by several partisans. According to Christopher Sykes, the fugitives left on horseback while reciting the first chapter of the Koran for good luck.

Multiple arrests and escapes

To fool the British, who were hot on his tail, Wassmus wore European clothes and adopted the identity of Mr Witt, a prospector for the *Anglo-Persian Oil Company*. In April 1919, however, he made the mistake of attending the *Nowruz* celebrations in Kashan. Recognised and betrayed by an Armenian telegraphist, he was arrested and beaten up on the road to Qom. He was imprisoned in Qazvin, the former capital of the Persian Empire, located north east of Tehran. But the wretched fellow managed to escape again! He headed for Tehran this time. Two weeks later, after having crossed the Alborz mountain range on foot, he arrived famished and in rags at the headquarters of the German legation. After much negotiation, the British decided to repatriate him under escort. The return journey was long and complicated. At each stop - Baku, Alexandria, Marseilles- he was jailed while the authorities awaited orders regarding his case. In the autumn of 1919, the occupying troops in Cologne, having received no orders concerning his case, placed him in detention. So he escaped again!

Return to Persia and disillusion

Wassmuss married in 1921. He was soon appointed head of the

Weimar Republic's[122] Department of Eastern Affairs. The Tangestani tribal chiefs wrote to him to claim the money he had promised them for their support but, crippled with debt, the German government refused to pay. Mortified by what he considered to be a breach of German honour, he left Germany in 1924 to spend his honeymoon in Bushehr. He wanted to announce the bad news to his friends in person.

In Tangestan, he explained to the tribal chiefs that his country, defeated, was temporarily unable to honour its debts. But he assured them that he would personally see to it that they were reimbursed as soon as possible. A chance meeting with a German farmer, who sought to move to Persia, gave him an idea.

Back in Berlin, he made a formal request to be appointed consul to Bushehr, but this was refused, as his appointment would have offended the British. So he resigned. In the end, the government gave him 5000 pounds but, instead of reimbursing the sheikhs, he invested the money in the construction of a farm in Tangestan. He was convinced that he could turn the area into a prosperous farming region, thereby allowing him to repay in instalments the debt owed to his Persian friends. A tribal chief rented him some land in Chahgoudak, not far from Shiraz. He bought some agricultural machinery – tractors, ploughs, seeding and threshing machines – and got down to work, helped by the wife of the German farmer he had met.

Unfortunately, those who fought beside him died of old age, one after

---

[122] Following the German Empire, the Weimar Republic was established. It was named after the city, where its constitution was drafted.

the other. The new generation could not understand why their parents had backed the wrong horse during the war. Some of them wondered whether the farm in fact had a darker purpose, and began to suspect that Wassmuss was playing on their naivety to make his fortune. Though urged by all to abandon his project, Wassmuss refused and ended up losing all the money he had invested.

The sheikhs then demanded they be repaid in full and brought legal proceedings against him. In Bushehr, an unfavourable verdict was returned. Fearing reprisals, the judged declared he was guilty. He then made an appeal in Shiraz, but the jury upheld the judgement, again for fear of reprisals. Wassmuss made another appeal, this time in Tehran, but the trial was severely delayed. He returned to Germany in April 1931 and fell gravely ill. Shortly after having learnt that the Persian court had finally ruled in his favour, he died.

Chapter IX

ST JOHN PHILBY, THE SPY WHO CHOSE WAHHABISM

While T.E. Lawrence, lost in his dream of a great Arab kingdom, was busy defending Hussein, the Sharif of Mecca and King of Hejaz, Harry St John Philby (Jack to his friends), an intelligence officer for the British Colonial Office, was working to make the Emir of Najd (Ibn Saud) the King of Arabia. Though not as famous as the author of the *Seven Pillars of Wisdom*, Philby's mark on the history of Arabia is greater than that of his rival. He had an enormous influence on Anglo-Saudi relations, and played a key role in the war for oil. For a long period, his publications[123] were considered to be the key source for reliable historical, geographical, botanical and archaeological data on the kingdom.

But there was another side to the man. He condemned British policy in Arabia which he viewed as hypocritical and short-termist. His activism, which today would be termed subversive, was considered by London to be a form of dissidence, treason even. Indeed, his activities earned him a prison sentence at the beginning of the Second World War. Some, including his friends, sensed he was playing a double game. He was

---

[123] Philby had written thirty eight books, seventeen of which were published.

suspected not only of being a spy but also a communist, a fascist, a Nazi and even a Zionist. Albert Londres, a prominent French journalist who had met Philby in the 1930s while in Jeddah, described him as being the most inscrutable of all the British diplomatic figures in the Middle East, a Janus-like character.[124] As Philby himself once claimed, he was one of the first to publically advocate that the region be freed from all form of foreign control.[125] Comparatively speaking, the various charges which have been made against him are trifling.

An Islam fuelled by nationalism

Ibn Saud was the chief of the powerful Arabian Wahhabi sect. His father had been driven out of Riyadh by the family's hereditary enemy, Saud Ibn Rashid, leader of the Shammar tribe. But in 1902, aged just 18, Ibn Saud recaptured Riyadh. At the time, Najd, a desert region in the heart of the Arabian Peninsula, was divided along political, religious and tribal lines. In the north, Emir Rashid, barricaded behind fortress walls in Ha'il, recognised the absolute power of Abdul Hamid, the Sultan of the Ottoman Empire. In the south, Ibn Saud and his supporters wanted to seize control of Mecca and impose, by force if necessary, their fundamentalist version of the Koran and the Hadiths on the whole of Arabia. To this end, he had created the *Ikhwan*, an army of Bedouin tribesman, who had been indoctrinated by Wahhabi *ulamas* (scholars)

---

[124] Anthony Cave Brown, *Philby, père et fils, la trahison dans le sang*, Pygmalion, Paris, 1987.

[125] Quoted in Daniel Yergin, *Les hommes du pétrole* (tome I.), Stock, Paris, 1991.

and trained to fight to the point of martyrdom[126].

Ibn Saud hated the chief of the Hashemites, Hussein, appointed Sharif of Mecca some years previously by Istanbul. It is likely that he detested him even more than he detested the British or the Turks! As far as he was concerned, the Hashemites, the Prophet Muhammad's tribe, were miscreants who should be forced to adhere to Wahhabism, which he considered to be the true path of Islam. Those who refused to live in accordance with Wahhabi principles were to be killed! The very thought that Hussein could one day govern Arabia and be considered the *Amir al-Mu'minin* (Commander of the Faithful) was unbearable for Ibn Saud.

The British created and exploited tribal enmities in order to further their interests. For them, Arabia was a strategically important region, the control of which was essential for the protection of the main routes into India. The growing influence of Wahhabism had been worrying the British for some time. Indeed, Wahhabi imams would frequently attempt to convert the Muslim communities in India and Malaysia. In the early 20th century, London and Shimla (the capital of British India) were not the only ones to covet this region. The Gulf was infested with German and Russian spies. British intelligence possessed several advanced observation posts in the region: Kuwait, Basra (Mesopotamia) and Bushehr (Persia).

Suitcase stuffed with sterling

---

[126] Osama bin Laden's Islamic movement was not too dissimilar to the *Ikhwan*. Both fought against the corruption of Saudi princes.

Philby, whose father owned a coffee plantation in Sri Lanka, was barely thirty when, in November 1915, he arrived in Basra as an intelligence officer for the British Colonial Office. His first mission immediately confronted him with the harsh realities of the British game in Arabia. Sir Percy Cox asked him to raise 20 000 pounds to finance the emir of Najd[127]. Cox, the British Consul-General for southern Persia (an area which encompassed the oil region of Arabistan and the Gulf islands) had been appointed Chief Political Officer for General Townshend's *Indian Expeditionary Force*, which had just landed at Fao in preparation to invade Mesopotamia.

Cox had met Ibn Saud on Tarout Island, close to the Al-Ahsa[128] region's coastline, and promised him substantial aid if he attacked Emir Rashid, a key ally to the Turks. It was here that Philby first heard about T.E. Lawrence, who was said to be roaming about the region with a suitcase stuffed full of pound notes. Lawrence had planned to bribe the chief of the Turkish forces and turn the tribal chiefs to the British cause. Philby considered that this was not the best way to proceed and that Lawrence had no chance of rescuing the Anglo-Indian expeditionary force, surrounded in Kut[129]. He was right: the British suffered a dreadful defeat, an unprecedented humiliation for the British Empire.

Following the capture of Baghdad by General Maude on 11 March 1917,

---

[127] Elizabeth Monroe, *Philby of Arabia,* Faber and Faber, Londres, 1973.

[128] When Ibn Saud conquered the region of Al-Ahsa in 1913, it became part of his kingdom of Najd. The majority of Arabs in this region are Shiites.

[129] During the Siege of Kut Al Amara (7 December 1915 – 29 April 1916), the British suffered 23,000 casualties. General Townshend was taken prisoner, along with 13,000 of his men.

Philby was put in charge of the secret service accounts. This post gave him an unparalleled view of all the various schemes, notably those aiming to annex the oil-rich vilayet of Mosul, which, according to the terms of the *Sykes-Picot Agreement*, belonged to the French. To keep abreast of developments in the conflict, but also mainly to further his own career plans, he would secretly study the confidential files in Percy Cox's office[130]! In the evening, disguised as a beggar, he would sneak off to the souks, on some unknown mission.

To Najd on camel-back

Cox needed a representative for his dealings with Ibn Saud. His secretary at the Arab Bureau, Gertrude Bell (nicknamed the *Desert Queen*), ensured that Philby, whom she found to be both competent and likeable, was given the post. For Philby, it was just the ticket. In December 1917, he arrived in Riyadh on camel-back. The Saud dynasty was, in principle, indefinitely beholden to Britain via a treaty which Ibn Saud had signed the year previously with Cox[131]. But the treaty made no mention of oil. It vaguely alluded to British interest in treasures buried beneath the sand[132]. The emir may well have adhered to the rigourous precepts of Wahhabism, but he was perfectly prepared to make an alliance with Christians in order to further the interests of Islam.

---

[130] Letter to May Philby, 11 November 1917, in *Philby, père et fils, la trahison dans le sang*, Anthony Cave Brown, Pygmalion, Paris, 1987.

[131] In 1912, Ibn Saud was, politically speaking, still manoeuvring between the Turkish and the British.

[132] *Philby, père et fils, la trahison dans le sang*, Anthony Cave Brown, Pygmalion, Paris, 1987.

As a true Bedouin, water was the only treasure he wanted to discover in the desert...

In January 1915, Captain William Shakespear, one of Britain's most illustrious secret agents, arrived in Nadj. His mission was to persuade Ibn Saud to support the British expedition in Mesopotamia. But not long after his arrival he was killed during the *Battle of Jarrab*. His remarkable bravery had impressed even the *Ikhwan*. Glubb Pasha, founder of the Arab Legion, would later portray him as something of knightly figure, a Richard Lionheart of the Nadj[133].

Ibn Saud, who kept a close eye on Hussein's game with the Arab Bureau in Cairo, was very happy to welcome a new British agent and guide him through the maze of Arab affairs. The emir of Najd, reputed to be a shrewd judge of character, was willing to trust this envoy who had carefully listened to him for hours and given him honest advice. The British in Arabia, he knew, always had several irons in the fire, and they had a very clear preference for Hussein who, they believed, would allow them to rule the country. But they hadn't banked on St John Philby.

Mission in Cairo

To secure the emir's friendship, Philby gave him 10 000 pounds, double his usual tribute. In the course of private conversation, he had promised to make him the King of Arabia. Without official approval – and this was

---

[133] Sir John Bagot Glubb (Glubb Pasha), *War in the Desert*, Hodder and Stoughton, London, 1960.

to later earn him much criticism - he proposed to persuade his Arab Bureau colleague, Ronald Storrs, responsible for leading negotiations with Hussein, to come to Riyadh, so he could see for himself that Ibn Saud was the only legitimate Arabian interlocutor for Britain. But since Storrs was absent, he had to go to Cairo with the archaeologist and part-time spy, David George Hogarth, in order to defend his views.

The First World War was coming to an end. The Bolsheviks had overthrown the Tsar. Leon Trotsky, their foreign affairs commissar, had revealed to the world the terms of the secret *Sykes-Picot Agreement*, which divided the Near East to the advantage of the great powers, but to the disadvantage of the Arabs. In Cairo, what Philby had to say was taken seriously. But he was told that supporting anybody other than Hussein was out of the question. The Emir of Najd would not be given the gold and guns he wanted. Indeed, London was in fact preparing to turn Ibn Rashid against the Turks. Hogarth, an influential member of London's secret *Round Table*[134], vehemently opposed Philby's proposals. To his mind, Philby was an inexperienced "young man"[135], who lacked discipline and a sense of commitment to the British Empire.

Philby felt betrayed. He loved his country, but not the way it was governed. What's more, he loathed the British establishment. Rebel and republican at heart, he found it increasingly difficult to conceal his

---

[134] The *Round Table* was a think-tank, as it would be termed today. It was founded in September 1909 by Lord Alfred Milner (1854 – 1925) to defend the British Empire and promote the expansionist ideas of Cecil Rhodes. It continues its activities today under various guises, the most notable of which is the *Royal Institute of International Affairs* (RIIA).

[135] Joseph Kostiner, *The Making of Saudi Arabia,* Oxford University Press, 1993.

contempt for the deceit and perfidy which was often said to characterise British leaders. Since Philby had been forbidden from entering the Hejaz region by Hussein, who did want a foreign agent supporting his worst enemy on his territory, he was forced to return to Najd via Bombay and Kuwait. He had failed to convince his superiors that Ibn Saud was worth meeting and was forced to tell the truth to the emir: a Wahhabi war against the Hashemites was of little interest to the British. Ibn Saud was outraged. Philby, despite his orders from Cairo, gave him 20 000 pounds to capture Ha'il, the capital of Ibn Rashid. But the assault failed.

On the front, the Ottoman Empire was collapsing. In Mesopotamia, the Anglo-Indian forces were rapidly advancing towards Mosul to create a *fait accompli*. Philby's mission in Najd was completed, and Cox ordered him to return to Britain. Instead of taking advantage of a long break in London, he made a bid to persuade the Foreign Office that it was better to support Saud than Hussein. This was in vein. The British were convinced that they could find not only oil in the Hejaz region but also King Solomon's mines! At the very most, they were prepared to pay Ibn Saud an annual tribute of 5000 pounds, a sum considered sufficient to pacify him.

The Foreign Office only took Philby's views seriously when the Ikhwan stormed the oasis of Al- Khurma in 1919, forcing the Sharif of Mecca's youngest son, Abdullah, to flee in his nightshirt. The moment had come for the Wahhabis to conquer Arabia. Philby received orders to immediately take the plane for Cairo and Jeddah. But Lawrence, who at the time was making a stopover at the Greek island of Heraklion, would not have a rival stand in the way of his ambitions. He pulled a few strings and had Philby sent back to Britain.

Return to Mesopotamia

Follwing the 1920 Iraqi revolution (financed by Rockefeller's[136] *Standard Oil*, according to *The Times*), Sir Percy Cox asked Philby to become adviser to Sayid Talib, the *Naqib*[137] of Basra and first Iraqi minister of interior. Bored by London life, he gladly accepted.

Before arriving by boat in Basra, he took advantage of a stopover in Uqair, a fortified port in the province of al-Hasa, where Cox had decided to meet Ibn Saud to convince him to capture the city of Ha'il and eliminate Ibn Rashid. The British no longer blamed him for having supported the Turks in the past and were determined to win him over. A year later, the Wahhabis murdered the Shammar leader, together with members of his family.

Though happy to see Gertrude Bell once again, his time in Baghdad was far from serene. Indeed, he had arrived in the city at a time of great turmoil. The British had hoped to quell public unrest by granting the country a semblance of independence. Prince Faisal, driven out of Syria by the French, was supported by Gertrude Bell and Lawrence, both of whom campaigned for him to be made the country's king. Opposed to this plan, Philby proposed the establishment of a republic with Sayid Talib[138] as its president. Talib had planned to annex Arabistan, believing

---

[136] Anthony Cave Brown, *Philby, père et fils, la trahison dans le sang*, Pygmalion, Paris, 1987.

[137] The British chose to negotiate with the *Naqib* as he was the political chief appointed on behalf of the Ottoman Empire.

[138] Lyon, W.A. *Kurds, Arabs and Britons*, Tauris Publishers, London, 2002. Colonel Wallace Lyon was the British Provincial Administrator and Administrative Inspector

that people on both sides of the Shatt al-Arab river belonged to the same tribes and that they were united in their hostility to the Persians. He ought to have kept this proposal a secret, because it was far too dangerous for the masters of the *Anglo-Persian Oil Company* and *The Iraq Petroleum Company*. In Cairo, Churchill, appointed Secretary of State for the Colonies, decreed that Iraq be led by Faisal and that Jordan be led by Abdullah.

Rigged election

The *Naqib's* influence was inconvenient for the British: he had to be removed from the Iraqi political arena. Percy Cox's wife and Gertrude Bell had the idea of inviting him to take afternoon tea. When he arrived, he was arrested and then immediately sent into exile in Ceylon. Philby was furious. They had cut his telephone so he could not stop Talib's arrest[139]. To get even, he immediately told Faisal, who had just arrived in Basra, that he was unwelcome in Iraq. He let his superiors know that Britain's rigged election was against his principles[140]. Faisal was, of course, elected king by 96% of the voters, most of whom had either been paid or subject to some form of pressure.

Philby never spoke to the *Desert Queen* again. Oil interests, he claimed, had taken priority over the promises of democracy made by General

---

for the Kurdish north of Iraq.

[139] Philby struggled to find a publisher for his *Mesopotage*, a book which exposed a number of secrets about British policy in Mesopotamia.

[140] Anthony Cave Brown, *Philby, père et fils, la trahison dans le sang*, Pygmalion, Paris, 1987.

Maude after his forces had captured Baghdad[141]. Iraqi oil remained British owned until the day it was nationalised by General al-Bakr in 1972[142]. But, with the second Gulf War in 2003, the sovereignty of Iraqi resources was once again jeopardised in a scenario not too dissimilar to that played out in the days of British Iraq.

Mission in Amman

Since his presence in Iraq was inconvenient for the British, Philby was posted to Amman in October 1921. His was to help Abdullah, Sharif Hussein's son, transform a piece of desert –given to him by way of consolation prize – into a nation, a country which later came to be known as Jordan[143]. In December 1922, he accompanied the king to London. The monarch requested that his kingdom be granted full sovereignty as well as membership of the *League of Nations* (LN). In addition, he proposed the creation of a union between Jordan and Hejaz. Needless to say, his suggestion was rejected. Being shrewd, Philby had understood that Ibn Saud would one day rule Arabia and would have swiftly put paid to a confederation of this sort.

Philby's relations with Abdullah soured when the king demolished a sixth-century Byzantine basilica in Amman, in order to construct a mosque. Enraged, Philby accused him of vandalism[144]. The British

---

[141] General Maude had promised Iraqis democracy and the right to self-governance, just as George W. Bush had done in 2003.

[142] General Ahmed Hassan al-Bakr (1912 – 1982) was the president of Iraq from 1968 to 1979.

[143] Jordan was known as Transjordan at the time.

[144] Elizabeth Monroe, *Philby of Arabia*, Faber and Faber, London, 1973.

authorities discovered that Philby had been sending messages to Ibn Saud without the necessary permission[145]. The British High Commissioner in Jerusalem, Herbert Samuel, was Philby's supervisor. Philby had taken a disliking to him, as he believed he promoted the Zionist colonisation of Palestine[146]. Unable to bear the situation any longer, he resigned in January 1924 and returned to Britain, infuriated and disillusioned.

Attempted poisoning?

Philby urgently needed to find a new job. By chance, Remy Ernest Fisher, an old acquaintance from his days in Cairo, was looking to obtain an oil concession in Hejaz. Ibn Saud had not yet taken a keen interest in oil. In 1922, the New Zealand born British geologist Frank Holmes, nicknamed *Abu Naft* (the Father of Oil) by the Arabs, had tried to convince the emir that the oilfield he discovered in Bahrain extended as far as the Al-Hasa province. Holmes had connections to the Texan oil industry and was an associate of the US Secretary of Commerce, Herbert Hoover[147], who urged American companies to cross swords with the British in Mesopotamia. Sceptical and more interested in the exploration for water, Ibn Saud awarded him a concession. Philby, too, discussed oil with the emir, but only to advise him to never get involved with British companies if he wished to remain independent.

---

[145] Anthony Cave Brown, *Philby, père et fils, la trahison dans le sang*, Pygmalion, Paris, 1987.

[146] *The Balfour Declaration* announced Britain's support for the creation of "national home for the Jewish people" in Palestine.

[147] The Republican Herbert Hoover was elected US president in November 1928.

They were, he told him, too closely linked to the Crown and often confused finance with politics[148]. Philby, nontheless, ensured that Fisher obtained the concession.

Philby learnt that Ibn Saud had captured Ha'il and that Ibn Rashid, together with his family, had been killed. The emir was now determined to take Mecca, the justification for this being that the Wahhabis had been banned from making their *hajj*. Sharif Hussein had abdicated in favour of his eldest son, Ali, and had set sail for Aqaba, his treasure hidden on his yacht in an oil barrel[149]. Perfidiously, the British had ordered both of Hussein's sons, who ruled Jordan and Iraq, not to grant him refuge. A few days later, Mecca was captured, but there was no bloodshed. In Jeddah, the British consul kept a watchful eye on Philby, who was warned that his pension would be withdrawn if he attempted to support Ibn Saud.

We will never know if Basra's former *Naqib*, Sayid Talib[150], who had defected – yet again - to become Ali of Hejaz's adviser for Iraqi affairs, had attempted to kill Philby by serving him poisoned caviar on Christmas Eve. Nor will we ever know if the doctor, who had been called to relieve Philby's agony, had deliberately used an infected needle. But one thing is certain: Philby was violently sick and suffering from the early stages of gangrene. He was rushed to hospital in Aden. After having made a recovery, he returned to London, broke and crippled

---

[148] Jean Lartéguy, *Tout l'or du diable*, Presses de la Cité, Paris, 1974.

[149] Anthony Cave Brown, *Philby, père et fils, la trahison dans le sang*, Pygmalion, Paris, 1987.

[150] Before the British occupation of Mesopotamia, Sayid Talib had been a fervent supporter of the Ottoman Empire.

with debt.

Sharqieh Ltd.

Philby again made contact with Fisher who, upon his advice, created *Sharqieh Limited* to carry out the exploration of the Saudi subsoil. He returned to Arabia in November 1925 to ask Ibn Saud for a concession. As a token of their friendship, the emir gave him *Beit Baghdadi*, the palace of the former Turkish governor. But as far as other matters were concerned, he asked Philby to wait. The emir was preparing to attack both Medina and Jeddah, and he needed to reassure the *Ikhwan* who were against any dealings with the West.

At the same time, the emir had to allay the fears of the Muslim world, which dreaded a repeat of the sort of sectarian violence seen in 1805, when the Wahhabis desecrated the *Al-Masjid an-Nabawi* (the Prophet's Mosque) in Medina and plundered its treasure. During the raid, they destroyed the tomb of Muhammad's first wife (Khadija) and that of one of his uncles (Abu Talib, worshipped by the Shia Muslims), who had raised Muhammad following his father's death. In the end, they were dealt a decisive blow by the Khedive[151] of Egypt, Muhammad Ali, who led an expedition to recapture the holy sites. Diriyah, the Wahhabi capital, was razed to the ground in 1818 by a battalion commanded by Vaissière, a French army officer. Abdullah bin Saud, their emir, surrendered. Taken to Istanbul, he was beheaded before a baying crowd. His corpse was then fed to the dogs. A cousin of the emir, Turki,

---

[151] The Khedive was the viceroy of Egypt under Ottoman rule. The title became hereditary.

restored Wahhabism and adopted Riyadh as the new capital.

On 6 December 1925, Medina was captured, followed by Jeddah on the 28th. Philby obtained Ibn Saud's permission to open a branch of *Sharqieh Ltd*[152] in Jeddah. At first, his commercial activities were minimal. Always on the look-out for opportunities to coax Arabia out of its isolation, he persuaded the emir to accept the letters of credence of Hassim Hakimoff Khan, Moscow's man in Jeddah. One can just imagine the Foreign Office's reaction!

The *Ikhwan*, increasingly critical of Ibn Saud, staged a revolt. They accused Ibn Saud of favouring Christians as well as promoting modernist views. In 1929, they suffered their first defeat. Their leaders were imprisoned and one of their towns, al-Ghat, was destroyed[153]. By 1930, following a battle personally led by Ibn Saud, they had been completely eliminated from the political game. Philby, now having the necessary leeway, went to Cairo to convince the United States to officially recognise the Saudi kingdom. But it was still too early.

Abdullah Philby

After having been circumcised, Philby converted to Wahhabi Islam in Mecca. The ceremony took place before the king who gave him the name of Abdullah, "the slave of God" and appointed him to his private

---

[152] The company was not alone in its exploration efforts. *Midian Ltd* also believed it could find oil in the northern Arabia, in an area once surveyed by Richard Francis Burton, the 19th century British explorer who, disguised as an Afghan doctor, made a clandestine pilgrimage to Mecca in 1853.

[153] Gary Troeller, *The Birth of Saudi Arabia,* Frank Cass, London, 1976.

council. In 1931, accompanied by Ibn Saud, he made his pilgrimage to Mecca, the fifth pillar of Islam.

The British consul in Jeddah, convinced that Philby's conversion to Islam would increase his potential to undermine British policy in the region, hurried to alert the Foreign Office. Philby was accused of being a supporter of Pan-Arabism, a movement which sought to restore the Arab Empire under one leader[154]. How could London bring him to heel? Threatening to withdraw his pension hadn't worked. Arrest him for treason, assassinate him? The British were far from adverse to these ideas and, as we will see, were just waiting for the right moment.

Philby's conversion to Islam meant he could freely trade under the nose of what remained of the *Ikhwan*. He set up a *Ford* dealership in Arabia. In addition, he worked as a sales representative for *Singer*, the sewing machine manufacturer, and *Socony-Vacuum* (later renamed *Mobil*). He even set up the first Saudi radio station. But Philby was certainly in no rush to make a profit. Indeed, the contracts he signed with the kingdom were only paid some twelve years later, during the Second World War.

American infiltration

Badly managed and broke, Ibn Saud's kingdom was on the verge of bankruptcy. Only the Soviet Union, upon the advice of Hassim Hakimoff, agreed to supply petrol and other essential manufactured goods. During a car journey made with the emir, Philby, who had resigned from his

---

[154] Anthony Cave Brown, *Philby, père et fils, la trahison dans le sang*, Pygmalion, Paris, 1987.

private council to protest at the kingdom's disastrous economic policy, assured him that the country was a potential gold mine. The only way the country could make a solid economic recovery was by exploiting its mineral assets. Since Ibn Saud lacked the financial and technical means to do so, he would be obliged to rely on the help of foreign companies. But Philby reassured the king by quoting the Koran[155]: *"Allah will not change the condition of a people until they change what is in themselves."* With this, Ibn Saud agreed. Philby immediately suggested that he invite Charles Crane, an American multi-millionaire and philanthropist.

In July 1919, President Woodrow Wilson had appointed Crane to head an official inquiry into what the different ethnic groups in the Near East thought about national independence. Concealed behind the American rhetoric of self-determination, however, lay the ambition to take the place of the European powers. The British had stopped Crane's commission from visiting Mesopotamia. Despite this, the commission relayed the demands for independence made by the Kurdish and Arab communities in the region. Furthermore, it recommended that Lebanon, which enjoyed a certain degree of autonomy, remain within Syria, and criticised the *Balfour Declaration*. In 1929, Crane had attempted to enter Arabia via Kuwait, but he was ambushed by the *Ikhwan* and one of his friends was killed.

In 1931, Crane accepted the king's invitation. Psychologically astute, he made no mention of oil and discussed water instead. After having made a presentation at *Beit Baghdadi*, Philby's residence, he asked Ibn Saud

---

[155] St John Philby, *Arabian Jubilee*, Robert Hale Ltd, London, 1952.

to support his engineer, Karl Twitchell, in his efforts to locate groundwater sources in the Jeddah region. A month later, it was done. The city soon had running water, and Twitchell was authorised to continue drilling, but this time for oil.

Rub–al-Khali

Charles Crane's visit marked the beginning of American infiltration into Arabia. Satisfied at having once again clipped the British lion's claws, Philby embarked upon a long cherished dream: cross the *Rub-al-Khali* (Empty Quarter), a hostile and largely unexplored desert, whose surface area exceeds that of France. It was here that archaeologists had attempted to locate the fabled lost city known as *Iram of the Pillars*, founded, according to the Koran, by Noah's great-grandson.

In February 1932, having had no news from Philby for over two months, it was thought that he had died of thirst during his exploration. But he made it back in the end, accompanied by his Wahhabi escort. They had survived over fifty days without water by drinking the sap of rare desert plants, pouring the last drops of their brackish water reserves onto the nostrils of the camels to keep them moving. The British media heralded his exploration as a triumph, an exploit comparable to Lindbergh's solo transatlantic flight. On his way back to Arabia, he visited various European capitals, including Berlin and Rome. According to documents found among the KGB archives following the collapse of the Soviet Union, Philby had met Hitler and Mussolini[156].

---

[156] Anthony Cave Brown, *Philby, père et fils, la trahison dans le sang*, Pygmalion,

Oil concessions for the Americans

At a time when *Sharqieh Ltd* was acting as a representative for *Marconi* in order to bolster its revenue, the United States introduced Philby to their Assistant Secretary of State, Francis Loomis, who wanted Ibn Saud to open the doors of his kingdom to American oil companies.

While in Jeddah, Philby started to communicate with *Standard Oil*, using a secret code. In May 1932, oil had been found in Bahrain, and this discovery suddenly increased interest in the desolate Al-Hasa region. Philby, in liason with Twitchell, contacted *Standard Oil of California (Socal)*, which was not bound by the *Red Line Agreement*[157], according to which a company needed the unanimous approval of all the other signatories before undertaking exploration in the region. Before allowing the Americans to drill for oil, Ibn Saud stipulated certain conditions, which were exorbitant for the time: a loan of £100 000 in gold and an annual stipend of £5000. The king was prepared to give priority to the British if they accepted these terms. In May 1933, a contract was signed with *Socal* which included commission for Philby. He duly informed the British Minister to Saudi Arabia that an American and not a British company had secured the concession. Upon hearing the news, the minister reacted as if he had been *"thunderstruck"* and it was said that

---

Paris, 1987.

[157] Since Kuwait was generally considered to be Britain's domain, it was excluded from the terms of the *Red Line Agreement*, which otherwise applied to all countries in the Near East.

"his face darkened with anger and disappointment."[158]

The next day, the kingdom - twinned with both Hejaz and Najd as well as its dependent regions - became officially known as *Saudi Arabia*. In August 1933, a ship came to dock at Jeddah. Chartered by *Socal*, its cargo of gold sovereigns was deposited at the state-owned bank, which had been specially created for the occasion. In 1936, *Socal* joined forces with the *Texas Company* (later known as *Texaco)* to form the group *California-Texas*, or *Caltex*. Two years later, an oilfield of vast potential was discovered in Dhahran. In 1944, the company changed its name to become the *Arabian American Oil Company*, better known as *Aramco*[159].

Philby's plan for Palestine

Philby was brimming with energy and ideas. In 1938, thanks to his good relations with fascist Italy, he had weapons and ammunition delivered to the Saudi kingdom. A year later, at his home in London, he brought together Chaim Weizmann, president of the *World Zionist Organisation*, and David Ben-Gurion, leader of both the *Haganah* and the *Jewish Agency*. He informed them that Ibn Saud was prepared to accept the presence of a large number of Jewish settlers in Palestine, provided that his son Faisal be made king. A month later, in the presence of Fuad Bey Hamza, the Saudi foreign affairs official, he explained that, should they agree to his proposal, he would need £20 million to

---

[158] Quoted in Daniel Yergin, *Les hommes du pétrole* (tome I.), Stock, Paris, 1991.

[159] In 1948, *Aramco* opened its capital to *Standard Oil of New Jersey* (later known as *Exxon*) and *Socony Vacuum* (later *Mobil*).

establish a new home for the Palestinians.

Leaked to the press, this curious initiative failed and the Saudi king, embarrassed, was forced to deny all knowledge of the affair. Was this an attempt to isolate Weizmann in the Zionist movement? Or was this an attempt to help British troops, battling with *Irgun* terrorists? In any case, this strange episode was later used by Philby's enemies to claim that he was a Jewish spy.

Three months prison

In 1939, Philby stood for election as a member of the *British People's Party* (BPP) which campaigned for peace with Germany and negotiations with Hitler[160]. He failed to win a seat in Parliament. Interestingly, at the end of the Second World War, even though the *Colonial Office* had given serious though to having him shot, the *Secret Intelligence Service* sought to recruit him to oversee British counter-espionage operations in the Middle East! But this idea was soon abandoned.

In Arabia, exactly as Ibn Saud had requested, he provoked the French Minister Plenipotentiary to Jeddah by declaring that Hitler was *"a great man"*, comparing him to Jesus and Muhammad! As an invitee of the *California Standard Oil Company*, he left for the United Sates, in order to campaign against the war. *The Indian Office* then sent London a report, according to which Philby was a *"... reptile who had long been a critic of British policy in the Near East."* On 29 July 1940, while stopping-

---

[160] Not to be confused with Oswald Mosley's *British Union of Fascists*.

over in Bombay, he was arrested, repatriated and imprisoned on the grounds of his alleged support for the Nazis[161]. He came in for severe criticism for his comments and, in particular, was condemned for having urged Ibn Saud to withdraw his assets from London banks.

He was finally released in February 1941[162], after having appeared before a special tribunal. During his hearing, he detailed the damage done by British imperialism in the Middle East. The jury ruled that he was neither disloyal to his country nor politically dangerous. Nonetheless, his passport was confiscated until the end of the war.

Prior to the conflict, the British had been somewhat parsimonious in granting financial aid to Ibn Saud. However, fearing that the United States would take advantage of the war to secure a foothold in the region, Britain decided to pay generous sums to Ibn Saud. The Americans did likewise. This marked the beginning of the Anglo-American version of the *Great Game* in the Middle East.

For much of the Second World War, Arabia chose to be neutral. It was only much later that Arabia declared war against Germany so as to figure among the victors! In July 1945, the Home Office, responsible for the supervision of British counter-espionage efforts, agreed to give Philby his passport back. With this, he immediately left for Cairo, where he made the flight to Jeddah in Ibn Saud's plane. He resumed his duties as a member of the king's private council. Happy to see him again, the

---

[161] Bruce Page, Philip Knightley et David Leitch, *Philby, l'Intelligence Service aux mains d'un agent soviétique*, Robert Laffont, 1968.

[162] According to some, he was released thanks to the intervention of George Lloyd, Secretary State for the Colonies.

king offered him Rozy, a young Baluchi slave, chosen among his harem. As authorised by Sharia[163], she became his second wife.

The Quincy Agreement

On 14 February 1945, Franklin Roosevelt, returning from the *Yalta Conference*, met Ibn Saud aboard the cruiser *US Quincy*, docked in the Suez's Great Bitter Lake[164]. According to the only interpreter aboard, oil was scarcely mentioned oil, as if the agreement which would come to bind Arabia to the United States was purely a matter of friendship. The American president offered Ibn Saud an aircraft, a *DC3*[165] equipped with a swivel-chair so that he could always face Mecca. Roosevelt broached the question of Jewish immigration into Palestine. The king believed that, once the war was over, all settlers should return to their respective home countries or to the Axis countries, adding that reparations should be paid by the war criminals and not the Palestinians who were not to blame for this conflict[166]. Back in Washington, Roosevelt wrote to Ibn Saud, confirming that nothing would be decided on Palestine without

---

[163] After marrying in Britain, Philby had several children. His son Harold, better known as Kim, became internationally famous when it was revealed that he was a member of a Soviet spy-ring known as the *Cambridge Five*.

[164] Aboard the *USS Quincy*, Roosevelt also held meetings with King Farouk of Egypt and Emperor Haile Selassie of Ethiopia. The future kings of Saudi Arabia, Prince Faisal and his brother Prince Khalid, had met Vice-President Harry Truman the previous year in the US.

[165] In 1936, Prince Faisal was officially received in Italy, where he had signed an aeronautical agreement.

[166] Hamadi Redissi, *Le pacte du Najd*, Le Seuil, Paris, 2007.

having first consulted the Arabs.

Roosevelt died two months later, just after having appointed Colonel William Eddy as the American consul in Jeddah. Eddy, who acted as the interpreter aboard the *Quincy*, was born in Lebanon (Tyre). During the war, he was the operations chief for the *Office of Strategic Services (OSS)*, the CIA's predecessor. In 1947, he worked as a consultant for *Aramco* and returned to work for the intelligence service during the 1958 American invasion of Lebanon. Harry Truman, successor to Roosevelt, supported the creation of Israel, a decision he justified by explaining that there were not a sufficient number of Arab voters in America for their objections to be properly taken into consideration!

The Explorer

Though having passed sixty, Philby had hardly settled down. He continued to carry out short missions abroad for the king and threw himself into the exploration of Arabia. In 1947, he was sent to India where he was welcomed by Lord Mountbatten, the viceroy. To Philby's delight, Mountbatten was preparing for the independence of the country, which was soon to be divided with the creation of Pakistan. In Arabia, he methodically explored the north of the kingdom in order to map its contours, and searched for traces of both lost civilisations and pre-Islamic Jewish tribes. In 1951, accompanied by Canon Ryckmans from the University of Louvain, he penetrated into the heart of Yemen's Hadhramaut desert region. Together, they covered some 5400km and saw from afar the ancient ruins at Marib, which was once the capital of the Sabaean kingdom. But they were unable to explore the site, as the

142 | P a g e

Imam of Yemen had forbidden all foreigners from entering the area, an exclusion which applied particularly to friends of Ibn Saud! They brought back photos of some 15 000 pre-Islamic and Sabaean inscriptions[167].

Banished from Arabia

Ibn Saud, considered by Philby to be the greatest Arab since the Prophet Muhammad[168], died on 9 November 1953. Following his death, Philby's relations with Prince Saud, the king's successor, soured. Philby disapproved of Arabian princes who mimicked the worst of Western practices and criticised the corruption triggered by the sudden inflow of petrodollars. His relations with *Aramco* deteriorated, too, as he severely condemned the company's control of the country[169]. His highly critical article published by *Foreign Affairs* in April 1954, followed by a conference given to *Aramco* directors in Dhahran, enraged King Saud. Philby had gone too far: he was banished from Arabia. He moved to Lebanon, but he found that the world had changed. An article he wrote for *The Sunday Times* decried how oil had sullied the wellspring of Arabian chivalry[170].

During a conference at the *American University of Beirut*, Philby had excoriated King Saud's management of the country. But the monarch had understood that Philby would do less harm in Riyadh where he

---

[167] Jacques Benoist-Méchin, *Ibn Saud ou la naissance d'un royaume*, Albin Michel, Paris, 1970.

[168] St John Philby, *Sa'udi Arabia,* Ernest Benn, London, 1955.

[169] In 1980, the Saudi government finally took control of *Aramco* and, in 1988, changed its name by royal decree to *Saudi Aramco*.

[170] André Falk, *Visa pour l'Arabie,* Gallimard, Paris, 1958.

could keep an eye on him. After two years of exile, then, Philby was welcomed back into the kingdom and reappointed to the king's private council.

God, I'm bored!

In the summer of 1960, Philby, as a member of the *Royal Geographical Society*, was invited to Moscow to attend the *25th International Congress of Orientalists*, suspected by the Western intelligence services as being a conference for Communist spies. On the return journey, he stopped over in Lebanon to see his son Kim, a correspondent for the *Observer*. On 30 September 1960, following a rowdy party organised in his honour, he collapsed with a heart attack. He was 76 years old. In hospital, his dying words were *"God, I'm bored!"*. He was buried by his son in the Bashura cemetery in Beirut. His gravestone bears his son's short inscription *"Greatest of Arabian explorers"*.

Chapter X

THOMAS EDWARD LAWRENCE, THE OVEREXPOSED SPY

Thomas Edward Lawrence – *Lawrence of Arabia* – ought to have been named Chapman of Arabia. Indeed, it was only later in life that he discovered that his father, Thomas Chapman, a landowner in the Irish county of Westmeath, had in fact changed his name to leave his wife who refused to divorce. His parents were therefore not married. What's more, his mother was none other than the former nanny to his five half-sisters. Lawrence was born on 16 August 1888 in Tremadog, Wales, where his father lived at the time. The family frequently changed homes, moving from Scotland to Dinard in Brittany before finally settling in Oxford, where Lawrence completed his education.

From a very early age, Lawrence was fascinated by archaeology, heraldry and medieval monuments. In 1906, he cycled around Brittany and the northern Loire region in search of cathedrals and castles. His spiritual outlook had no doubt been shaped by the gospel teaching of Canon A.M.W. Christopher, a close friend of the family, and his time in the Scouts. In 1906, after having attempted to join the army, he began his studies at Jesus College, Oxford, where, upon the request of his father, the archaeologist David Hogarth and David Margoliouth (Laudian

Professor of Arabic) watched over him. Both were to have a decisive influence on his life.

David Hogarth, spiritual father

Hogarth, in his late forties at the time, would often advise British intelligence on the countries he had explored. Fluent in several languages, including Arab and Turkish, he had covered the Turko-Greek war for the *Times*. In addition, he had carried out several archaeological expeditions in Egypt and Asia Minor, and worked as a curator at the *Ashmolean Musuem*. He belonged to the *Round Table*, a somewhat esoteric society created in 1881 by Cecil Rhodes, the magnate who founded Rhodesia (modern-day Zimbabwe) and who, behind the scenes, advocated the establishment of a "new world order", led by an Anglo-Saxon government. This programme for the world brings to mind the speeches made by George H.W. Bush during the first Gulf War. Following the death of Rhodes in 1902, Lord Milner, former governor of South Africa, succeeded him, and the *Round Table*, recruiting its members uniquely from the upper echelons of society, became a secretive and powerful lobby group - as well the source of all nightmares for conspiracy theorists!

David Hogarth held democracy in some contempt, believing that the world was akin to a chessboard upon which the British Empire found only interests. For Hogarth, the end always justified the means. Today's allies should be viewed as tomorrow's enemies. He used his contacts and position at Oxford to recruit what the historian Arnold Toynbee termed 'human tools'[171] capable of securing the supremacy of the British Empire. Lawrence, whose hidden qualities had been accurately gauged by Hogarth, was to be one of these tools. With this in mind, Hogarth trained him. He supervised his studies, immersing him in the Arthurian legend.

He then directed him to study manuals of chivalry and the finer tactical aspects of the great battles, the details of which he then had to discuss with experts in the field. This knowledge, unknown to those who would later question his military capabilities, allowed him to command the Arab tribesmen who captured Aqaba and harassed the Turkish army along the Hejaz railway.

In 1908, after having toured France in search of castles and battlefields, Lawrence chose as the theme for his thesis the influence of the Crusades on military architecture. He learnt Arabic to a rudimentary level and sought the advice of Charles Doughty, famous for his *Travels in Arabia Deserta*, and set off for Syria the following year.

It is often thought that Lawrence began his career in British intelligence in 1911 before his departure to Carchemish where, using the cover of archaeological research, he would photograph the progress of the Berlin-Baghdad railway. Others say he began his intelligence career later in 1914, when he joined the army. But nothing could be further from the truth. In fact, Lawrence left for Syria with various safe conduct passes, signed by the former Viceroy of India, Lord Curzon, who tended to view the Persian Gulf as a British inland sea. In addition, British

---

[171] Arnold Toynbee, *Acquaintances,* Oxford University Press, London, 1967.

intelligence had handed Lawrence various maps to be redrawn. Lawrence covered some 1700 km by foot, and updated the service's maps en route[172].

Lawrence successfully completed his studies in 1910. Thanks to a research grant, he travelled with Hogarth and Leonard Woolley to Carchemish, where, aside from executing his intelligence mission, he refined his Arabic, learnt Bedouin customs and became familiar with the ways of desert life.

When war was declared against Germany in 1914, he was selected, along with Woolley, to assist Captain Newcombe, an officer from British military intelligence in Cairo. He was to update maps of Sinai and Negev and then carry out a reconnaissance mission in the Taurus Mountains, where the Germans had built a road to facilitate the construction of their Berlin-Baghdad railway. In August, Hogarth found him a post in *MO4*, the *British War Office's Geographical Section*, one of the numerous guises of British intelligence.

Antonin Jaussen, Dominican Father on Her Majesty's Service

Hogarth and Lawrence were not the only ones interested in Ottoman railways. In 1907 and 1910, two Dominican Fathers, Antonin Jaussen and Raphael Savignac, both educated at the *École biblique de Jérusalem* (EBJ), used their archaeological explorations at the oasis in

---

[172] Phillip Knightley et Colin Simpson, *Les vies secrètes de Lawrence d'Arabie*, Robert Laffont, Paris, 1970.

Mada'in Saleh, in northern Arabia, to mask their surveillance of the Hejaz railway construction. France was determined not to be left out of the game ever since their *Deuxième Bureau* (military intelligence) had learnt that the Austrian Alois Musil[173], an EBJ educated priest and spy, had reconnoitred these regions on behalf of the Emperor of Austria. Using the diplomatic bag, weapons were supplied to the Dominicans, who then passed these to the Bedouin chiefs.

When the conflict broke out in December 1914, the Turks expelled Jaussen from Jerusalem, together with 300 monks and nuns from enemy countries. While heading for Palermo, his boat was seized by the British. Since the intelligence officers found him to be particularly well-informed, they had him transferred to another boat, headed for Egypt. Aboard, he recounted to British military intelligence officers all he had seen in Syria[174]. With a certain relish, he reassured a British colonel that his sources were better than his. His informants helped him for the love of France, whereas those working for Britain or Turkey were motivated uniquely by profit, spying for the highest bidder. He was invited to join British intelligence. He accepted immediately, without even waiting for the necessary authorisation from his superiors[175], and left his religious order to join the French army. Today, we have the proof that he had in fact been in contact with Leonard Woolley for quite a while.

---

[173] Aloïs Musil, Czech orientalist and explorer, abandoned his theological studies in Jerusalem in order to focus on the study of ancient Islamic sites in Syria.

[174] *Bulletin assomptionniste*, n° 86, 12/1/1915.

[175] Dominique Avron, *Les frères prêcheurs en Orient,* Cerf, Paris, 2005.

The Arab Bureau

In 1915, Lieutenant Lawrence stood out in Cairo mostly due to his capacity for hard work and his somewhat scruffy appearance. He had gathered vital topographical data and created a network of informants. In addition, he maintained regular contact with Arab nationalists and interrogated prisoners of war, asking them not only for details on the Turkish army but also – and this is what interested him the most - on the attitude of the various religious sects and secret societies in Arab countries[176]. Masonic lodges in Turkey had been used to great effect by the *Young Turks* to stage their revolution. While they attempted to promote Freemasonry in the Ottoman provinces, the Arabs founded in Constantinople their own secret society, known as *Al-Mountada al-Abadi*, which, aside from its ostensible cultural and social aims, secretly led nationalist activities in Syria[177].

On 1 January 1916, General Clayton officially announced the existence of the Arab Bureau, presenting it as an agency tasked with the provision of information to the Foreign Office. Immediately, to great surprise, Field Marshal William Robertson, Chief of the Imperial General Staff, sent Lawrence to bribe Halil Pasha, whose forces had encircled General Townshend's 6th Poona Division in Kut. His selection for the Kut mission was in no small part due to the intervention of the Arab Bureau's director, David Hogarth, who continued to promote his protégé. Lawrence was to hand over a million pounds to Halil in exchange for

---

[176] Janet Wallach, *La reine du désert*, Bayard Éditions, Paris, 1997.

[177] Joseph Hajjar, *L'Europe et les destinées du Proche-Orient* (tome IV), Éditions Tlass, Damas, 1996.

the conditional surrender of the British troops, i.e. their liberation. Halil refused, even though the sum offered was doubled.

Based in Cairo's Savoy hotel, the Arab Bureau opened the Sharif of Mecca's letters, as well as those of his sons, and recruited nationalists prepared to support the British. Money being the sinews of war, the Arab Bureau's coffers overflowed with sovereigns and pounds, and this cash came to play a vital role in the seduction of recalcitrant Arab tribes refusing to deal with the British infidel[178]. Hogarth penned a poem[179] describing his secret service fiefdom:

> *Do you know the Arab Bureau? Clayton stability, Symes versatility, Cornwallis is practical, Dawnay syntactical, Mackintosh havers, And Fielding palavers Macindoe easy, And Wordie not breezy, Lawrence licentiate to dream and to dare, And yours faithfully* bon à tout faire.

The Arab Revolt

Lawrence's mission in Mesopotamia failed. General Townshend and his troops were forced to surrender and were interned in a Turkish prison camp. In Basra, Lawrence had asked various politicians to support the British, but they all refused. A turning point, however, came on 10 June 1916, not long after Lawrence had returned to Cairo, with news of the Arab Revolt led by Hussein, the Sharif of Mecca.

---

[178] Hogarth had originally wanted to call the Arab Bureau the "Islamic Bureau", so as to distinguish it from similar bodies in North Africa.

[179] *Clayton to Hall*, 13 January 1916, PRO, Foreign Office. 882/2, ARB 16/5. Quoted in Bruce Westrate, *The Arab Bureau*, Pennsylvania State University Press, 1992.

In October, Lawrence was sent to Jeddah, as part of a mission led by Ronald Storrs, to probe the intentions of the Emir Abdullah, the Sharif of Meccca's eldest son, close to the Arab nationalist movement. In 1909, the Egyptian nationalist Aziz al-Masri, an army officer who helped establish the *al-Muntada al-Adabi* (The Literary Club), created the secret group known as *Al-Qahtaniyya* - named after Qhatan, the legendary forefather of the Arabs – and then another nationalist organisation named *Al Ahd* (The Covenant Society), whose membership was made up largely of Iraqi officers. Around the same time, in 1911, a group of young Arab nationalists in Paris created *Al Arabiyya al-Fatat* (The Young Arab Society). From a distance, Lawrence kept a vigilant eye on the activities of these Arab secret societies which, in 1915, unified their efforts to break free from the Ottoman yoke[180], accusing the Turkish nationalists of seeking to "Turkify" the Arab population.

Lawrence did not get along with Abdullah, finding him to be a hedonist and too intelligent for his designs. So he chose Faisal, whom he found to be more pragmatic and open to the world[181]. The Hejaz army was formed with the Hashemite prince as its commander. But Lawrence was not the only foreigner in this unit. He was obliged to cooperate with Colonel Edouard Brémond[182] and a French detachment, comprised mainly of North African riflemen and spahis. For Lawrence, the *Quai*

---

[180] Mahmoud Kamel, *L'arabisme*, Organisation Égyptienne Générale du Livre, Le Caire, 1977.

[181] Lawrence, T. E., *Les Sept Piliers de la sagesse*, Payot, Paris, 1936.

[182] Born in 1868, Colonel Edouard Brémond, France's mission commander in Hejaz, had served in Madagascar, Algeria and Morocco, where he ran the Moroccan port police. In 1913, during France's Moroccan campaign, he was appointed chief of military intelligence by General Paul Prosper Henrys.

d'Orsay was an obstacle to the creation of an Arab kingdom. He therefore systematically sidelined the French contingent.

Lawrence's career as the self-proclaimed champion of the Arab cause began with the capture of Aqaba on 6 July 1917. Determined not to have what he viewed as being his victory snatched from him, he dashed to Cairo, covering 250km in 48 hours, so as to announce the news in person. In truth, however, the victory belonged to the Howeitat leader Auda Abu-Tayeh, who had planned the attack and convinced the tribes to join him. Of course, Lawrence had valiantly participated in the first assault. But firing somewhat haphazardly, he had accidentally shot his own camel and fell to the ground, remaining unconscious during the entire battle.

In August, General Allenby took control of Faisal's army. He gave Lawrence carte blanche to harass the Turkish and two thousand pounds in gold for his propaganda campaign. While planning various raids on the Hejaz railway line, Lawrence also found the time to write a manual entitled *27 Articles*, his guide on how to manipulate the Bedouin.

France demands its share of Syria

As Allenby's expedition force and Faisal's army drew closer and closer to Damascus, the *Sykes-Picot Agreement* increasingly came to be called into question. So an Anglo-French committee was created to ensure that the terms were respected. In 1917, Allenby was appointed to work for François-Georges Picot and Sykes.

On 8 August, Louis Massignon made his first encounter with Lawrence, who, upon meeting him, quipped that they were both "masked archaeologists", i.e. spies. Lawrence had made some enquiries into Massignon's background, for he feared that Faisal would favour him. In October, when General Allenby approved Massignon's appointment to Faisal's general staff, Lawrence vetoed the decision and even threatened to resign.

Georges Picot asked the *Quai d'Orsay* for a generous line of credit so that Massignon could, via the allocation of subsidies, lead the Arabs to believe that France was fully engaged in the conflict! Moreover, Massignon was temporarily promoted to captain, so as to give him the same rank as Lawrence. But Lawrence, who already objected to the conspicuous presence of other British officers, certainly did not want a French rival close by in Damascus. Massignon, then, was dispatched to advise the general staff of a short-lived Anglo-French Arab Legion. Like Lawrence, some of his time was spent interrogating prisoners of war. Arab members of the Ottoman army were persuaded – or paid where necessary - to defect. In his report sent to the *Quai d'Orsay* in late October, Massignon highlighted the resurgence of nationalist sentiment among the members of the Arab Legion. Their dream was to liberate Arab countries, including those of North Africa. This demand, he wrote, was idealist and, therefore, difficult to support[183].

The case of Louis Massignon

It was ill-advised to insinuate that Massignon's archaeological research in Arab countries on behalf of the *Quai d'Orsay* and the French Ministry

---

[183] Keryell, Jacques, *Louis Massignon et ses contemporains*, Karthala, Paris, 1997.

of Colonies[184] was mererly a cover for espionage. The professor would fly into a rage. Nonetheless, he had been suspected of being a spy ever since his first visits to Egypt and Mesopotamia in 1907 and in 1908. He was appointed in 1906 to Cairo's *French Institute for Eastern Archaeology*. Excavations interested him less than the activities of the Senussi[185] sect, a Sufi order which had radical anti-colonial tendencies. He would often dress as a *fellah*, in order to frequent various insalubrious bars where, as he later revealed, he made his first homosexual encounters. A year later, in Mesopotamia, he turned to religion. For his thesis, he chose to study Mansur al-Hallaj, a Persian Sufi preacher who, in 922, was decapitated for heresy in Baghdad.[186] He travelled to Baghdad with a bursary granted by General Léon de Beylié, known for his intelligence operations in the Caucasus and Central Asia, carried out in 1888[187] under the cover of archaeological

---

[184] The accusation of espionage, more or less justified, haunted Massignon all his life. In March 1953, an article published in the Cairo university journal *Majallat al-Ahzar*, claimed he was a missionary Christian agent whose interest for mysticism was purely a ruse, calculated to turn Muslims away from the true faith. Certain Arab nationalists thought him to be a hypocrite who worked to further the interests of French colonialism.

[185] Founded by Sayyid Muhammad ibn Ali as-Senussi, born in Mostaganem, Algeria.

[186] Mansur al-Hallaj not only claimed God spoke through him but also that he had to be killed in order to escape the human condition and become part of the divine totality.

[187] In 1907, General Léon de Beylié had carried out excavations in Samarra and Kurdistan. He wrote *L'Inde sera-t-elle russe ou anglaise?* (Berger-Levrault, Paris, 1889) as well as *Mon journal de voyage, de l'orient à Samarcande* (F. Allier père et fils, Grenoble, 1889).

exploration.

When Massignon arrived in Mesopotamia, the French consul introduced him to the prominent Alusi family who took him under their wing, believing that they were dealing with a Frenchman on the path to Islamic conversion. He met eminent scholars, visited al-Hallaj's[188] cenotaph, and collected the data necessary for the preparation of his doctoral thesis[189]. His propensity to frequent the souks, under the pretext of wanting to improve his Arabic, intrigued the wali, the city's governor. Of course, Sultan Abdul Hamid II had approved his itinerary. Nonetheless, the police kept him under close surveillance as they suspected that his arrival might be connected in some way to the *Committee of Union and Progress* (CUP), which supported the *Young Turks* and was very active in Baghdad. The police also believed him to be one of the many geologists who had overrun Mesopotamia in search of oil.

Having entered into negotiations with the Kaiser, Abdul Hamid II was very keen to learn if any new oilfields had been discovered in the region. A month after his arrival, the German archaeologists Sarre and Herzfeld, experts on Samarra[190] culture, reported Massignon to the

---

[188] Mansur al-Hallaj's dismembered corpse was thrown into the Tigris. His disciples later constructed a cenotaph in his honour, a symbolically empty tomb.

[189] Louis Massignon defended his thesis in 1922. He is the author of *La Passion de al-Hallaj*, Gallimard, Paris, 1975, and *Al-Hallaj, Recueil d'oraisons et d'exhortations du martyr mystique de l'Islam*, J. Vrin, Paris, 1975.

[190] Samarra, located 125km to the north of Baghdad, was the Iraqi capital during the 9th century. Its vestiges stretch over 30km along the banks of the Tigris. The most well-known monuments include the Great Mosque with its spiral minaret (*Malwiya*) and the Al-Askari Shrine, close to the site where Muhammad ibn Hasan

Ottoman authorities, accusing him of espionage. In truth, Massignon was their intellectual rival, and they feared that his discoveries would eclipse theirs. Nonetheless, the rumour spread, and he was often accused in public of being a spy. What he sometimes wore when walking the streets –a mismatched Turkish uniform –only fuelled suspicions.

In March 1908, Massignon decided to explore the *Fortress of Al-Ukhaidir* and spend a few days touring the Shia holy cities of Karbala, Kufa and Najaf. He had also planned a visit to Wasit, not far from Kut, where the *Muntafiq* had staged an uprising against the Ottoman regime. The questions he asked the tribal chiefs seemed to suggest that he had been assigned by French intelligence to assess whether the Shia community would be prepared to overthrow the sultan.

On the way back, on the 1st May, the *kaimakam* (deputy governor) had him arrested for espionage. He was held in custody on the *Burhaniye*, a steamship which was making its way up the Tigris. Massignon threw overboard an official questionnaire, handed to him in France, on the noble families of Baghdad. Terrified, believing that he would be executed, he was seized by a fit of delirium. Having interpreted his seizure as the presence of God, he returned to the Christian faith. On 5 May, the French consul in Baghdad declared that he had in fact been suffering from sunstroke. He was released thanks to negotiations led by the Alusi family who, having welcomed him as a guest, considered

---

al-Mahdi, the Twelfth Shiite Imam (the Mahdi), entered into "minor occultation" in 874.

it their duty to protect him in accordance with Arab tradition.

The capture of Damascus

In the end, Lawrence came to appreciate French military support, but he would not have any talk of France's immemorial rights to Syria. He raised no objections to his sabotage squads being trained by Captain Pisani[191] and his Algerian non-commissioned officers. Moreover, he did not refuse the 65- mm mountain guns, delivered in February 1918. He refused to listen, however, to Colonel Brémond's advice, and would even make a point of doing exactly the opposite of what he recommended. So when Brémond warned him against Abd el Kader, whom he suspected of being a Turkish agent, it was no surprise that Lawrence immediately placed the Algerian under his protection. It is likely that Brémond had expected that this is precisely what Lawrence would do. Abd el Kader deserted in the end, and Lawrence blamed him for the sabotage of the Yarmuk railway bridge, a vital supply line for Ottoman forces in Palestine. He also believed him to be behind his arrest at the Syrian town of Deraa, at the railway junction leading to Medina. Abd el Kader is said to have given his description to the Turkish authorities. He was arrested, tortured and – if we are to believe his account of events – raped[192]. Nevertheless, he managed to escape.

---

[191] Captain Rosario Pisani, born in Algeria in 1880, led the detachment of 65mm mountain guns. He had served in Morocco (under the orders of Edouard Brémond, captain at the time) and participated in the repression of the Fez Riots in 1912.

[192] Lawrence had masochistic tendencies. His claim that he was raped at Deraa has been called into question. Indeed, he gave several versions of the incident and even admitted that he had lied in his *Middle East Diary 1917-1956*, published after

The legend, perpetuated by Lowell Thomas and the *Seven Pillars of Wisdom*, portrays Lawrence as being the first to enter Damascus, which had been abandoned by the Turks. In fact, however, when he arrived, he was greatly surprised to find Abd el Kader and his brother, Muhammad Saïd, at the head of a provisional government which had been formed to outwit the British. He had the Algerian brothers arrested by Ruwallah tribesmen, led by Sheikh Nuri Shaalan, and gave the order for their execution. He appointed Shukri Pasha Ayubi as acting governor of the city, but the Algerians were not executed, as Faisal had decreed a general amnesty.

What happened next was not exactly what the Arab Bureau had planned. General Allenby brought together the two expedition leaders to announce that Syria would be placed under *French* control and separated from Palestine and Lebanon. Faisal was stunned. Allenby was surprised that Lawrence had not told them what had been decided[193], and tersely reminded him that he must execute his orders while awaiting a final resolution. For Lawrence and his Arab Bureau friends, who had hoped for a British government in Damascus, the operation was a failure. Their last hope was to reduce the *Sykes-Picot Agreement* to its simplest expression at the forthcoming peace conference. Greatly vexed, Lawrence left Syria, but he was determined to have his views heard at the Foreign Office.

---

his death.

[193] Following the October Revolution, Leon Trotsky publicly revealed the terms of the secret Sykes-Picot Agreement. The British, therefore, strove to lull Sharif Hussein into a false sense of security by reassuring him that both the French occupation of Syria and the British occupation of Mesopotamia would be temporary.

The dream shatters

Talks at the *Paris Peace Conference* began on 16 January 1919. Lawrence was determined to ensure that Faisal did not lose face. But his efforts were in vain because he was obliged to safeguard the higher strategic interests of Britain and, at the same time, accommodate the demands of the French who, according to his letter to Hogarth, wanted to hand Syria over to Senegalese troops[194]. For the Western powers, the question of who was best placed to lead their people – Sharif Hussein, Prince Faisal, Emir Ibn Saud or a future king of Iraq – was to be answered almost exclusively in reference to the oil potential of each country. The British laid claim to the vilayet of Mosul, very promising in this respect.

Another key issue was the Palestinian question. In June 1918, the British had already prepared the ground by arranging a meeting with Faisal and Chaim Weizmann, the future president of the *World Zionist Organisation*. The Zionist leader had, it is said, convinced Faisal that the creation of a Jewish Palestine would allow the Arab kingdom to obtain the necessary finance for its development. Close to Weizmann, Lawrence, who believed that anti-Zionism was detrimental to British interests, prepared the text for the agreement, which was signed six months later. But Faisal then backtracked, explaining that welcoming Jewish refugees did not mean granting them sovereignty. He feared that their presence would spark a violent conflict. Infuriated, Lawrence wrote a letter to an American Zionist leader and signed it in Faisal's

---

[194] Knightley, Phillip et Simpson Colin, *Les vies secrètes de Lawrence d'Arabie*, Robert Laffont, Paris, 1970.

name! Published by the *New York Times*, the letter wished the Jews *"a most hearty welcome home."*[195]

As for the French, Georges Clemenceau handed over the vilayet of Mosul, together with its oilfields, to the British. This was exactly what he had secretly promised Lloyd George following the armistice of 1918[196]. In April 1920, at the *San Remo Conference*, Mesopotamia and Palestine were placed under British mandate, a decision which enraged Arab nationalists, as they had sincerely believed the promises of self-determination. In exchange, France was given the green light to occupy Syria and Lebanon. The French colonial lobby, which regarded the Levant to be a sacred heritage of the Crusades, rejoiced. Louis Massignon, though he often disagreed with what was happening, had got even with Lawrence. He was appointed the French government's representative for Syria.

---

[195] *New York Times*, 5 March 1919. Asked whether he had really made such a declaration, Faisal was adamant: he had no recollection of having written a letter of this sort.

[196] At the 1920 *San Remo Conference*, Mesopotamia and Palestine were placed under British mandate, a decision which greatly angered Arab nationalists who had believed the promises of self-determination. Georges Clemenceau relinquished the vilayet of Mosul and surrendered all claims to its oil reserves, exactly as he had secretly promised the British following the 1918 armistice. Maurice Hankey, Secretary to the Imperial War Cabinet, was present at the meeting. He had made a record of Lloyd George's famous conversation with the French prime minister in his diary. Clemenceau spoke first: *"Tell me what you want."* Lloyd George: *"I want Mosul."* Clemenceau: *"You shall have it. Anything else?"* Lloyd George: *"Yes, I want Jerusalem, too."* (Henry Laurens, *La Question de Palestine*, tome I, Éd. Fayard – Paris, 1999).

After Faisal had been named king by the *Syrian National Congress* in March 1920 (a hostile take- over, according to Massignon[197]), Clemenceau appointed General Henri Gouraud to the post of French High Commissioner in Syria. He took control of Damascus and asked the king to leave the country. Then, in a historically symbolic gesture, he went to Saladin's mausoleum, kicked his tomb and exclaimed: *"Awake Saladin, we have returned!"*

A living legend

While Lawrence slipped further into the depths of depression, his media image as the uncrowned king of Arabia took on stratospheric proportions. Behind this craze was an American journalist, Lowell Thomas. In August 1919, Lowell had given in Convent Garden a series of lectures, entitled *The Last Crusade*, portraying Lawrence as the most powerful figure in Arabia since Harun al-Rashid. Lowell's show was so successful that even King George V requested a private viewing.

Lowell Thomas had first met Lawrence in February 1918 when, with the approval of the Foreign Office, he came to Palestine to film the capture of Jericho. Ronald Storrs, military governor of Jerusalem at the time, introduced them both. The journalist had read of his exploits in the local press. He was immediately convinced that this short man of five-foot five with his sun-furrowed face, dressed like a Prince of Mecca,[198] would

---

[197] Louis Massignon, *Éléments arabes et foyers d'arabisation*, Revue du monde musulman, 1924.

[198] Joel Hodson, *Lawrence of Arabia and American culture: the Making of a Transatlantic Legend*, Greenwood Press, Westport, 1995.

make the ideal subject for a documentary he was planning to have screened in the United States. Lawrence agreed to accompany him to Aqaba, so that he might be filmed and photographed with the Bedouin soldiers who had captured the port.

At the time, the proposition flattered his ego, and he believed that the documentary would portray the Arab Revolt in a favourable light. He was very far from imagining all the problems that the media coverage of his actions would later cause him! In late March, Lowell Thomas, having obtained the necessary authorisation, arrived in Aqaba where Lawrence, who had been promoted to colonel, awaited him. He filmed the princes Faisal and Zeid, together with Bedouin soldiers on their camels, and made a visit to Petra. When Lowell Thomas returned to the United States, he claimed that he had witnessed firsthand the raid on the Hejaz railway, whereas in fact he had spent only three days in the company of Lawrence. Ten years later, he even told a journalist from Detroit that he had spent over a year with the Hejaz army!

It is thought that over million people saw Lowell Thomas' documentary on Lawrence who, in a matter of a few months, became one of the most famous personalities of his time. Lawrence captured the imagination of silent film directors, and no doubt inspired productions such as *The Sheikh* (1921) and the *The Son of the Sheikh* (1926), both of which starred Rudolph Valentino.

The British press piled on the pressure, publishing a series of revelations, all of which proved to be false. Hounded by the press, Lawrence would often hesitate before opening his front door. Though largely due to Lowell Thomas, the craze was also in no small part due to Lawrence himself. To counteract all the media hype, he rushed to finish his *Seven Pillars of Wisdom*, a title he had already used in 1911 for an aborted book[199]. If we are to believe Gertrude Bell, whose advice Lawrence had sought, his dilemma when writing his personal account was to strike an appropriate balance between the exaggerated media claims, fuelled by Lowell Thomas, and an austere account of mundane events[200]. His chosen solution was to write an historical novel which allowed him to save face. A small number of private editions were printed in 1922 (8 copies) and in 1926 (120 copies). The public version was only published after his death. It was an instant success[201]. Ever since, there have been an almost infinite number of books and articles devoted to the legend of Lawrence.

Incognito in uniform

With the situation worsening in Iraq, Lawrence suggested the use of

---

[199] The source of the title is the Book of Proverbs (Proverbs 9:1) *"Wisdom hath builded her house, she hath hewn out her seven pillars."* It is also the name of a rock formation in Wadi Rum, Jordan, close to where Lawrence traversed the desert with Faisal's army.

[200] Being bound by the British *Official Secrets Act*, Lawrence could not reveal the exact details of the Arab Revolt.

[201] *The Seven Pillars of Wisdom* is dedicated to *"S.A"*. According to Dr Ernest Altounyan, a friend of Lawrence, the initials are those of Sarah Aaronsohn, a member of the Jewish spy network NILI (acronym of the Hebrew phrase *Netzah Yisrael Lo Yeshaker* – "the Eternal One of Israel will not lie") who collaborated with British intelligence. Arrested by the Turks in 1917, she is said to have committed suicide rather than reveal secrets under torture. According to others, however, the initials simply refer to Syria and Arabia.

chemical weapons to curb the uprising. Churchill, Secretary State for War at the time, gave this idea some serious thought. To quell public outrage, Churchill declared that he could not understand those who were squeamish in this regard and that he was strongly in favour of using poisoned gas against *"uncivilised tribes"*[202]. He made Lawrence his Arab affairs adviser and together they organised the 1921 *Cairo Conference*, which mandated Faisal's appointment as king of Iraq. Transjordan was created for Faisal's brother, Abdullah, who, as Philby wrote, had clearly resigned himself to playing the role of a puppet[203]. Lawrence's reaction to the news that Ibn Saud had overthrown Sharif Hussein was somewhat apathetic. In 1918, he had recommended that Muslim troops from India be sent in to curb the Wahhabi advance, but this affair was now ancient history for him. The role he played in the creation of two pseudo independent states for Hussein's son almost gave him a clear conscience.

In 1920, perhaps recalling his father's Irish origins, Lawrence, though a Protestant, met Michael Collins[204], the *Sinn Fein* and IRA leader, who had come to London to negotiate the independence of his country. He advised Collins to reach an agreement with the British, believing that a hard-line attitude would lead to nothing. In 1922, there were rumours that Collins, seeking to exploit Lawrence's popularity, had asked him to take command of an IRA unit, which was preparing to enter Ulster[205].

---

[202] Martin Gilbert, *Winston S. Churchill* (Official Biography – volume IV), Heinemann, London, 1976.

[203] St John Philby, *Forty Years in the Wilderness,* Robert Hall, London, 1957.

[204] Michael Collins was leader of the IRA and a special squad nicknamed the *Twelve Apostles*, a unit set up to assassinate traitors.

[205] Knightley, Phillip et Simpson Colin, *Les vies secrètes de Lawrence d'Arabie,*

A few days later, Collins was assassinated by somebody whose views were more radical than his.

With *The Seven Pillars of Wisdom* close to completion, Lawrence joined the RAF, using the pseudonym of John Hume Ross. But his cover was blown and he was forced to leave. Indeed, groups of journalists would often crowd round where he was based. Depressed to the point of practising self- flagellation, Lawrence nonetheless succeeded in joining the *Royal Tank Corps* by using the name of Thomas Edward Shaw. He was later transferred to the RAF and left for India and Afghanistan. When he returned, he withdrew to the tranquillity of a cottage in Clouds Hill, Dorset.

The black car mystery

As a member of the British armed forces, Lawrence refrained from expressing his political views. Nevertheless, it is known that he was favourable to the formation of an anti-Communist alliance with Hitler and Mussolini. When he was demobilised in February 1935, his views were shared by the members of *The Round Table*, including Lady Astor (Britain's first female Member of Parliament) and Oswald Mosely, leader of the *British Union Fascists* (BUF). But Lawrence's closest friends were people such as the socialist writer George Bernard Shaw and Henry Williamson, a member of Mosely's *Black Shirts*, both of whom were unpopular with the Conservative government. Williamson urged Lawrence to meet Hitler. Having got wind of this, the press besieged his cottage. He was repeatedly asked the date of the meeting and

---

Robert Laffont, Paris, 1970.

whether he intended to become the dictator of Britain! Obstinately refusing to answer, tensions mounted to the point where the police were obliged to intervene.

On 13 May 1935, Lawrence set off on his motorbike to the post office at Bovington, two kilometres from his cottage and not far from a military base. Having sent a telegram to Williamson, whom he had invited to lunch on the 14th, he made his way back home.

There were no eye witnesses to the accident. A solider, walking his dog, saw the motorbike appear at the top of a dip in the road and then disappear as it descended the slope. He also saw two cyclists and then a black car, travelling in the opposite direction. It was at this point that he heard a crash. He ran to the scene of the accident and found Lawrence lying in the road, his head covered in blood, and saw the black car driving away in the distance. He flagged down an army lorry, which happened to be passing at the time, and Lawrence was immediately taken to Bovington Camp hospital. Any information relating to Lawrence was classified secret and all articles, the government told the press, had to be approved by the War Office before being published. An intelligence officer's statement, confirming that nobody had witnessed the accident, gave a very bad impression to the public. Lawrence never regained consciousness and died on 19 May.

A cursory inquest into his death was carried out. The two cyclists claimed that they had not seen the car and did not know how Lawrence had come to collide with one of them. No attempt was made to identify the driver of the black car. The coroner had wanted to solve this mystery, but the jury ruled that Lawrence's death was accidental.

Neither the press nor his friends were satisfied with this verdict. Some believed he had been assassinated, while others claimed that the accident had been staged by the secret services so that Lawrence might carry out another mission somewhere. Clearly, it was very difficult to admit that the legendary Lawrence of Arabia had been killed in an ordinary motorbike accident.

Chapter XI

GERTRUDE BELL, THE HEARTBROKEN SPY

Gertrude Lowthian Bell, the first ever women to be awarded a first in Modern History from the University of Oxford, was highly intelligent, athletic, and possessed a determined character. Bell first discovered the Orient when in Tehran in 1892 thanks to Friederich Rosen, a German diplomat and orientalist, and Henry Cadogan, a junior official at the British embassy who was fascinated by Persian culture and history. She fell in love with Cadogan, learnt Farsi and translated the mystical poems of Hafez[206]. When Cadogan died in Persia, Bell was mortified.

To escape the stifling boredom of Victorian society, she spent several months in Jerusalem to learn Arabic, and then travelled to Greece where she developed a passion for archaeology in the company of historian and British agent David Hogarth, who was later to become the director of the Arab Bureau in Cairo. She made her first solitary[207]

---

[206] Hafez, born in the 14th century, is one of the greatest and most popular Persian poets. His compendium of poems, permeated by Suffi mysticism, is entitled the *Divan of Hafez*.

[207] Bell was not entirely alone. She was accompanied by several Arab servants to pitch tents, cook, and heat the water for her portable bathtub and hot-water bottle. Bell took with her a porcelain dinner set, cut crystal glasses, as well as her wardrobe and her perfume for special occasions.

journey on horseback in the Palestinian desert. She visited Petra and then, in 1900, the Jabal al-Druze mountains, defying the Ottoman interdiction. Published in 1907, *The Desert and the Sown*, Bell's account of her discovery of the Bedouin, was a success. David Hogarth regarded it as being one of the ten best works on the Orient.

A misleading reputation

Bell continued her travels in the Near East. In Syria, she participated in the restoration of churches dating from the early Christian period and, in 1909, made the journey across Mesopotamia, discovering Baghdad, Babylon, Karbala, and the country's various tribes. She conducted excavations at the Fortress of Al-Ukhaidir[208], some fifty kilometres from Karbala. She had planned to write a book on this mysterious fortification. Upon her return, however, she was immensely disappointed to learn that Louis Massignon had beaten her to it. His detailed record of Al-Ukhaidir had already been published in two leading French archaeological reviews. Over time, his commerce with the tribal chiefs made him an expert on Arab affairs.

Two years later, Bell returned to Al-Ukhaidir. She travelled up the Euphrates to Carchemish, the former Hittite[209] capital, where David

---

[208] The fortress of *Al-Ukhaidir* (green corner), located close to *Wadi Al-abyad* (the White Valley) is said to have been constructed during the late 8th century by Isa ibn Musa, former governor of Kufa who was to succeed Al-Mansur as caliph. When Harun al-Rashid became caliph in 786, ibn Musa agreed to confine himself to the fortress for the duration of his reign in exchange for a significant sum of money.

[209] The Hittites, an Indo-European people, had invaded Asia Minor and the Near East circa 1600 BC.

Hogarth had made a number of excavations. Since Hogarth was absent – he had been appointed the director of Oxford's *Ashmolean Musuem*[210] - she met his two assistants, the linguist Campbell Thomson, and a 23-year old student by the name of T.E. Lawrence. The young Lawrence wore a red tasselled belt of the sort worn by Assyrian young men in search of a wife. Lawrence had concealed his homosexuality from the Assyrians, who were numerous in the region. They would often introduce him to women who were keen to marry and believed that Bell, despite being 42 years old, was to be his bride. When he told them that she was too ugly to be his wife, they jeered him, and he was forced to leave!

The site at Carchemish, though of incidental archaeological interest, had become strategically important ever since the Germans began building their Berlin-Baghdad railway line, which was located some five hundred metres away. Using the cover of archaeological exploration, Lawrence and his colleagues closely monitored the progress of the line and made sketches of the bridges which they would one day, perhaps, have to destroy.

The letters she wrote to her friend Valentine Chirol, journalist for the *Times* and British intelligence agent, soon came to be read by those in the upper echelons of government, as they highlighted the threat which Wilhlem II's Berlin-Baghdad railway posed to British economic interests. Her reputation allowed her to meet major diplomatic figures such as Sir Percy Cox and Sir Mark Sykes, who immediately took a disliking to her,

---

[210] Oxford's *Ashmolean Musuem* was founded in 1683 by Elias Ashmole, alchemist, Freemason and member of King Charles II's court.

describing her as a "*bitch*" in one of his letters.[211]

The British press, which covered Gertrude Bell's adventures, misleadingly portrayed her as a gallivanting Amazon. However, having been born into a wealthy family of industrialists and being greatly influenced by her conservative upbringing, she was in fact very conformist. One might have expected her to be among the suffragettes, but, paradoxically, she campaigned against universal suffrage, believing that women were fit for raising children but unfit for government!

Ibn Rashid's Prisoner

In 1913, she fell in love with Richard Doughty-Wylie[212], a young diplomat who shared her passion for archaeology and the desert. Unfortunately, however, he happened to be married, and this only depressed Bell further, certain she would remain forever single. Her trip to Arabia, organised shortly after their separation, was not only the fulfilment of a long-cherished dream but also a form of therapy for her solitude.

She wanted to meet Ibn Rashid and Ibn Saud, rival Arabian sheikhs who were fighting for the control of the Najd region. She had hoped to convince them both to support Britain against the declining Ottoman Empire. In December 1913, she set off for Ha'il, a three-month journey on camel back. On the way, she gave out her calling card to Bedouin chiefs, requesting their protection. Her conversations with the sheikhs

---

[211] Janet Wallach, *La reine du désert*, Bayard Éditions, Paris, 1997.

[212] Richard Doughty-Wylie's uncle, still alive at the time, was Charles Doughty, author of *Arabia Deserta*, an essential reference for all orientalists.

meant that British intelligence was able to update its records of the tribal family trees and identify the issues which divided or united them.

On 24 February 1913, she arrived in Ha'il. In Ibn Rashid's absence, the city was governed by his uncle Ibrahim. Having carelessly told him of her intention to travel to Riyadh, she was detained for nine days in the *roshan*, the palace's reception hall. By the time she was released, it was too dangerous for her to meet Ibn Saud. Hostilities between the two chiefs had resumed, and Ibn Saud's Wahhabi troops were preparing to storm the city.

She left for Karbala and Baghdad, where she waited for news from Doughty-Wylie, who was in Ethiopia. Though she regretted not having been able to complete her journey, she learnt the truth about the Rashid family: a declining clan, marred by treason and murder. According to her, the future of Arabia belonged to the Saud family. In a letter to Chirol, her friend and *Times* journalist, she wrote that the idea of returning to London depressed her and that she would prefer to stay in Baghdad, which she considered to be the true heart of the Orient[213].

The death of Richard Doughty-Wylie

Gertrude Bell returned to London in May 1914, a month after the assassination of Archduke Franz Ferdinand in Sarajevo. It was the start of the First World War. The Near East and its oilfields were to become one of the key strategic issues of this conflict. Bell immediately wrote to Sir Edward Grey, Britain's foreign secretary. In her letter, she assured

---

[213] Janet Wallach, *La reine du désert*, Bayard Éditions, Paris, 1997.

him that Syria was willing to accept British control. London, she believed, ought to support Sayid Talib, an influential Iraqi nationalist in Basra, and form an alliance with Ibn Saud. She advised him to organise an Arab uprising against the Turks and proposed that she represent British interests on the ground. Her proposition, however, was rejected by the military chiefs of staff, who no doubt held the view that this was no place for a woman, and she joined the Red Cross in France.

While nursing the casualties of war in Boulogne, she learnt that Anglo-Indian expeditionary forces had landed in Al-Faw, not far from Basra. She asked Chirol to keep her up to date of their advance towards Baghdad which, she believed, would be captured with ease. Richard Doughty-Wylie had arrived in London, so she left France for Britain to enjoy a few moments of (chaste) happiness with him.

Churchill had dispatched 74 000 soldiers – British, Australians, French – to the Dardanelles to outflank Turkish forces and ease the pressure on British troops in Iraq. Doughty-Wylie, former British consul in Mersina and defender of the Armenian cause, was among the officers chosen to hold the region. The operation was disastrous[214]. Doughty-Wylie was killed on 25 May 1915, during the assault on Gallipoli. Gertrude Bell was devastated.

---

[214] The Ottoman forces were led by General Liman von Sanders. Among his ranks was Mustafa Kamal Pasha (later known as Atatürk), who commanded the unit which thwarted the Allied landing at Kabatepe on 25 April 1915. During the Dardenelles Campaign, in excess of 300,000 battle casualties were recorded among the British and French ranks.

The Great Game in Cairo

In November 1915, David Hogarth invited her to join his team. Under the direction of General Gilbert Clayton, he ran what was later to be officially known as the Arab Bureau. Staffed by a team of archaeologists, journalists and civil servants, this agency rose to prominence thanks to the quality of the intelligence it supplied to British secret service chiefs. Having been longing to play her part since the outbreak of the war, she gladly accepted the offer and no doubt reasoned, too, that being at the heart of the action would, perhaps, attenuate her sorrow.

In late November, she set off for Egypt. In Cairo's Savoy hotel, which had been commandeered by British intelligence, she met many familiar faces: T.E. Lawrence, the archaeologist Leonard Wooley, Philip Graves from *The Times*, Aubrey Herbert, Ronald Storrs, and even Fattuh, her faithful desert guide.

While Lawrence was busy inciting the Arabs to revolt against the Turks in the Hejaz region, Bell updated her knowledge of the various tribes in Najd, Syria and Mesopotamia. She analysed the character of their chiefs and described the topography of the regions under their authority. Arab nationalists, playing the British card - or perhaps a double-game - helped her complete her research. Victory had to be British! So, with Lawrence, she made plans to eradicate French influence in the region. The two great Western powers were to vie for the control of Syria and the oil-rich region of Mosul in a low-key version of *The Great Game*. The British, however, were divided on how to fight the war in the Near

East. Lord Hardinge, Viceroy of India, did not want an Arab kingdom swallowing Mesopotamia, which he had planned to annex. He believed that the Arab Bureau worked against British interests and that its activities were dangerous, as they were likely to trigger Muslim revolts in India.

Return to Mesopotamia

In January 1916, General Clayton sent Gertrude Bell to India. She was to meet the Viceroy, whom she had already met some years previously in Romania. In Delhi, with the support of Valentine Chirol, she skilfully resolved the conflict between the British Indian government and the experts at the Arab Bureau. She had succeeded in arranging matters in such as way that she was appointed to carry out a fact-finding mission in Mesopotamia, allowing her to consult secret files on British relations with prominent Arab figures.

In March, Gertrude Bell arrived at British headquarters in Basra, where she met up again with Campbell Thompson, who was responsible for the deciphering of Turkish code. The political advisers did not greet her with open arms. St John Philby was friendly, but Arnold Wilson, somewhat pigheaded, was less so. Wilson, already greatly angered by Arab Bureau interference in Mesopotamia, did not take kindly to a *woman* meddling in his affairs. What's more, as far as he was concerned, Anglo-Indian expeditionary forces were there for the express purpose of creating a colony, to be inhabited by peasants from the Punjab.

The Eyes of British Intelligence on Mesopotamia

With General Townshend's expeditionary forces besieged at Kut, Gertrude Bell was able to test her powers of political manipulation. She wrote to Nuri Said, an officer in the Ottoman army and member of the clandestine anti-Turkish group *Al-Ahd* (The Covenant), urging him to make his mark. She asked the tribal chiefs to cease their support for the Turkish army. Lawrence arrived from Egypt with a million pounds in a suitcase, in the hope to bribe General Halil, the commander of Turkish forces and nephew of the Turkish minister of defence, Enver Pasha. But Lawrence's efforts were in vain: the British Army suffered one of its most humiliating defeats in its entire history.

In Cairo, the existence of the Arab Bureau was finally made official, but Bell was now reluctant to continue her career there. Having experienced the reality on the ground, she felt that her views were more in line with those of Delhi. As she had become indispensible in Basra, Hardinge appointed her adviser to Percy Cox, whose remit covered Mesopotamia and the Gulf countries. Ibn Saud was impressed by Bell's knowledge and her determination when, in April 1916, he met her in Kuwait. Writing in the *Arab Bulletin*, the Bureau's secret in-house publication, she enthusiastically described the emir as being an exceptional man. Discreetly, she intimated her hope that he would eliminate Ibn Rashid and Hussein, the Sharif of Mecca.

After the British had taken Baghdad, Cox appointed her Oriental

Secretary. In other words, she was to be the *"eyes and ears"*[215] of British intelligence in Mesopotamia. Having earned the respect of Arab tribesman, she became known to many as *al-Khatun*, meaning the *"lady of the Court"*. She asked Fahad Bey, the chief of the powerful Anazeh tribe, to support Britain. He agreed after having justified his decision before his men in terms which are worth recalling: *"My brothers, you have heard what this woman has to say to us. She is only a woman, but she is a mighty and valiant one. Now we all know that Allah has made all women inferior to men. But if the women of the Anglez are like her, the men must be like lions in strength and valour. We had better make peace with them."*[216]

Secret agreement

At the same time as an enraged Percy Cox, Gertrude Bell discovered the existence of a secret agreement which divided the Near East into French and British spheres. Their plans were ruined. There was no longer any question of Mesopotamia becoming the bread basket of India or, indeed, of it forming part of an Arab kingdom. Worse still, the French had grabbed Syria and Mosul. While Ibn Saud represented what Cox and Bell considered to be the true Arabia, London and the Arab Bureau backed Prince Faisal, the Sharif of Mecca's son, believing him to be the man who would "set the desert ablaze"[217].

Lawrence marched on to Aqaba and Damas, and was lionised by the

---

[215] Janet Wallach, *La reine du désert*, Bayard Éditions, Paris, 1997.

[216] *Ibid.*

[217] *Ibid.*

press. In contrast, Gertrude Bell shunned the media limelight. And yet, it was thanks to the information she had obtained on the Howeitat tribe that Lawrence succeeded in his attempt to disable the Hejaz railway line. In 1917, however, she was less reserved, and spoke out against the *Balfour Agreement*, which promised the creation of a Jewish homeland. She condemned the project, claiming it was totally artificial, and wished it the *"ill success it deserves"*. The region was not suited, she opined, for what the Jews had in mind.

Turmoil in Mesopotamia

In 1918, tensions were mounting in Mesopotamia's southern Shia region. Persian spies, working for Germany, were not short of arguments when it came to inciting tribesmen, the majority of whom were pro-Turkish, to stage a revolt. After all, the British had requisitioned their livestock to feed the expeditionary forces, imposed an embargo on Turkish products, and forced them to pay taxes to finance their administration. Arnold Wilson, Percy Cox's deputy, had ordered the execution of the leaders of a secret anti-British committee.

Mesopotamia was plunged into turmoil by an accumulation of events: Cox's departure; General Allenby's entry into Damascus; the appointment of Faisal as Syrian leader; the Armistice of 11 November; and the Anglo-American declaration, according to which democratically elected governments would be established in the Near East.

Who would now govern Mesopotamia? Gertrude Bell had proposed Mesopotamia's borders, but opinions regarding its regime were divided. The British Indian government wanted to transform the country into a colony, while London wanted to back out, financially at any rate. The Arabs wanted their kingdom. The Shias demanded a religious state, while the Kurds hoped for independence. Meanwhile, the Assyrians and the Jews expressed their fears. They all agreed, however, to ignore the existence of the Turkmen, who formed a majority in Kirkuk and Erbil. The *naqib* of Baghdad, Abd Al- Rahman Al-Gillani, criticising Woodrow Wilson's *Fourteen Points*, believed that it would be absurd to hold democratic elections in Mesopotamia. The Americans, he claimed, were ignorant of the country's diverse cultures and customs[218], an opinion shared by Gertrude Bell.

How to create a nation-state

In 1919, Arnold Wilson dispatched Gertrude Bell to London in order to defend their vision of British interests in Mesopotamia. On the way, she made a stop in Paris to attend the peace conference. In the corridors and on the fringes of the main debates, there was much discussion about oil and the creation of a Jewish homeland in Palestine.

Faisal met Chaim Weizmann, the future leader of the *World Zionist Organisation*, and agreed to the terms of the *Balfour Agreement*. But he did so under the condition that the Western powers honour their promises to the Arabs. The creation of "independent" states was in the air. The pressure groups, however, were divided and the decision on the fate of the occupied territories – Syria[219], Mesopotamia and the

---

[218] *Ibid.*

[219] Before being geographically dismembered, Syria – the true Syria, as defined by its historical borders – included Palestine (transformed into a Jewish homeland),

vilayet of Mosul – was postponed.

On the way back, Gertrude Bell stopped over in Egypt. The Arab Bureau was in a sorry state. Gilbert Clayton explained that they were obliged to play the self-determination card and organise elections to maintain British presence in the region. Needless to say, these elections were rigged and the "elected" officials, mere puppets controlled by British intelligence, were selected in advance. Moreover, the oilfields remained in British hands. Gertrude Bell's stay in Jerusalem confirmed her fears: the *Balfour Declaration* had sown the seeds of eternal conflict.

In Damascus, she met members of *Al-Ahd* who had left the Turkish army to rally behind Faisal. She found both Nuri Saïd and Jafar al-Askari to be highly intelligent and Westernised. Indeed, she was so impressed that she later had Saïd appointed prime minister of the Iraqi kingdom and al-Askari defence minister. She returned from Baghdad convinced that the creation of an Arab state in Mesopotamia was both desirable and feasible, and that this would allow Britain to maintain its control of the country. It remained to be seen, however, how such a nation could ever be created, given that both the British Indian government and Arnold Wilson were not at all favourable to this idea.

Mesopotamia on the verge of disintegration

Tensions in the southern Shia region had been contained by the pro-British Grand Ayatollah Yazdi, but Gertrude Bell, being well-informed,

---

Jordan (an artificially created country) and Alexandretta, a region which France granted to Turkey.

sensed that there would soon be a nationalist uprising. Indeed, the situation was starting to slip out of her control.

It all started in 1919 when Ramadan al-Shallash, a member of the secret nationalist society *Al-Ahd*, captured the Syrian towns Deir ez-Zor and Abu Kamal. He was supported by Shammar, Dulaim and Jubur tribesmen. Faisal, who governed Damascus, had him immediately removed from his administration. But Mawlud Mukhlis, the Tikriti officer appointed to replace him, also joined the revolt. Al-Shallash had British officials in the region arrested, but he released them on Christmas Eve, demanding that the occupying troops move 70km away from the border. At the same time, Jamil al- Midfai, an officer and close associate of Shallash, marched into Mosul and captured Tal Afar, aided by Sheikh Ahmad Ajil al Yawar, the head sheikh of the Shammar tribe[220]. This was the last straw for the British. They crushed the revolt. But the Arabs had seen that British occupying forces were not invincible[221]. It was just the

---

[220] In Iraq, some 150 main tribes and 2 000 clans have been identified. Seventy five percent of the Iraqi population belongs to a tribe (*ashira*), subdivided into several clans (*fukhdh*). Its members identify with a common ancestor. A new clan is naturally formed once the original one becomes too large. Clans are divided into houses (*beit*) and then into extended families (*khams*). Tribes are united into confederations (*qabila*) which can sometimes simultaneously comprise Shiite, Sunni and Kurdish tribes. The Al-Bu Nasir, Saddam Hussein's tribe, comprises a Shiite branch, led by Hussein Sayyid Ali. The principal *qabila* are: Zubayd, Rubia, Dulaym, Shammar, Jubur, Ubayd, Anniza, Albu Mohammed, al-Tikriti, Ka'b, Bani Lam, al-Khaza'il. The names of confederations are often named after the towns close to where they live: Tikrit, Fallujah, Al-Dour, Rawa, etc.

[221] *Al-Assabiyah, ou la résistance des tribus irakiennes*, Gilles Munier, AFI-Flash, April 2007.

beginning.

Six months later, tensions mounted again when Grand Ayatollah Mohammed Taqi Shirazi, angered that his son, Mohammed Ridha, had been arrested and deported to Persia by the British, issued a fatwa calling for an uprising against the occupying forces. The Tamim and the Muntafiq tribes also staged a revolt and refused all direct contact with Bell, under the flimsy pretext that she did not wear the Islamic veil. Only the Anazeh remained loyal to her. But this loyalty was in no way a reflection of their support for British policy. It was, rather, a question of honouring the promises which their leader, Sheikh Fahad Bey, had made to her.

With Mesopotamia about to explode, the creation of an Iraqi state appeared to be the "least worst" option for the British, keen to protect their interests. So a dinner was held in honour of Sayid Talib, who happened to be passing through Baghdad at the time. Though Gertrude Bell despised him, he was the only nationalist leader willing to compromise himself by collaborating with the occupying powers.

The *Syrian National Congress*, held in Damascus, led to a more interesting development. Abdullah, the Sharif of Mecca's eldest son, was selected as the candidate to rule Iraq. British intelligence was behind this decision. As far as David Hogarth of the Arab Bureau was concerned, there was no other Arab capable of leading Mesopotamia. Not all Iraqi nationalists agreed. But Bell could not have cared less, believing that it was sufficient to present them with this *fait accompli* to pacify them. She disagreed with the decision to make Faisal the king of Syria, as she believed he would have better served the British in

Baghdad.

At the *San Remo Conference* in April 1920, Mesopotamia and Palestine were placed under British mandate. Arabia was recognised as being a British domain. France gained control of Syria, including Lebanon, and was given the assurance of a permanent oil supply for industrial and commercial purposes[222] in exchange for the vilayet of Mosul, which was handed to the British. Arab nationalists were outraged. For them, this decision proved that the right to self-determination was a lie, just like all the empty promises of democracy made by General Maude following the British capture of Baghdad. Good intentions could not resist the great powers' appetite for oil, whetted by the underhand influence of Henry Deterding, chairman of *Royal Dutch-Shell*.

The 1920 Revolution

On 30 May 1920, the death of an Iraqi nationalist, crushed by an armoured vehicle during a demonstration in the centre of Baghdad, triggered a general strike. In Tal Afar, the Shammar tribe and Turkomen, whose uprising had been brutally crushed a few months previously, staged an armed revolt. Several British officials and soldiers were killed. Arnold Wilson gave the order to shoot the rebels and destroy the city. The rebellion spread to the Shia town Kadhimiya[223] and the southern

---

[222] Janet Wallach, *La reine du désert*, Bayard Éditions, Paris, 1997.

[223] The Shiite shrine at Kadhimiya, separated from Baghdad at the time, contains the tombs of Musa al-Kadhim and Muhammad al-Jawad (the seventh and ninth Shiite Imams). It is one the main holy sites for the Twelver Shiite sect, but not for the Ismaili sect (the Seveners), who believe that Isma'il ibn Jafar (son of Ja'far al-Sadiq, the sixth Imam) had disappeared before his father's death and will one day

regions. Military convoys were attacked, and the British death toll soon rose to several hundreds.

The British were out of their depth. RAF bombings of villages and mass arrests only served to fuel anti-British sentiment, exacerbating an already explosive situation. News of the much-hated Colonel Gerard Leachman's death came as a blow for the British. Khamis, the eldest son of Sheikh Dhari al-Mahmud[224] (chief of the Zoba' tribe), killed Leachman in an ambush, close to Fallujah, and became the hero of the Iraqi resistance movement.

The 1920 revolution, which shook the country for over six months, claimed the lives of more than ten thousand civilians, and finally convinced the British to grant independence to Mesopotamia. Arnold Wilson completed his mission in Baghdad and, vexed by the turn of events, joined the executive board of the *Anglo-Persian Oil Company*...

On 11 October, the arrival of Sir Percy Cox, accompanied by St John Philby, marked a turning point in British policy on Mesopotamia. In his speech, Cox, the new High Commissioner, pronounced the word "Iraq" for the very first time and declared that he was prepared to discuss the future of this state with its representatives. In much of the country, however, the nationalists had not yet laid down arms. So, with the help

---

return to restore peace and justice.

[224] Following the American invasion of Iraq, Harith Sulayman al-Dhari, the son of the revolutionary hero Khamis, was appointed the chairman of the *Association of Muslim Scholars*. The rifle used to kill Leachman has become a highly symbolic token of Iraqi resistance to colonisation. It was used by Saddam Hussein during the anti-American military parades.

of Gertrude Bell and Philby, Cox urgently set about appointing prominent Iraqi figures to key government posts: prime minister (Abd Al-Rahman Al-Gillani, the *naqib* of Baghdad); minister of interior (Sayid Talib); minister of defence (Jafar al Askari); and minister of finance (Sassoon Eskell, a prominent Jewish financer). Each member of government was allocated a British adviser, who in fact held the powers ostensibly bestowed upon the ministers. The Ayatollahs had been excluded from the negotiations because, it was claimed, they were incompetent when it came to administrative matters. All that remained was to find a king or a president.

Kingmaker

Sayid Talib applied for the Iraqi leadership position. But since Gertrude Bell disliked him, she proposed Faisal, who had been driven out of Damascus in July by the French general Henri Gouraud. She knew perfectly well, however, that he would not suit the Iraqi nationalists or the Shias, who did not want a Hashemite from Mecca ruling the country. Britain's troubled occupation of Mesopotamia was a burden for the public purse. It was criticised by leading politicians, such as Herbert Asquith, the former prime minister, and was increasingly called into question by the press and public opinion.

To break the deadlock, Winston Churchill, Secretary of State for the Colonies, organised the *Cairo Conference* in March 1921. Forty or so experts on the Near East were invited, including Gertrude Bell, Percy Cox, Arnold Wilson, T.E. Lawrence, Kinahan Cornwallis[225] from British

---

[225] Kinahan Cornwallis was one of the key advisers to Faisal in Damascus.

intelligence, and Sir Herbert Samuel, the High Commissioner in Palestine. Humorously dubbed the conference of the "Forty Thieves" by Churchill, the event marked a personal triumph for Bell. She succeeded in having Faisal selected as the future king of Iraq, a choice approved by Jafar al Askari and Sassoon Eskell. What's more, this new state would include the oil-rich vilayet of Mosul.

Churchill abandoned the idea of granting the Kurds an autonomous status, believing that an RAF bombardment would be sufficient to quell the ardour of any rebels. The conference participants believed that Iraq would be held up as an example for the whole of the Near East. Of course, nothing went as planned. In Baghdad, Faisal was perceived as a foreign puppet, manipulated by the British. Sayid Talib, whose campaign slogan was "Iraq for the Iraqis", was deported to Ceylon. Meanwhile, the Kurds were just waiting for the right moment to stage their revolt.

Philby strongly disagreed with the choice of Faisal as king of Iraq. Even though his opinion on this matter was known, he was still chosen to greet him in Basra on 23 June! Seizing his opportunity to get even, he told the emir straight: he would have preferred to have seen Ibn Saud on the throne or the establishment of a republic. During the journey to Baghdad, the attitude of the Iraqis towards Faisal was cold, hostile even.

Gertrude Bell's problem was to have the various parties back Faisal. The *naqib*, though reluctant at first, finally endorsed him. The Jews, who had demanded that they be granted British citizenship should an Arab government be formed, gave him a standing ovation when he reminded those gathered of their shared Semitic roots. The Anazeh and Dulaim tribes pledged allegiance to Faisal, because he was approved by the British government[226]. The referendum held to see if the Iraqis would accept him as their king was a mere formality, as the fiercest opponents were not able to vote and not all the votes against were counted. On 23 August, to the tune of *God Save the King*, Faisal was officially declared the ruling monarch of Iraq. The British had won. Or rather, that's how it seemed...

Faisal I on a knife edge

While Gertrude Bell and Kinahan Cornwallis plotted against the French in Syria in the hope that one day the country would form part of Faisal's kingdom, the Arab nationalists put enormous pressure on the new king. They demanded that he refuse to sign the mandate imposed on Iraq and that a treaty alliance with Britain only be signed on a basis of equality. Churchill refused to listen to their demands. Iraq, he wrote to Faisal, was an *"ungrateful volcano"*, and the British were paying dearly for the privilege of living on top of it. Moreover, if Faisal did not respect the decision made by the League of Nations (LN), he would withdraw Anglo-Indian troops before the end of the year, abandoning the country to chaos. Lloyd George defused tensions. He pointed out to Churchill that Britain would lose its advantages in oil exploration if it were to abandon Iraq, and advocated patience. The French and the Americans would only take advantage of a British withdrawal to seize control of

---

[226] Janet Wallach, *La reine du désert*, Bayard Éditions, Paris, 1997.

some of the world's most promising oilfields[227].

After much tactical procrastination, Faisal finally acknowledged that he would never accept the British mandate, not least because he had no wish to be overthrown. A Muntafiq rebellion had already been murderously crushed. In Baghdad, there were non-stop anti-British demonstrations. The press was censored. In Kurdistan, supporters of Sheikh Mahmud Barzanji were bombed with mustard gas by the RAF. Churchill, fearing a revolt more violent than that of 1920, promised the king that he would rapidly secure LN membership for Iraq, explaining that this would be tantamount to abolishing the terms of the mandate. Gertrude Bell even went to see Faisal in hospital to convince him. Weakened by illness, Faisal made the mistake of agreeing...

In October 1922, the *Anglo-Iraqi Treaty* was signed during a period of immense instability for the country. The agreement guaranteed Britain's total control of Iraq and its oilfields for a twenty-year period. It forbade Iraq from appointing its own diplomats, though it was entitled to select its ambassador to London. Elsewhere in the world, however, Iraq was to be represented exclusively by the Foreign Office! In addition, Iraq was to cover 25% of British military costs. For the nationalists, whose opinion represented the majority, Iraq had been reduced to the status of a "vassal state".

Muhammad Mahdi al Khalisi, a Shia sheikh from Kazimiya, believed that Faisal had broken his promises to secure the independence of Iraq,

---

[227] Roger Adelson, *London and the Invention of the Middle East*, Yale University Press, London, 1995.

and thus declared that his oath of allegiance to him was null and void. In 1922, seven ministers resigned to mark their opposition to the treaty. Several days later, the prime minister did likewise. Without a government, Iraq now found itself under the direct control of the British High Commissioner, Percy Cox, who immediately deported al Khalisi to Tehran, along with a number of other nationalist leaders.

Ancient treasures and oil

Percy Cox left to take his retirement. Gertrude Bell found his successor, Henry Dodds, to be charming, though noted with some bitterness that he rarely sought her advice. In 1923, after a holiday in Britain, she grew bored. So she devoted her time to Britain's future ambassador to Baghdad, Kinahan Cornwallis, with whom she had fallen in love, and Mesopotamian archaeology. At Ur, she caught up with former Arab Bureau colleague Leonard Wolley, who had made a number of seminal discoveries here, including the burial site of the Sumerian royals. In her role as Honorary Director of the Department of Antiquities in Iraq, she inspected the major archaeological sites, had a number of collections placed under her trust, and then established the National Museum of Iraq.

In 1925, Gertrude Bell played a key role in the LN negotiations to determine the future of Mosul. She organised the Iraqi delegations with meticulous attention to detail, to the point of specifying where each participant would sit. She asked delegates to avoid all mention of oil and focus instead on the principle of self-determination. Her strategy paid off: it was decided that the region would be attached to Iraq.

Britain had grabbed the oil wealth in the north of the country. This had been one of the main aims of the invasion of Mesopotamia. Gertrude Bell would have been elated at this victory, but this was a difficult period for her, and Cornwallis' refusal to marry her, even though he had only recently divorced, intensified her depression. In Baghdad, she sensed she was somewhat *de trop*. Though always polite, Faisal proved to be aloof. Her parents had been ruined by the economic crisis. Her health was deteriorating. Was life still really worth living?

On the evening of the 11 July 1926 – two days before her 58th birthday – after a day spent in the scorching heat of Baghdad, Gertrude Bell asked her maid to wake her at six in the morning. But she did not awake that morning: her extra dose of sleeping pills proved fatal.

Chapter XII

GERMANY: THE MARCH TO THE EASTERN OILFIELDS

Drang nach Osten
Acte II: Hitler's Spies

In the beginning of his political career, Hitler had a narrow vision of the world: there were the Aryans, and then there were the others. He scarcely paid any attention to the Mediterranean countries, with the notable exception of Palestine, but only in so far as he wanted to deport German Jews. In August 1933, the *Haavara (Transfer) Agreement* was signed by Samuel Cohen, director of *Hanotea*, a citrus export company which settled Jewish immigrants in Palestine, and Heinrich Wolff, the German consul-general in Jerusalem. The slogan, popular in Berlin at the time, was *"Germany for the Germans: the Jews in Palestine."* In February 1934, German diplomatic missions in the Middle East were told that the creation of a Jewish homeland was an objective in keeping with German policy[228].

---

[228] *Le sionisme de Hitler*, France-Pays Arabes, n° 35, juin-juillet 1973.

When Hitler was conciliatory with the British

Hitler left the Arabs to Mussolini, who dreamed of recreating the Roman Empire in the Mediterranean region[229]. It is known that Hitler admired Atatürk for having opposed the terms of the treaties signed after the First World War, and that he had a weakness for the Persians and the Kurds, as they were of Aryan origin. But he was completely indifferent to the situation in India, even though the reversed Nazi swastika was derived from a Hindu symbol. As he had stated in *Mein Kampf*, he preferred to see India under British domination than under that of any other nation.

The Nazi party had contacts with the *League Against Imperialism*[230], but these were of no interest to Hitler. Its representatives were, in his view, pretentious windbags, clearly of "inferior race". He refused to meet Chandra Bose[231], an Indian nationalist who was prepared to form a strategic alliance with the Nazis. When Bose returned to Calcutta, he

---

[229] In 1934, Mussolini supported the Zionist movement and had declared that the Jews needed their own country with borders. In a meeting with the Chief Rabbi of Alexandria, the Italian David Prato, Mussolini stated that he preferred to see a Jewish homeland run by Ze'ev Jabotinsky, the Revisionist Zionist leader, as he considered him to be a true fascist. Jabotinsky admired Mussolini and had often sought Rome's assistance.

[230] Among the members of the *League Against Imperialism* were India, Egypt and the Baltic states.

[231] Chandra Bose was elected mayor of Calcutta in 1924, and was appointed president of the Indian National Congress in 1938. During the Second World War, in January 1941, he again sought the support of Hitler and Stalin, united by the Nazi-Soviet Pact. Disappointed, he moved to Japan.

wrote to Dr Franz Thierfelder in 1936, expressing his regret that *"the new nationalism of Germany is not only narrow and selfish but also arrogant."*[232] Hitler's views then shifted slightly in accordance with strategic, diplomatic and military needs. But his political evolution was also due to the discovery of cultures whose existence and influence he had never even imagined[233].

In November 1941, he radically revised his position on the Palestinian question. Indeed, he made a complete U-turn in relation to his views held during the 30s, and urged Haj Amin al-Husseini, Grand Mufti of Jerusalem, to lock what he had told him in the *"innermost depths of his heart"*. He would not make a public call for the Muslims to stage a revolt against the Allies, as long the *Wehrmacht* had not captured the Caucasus[234]. In his final political testament[235], Hitler held Mussolini responsible for the failure of his Arab policy, condemning the brutal manner in which he crushed the Senussi revolt in Libya. Moreover, he believed that Mussolini looked ridiculous in 1937 when, during a pompous ceremony held in Tripoli, he had himself made Protector of Islam *"by a few wretched brutes whom he had either bribed or terrorized into doing so."*

The Arabs were of no interest to Hitler, who wanted to avoid

---

[232] Chandra Bose's letter (25 March 1936) to Dr Franz Thierfelder, director of *Stuttgart's German Academy of Foreign Relations*.

[233] Hitler, Adolphe, *Libres propos sur la guerre et la paix*, Flammarion, Paris, 1952.

[234] Minutes of Hitler's meeting with Amin al-Husseini, 28 November 1941 - *Documents on German Foreign Policy 1918-1945, Series D, Vol. XIII, London, 1964*.

[235] Hitler, Adolphe, *Testament politique d'Hitler*, notes de Martin Bormann, Fayard, 1959.

encroaching on British territory. As he had stated in *Mein Kampf*, he believed Britain to be the natural ally of Germany. The Spanish colonisation of Rio de Oro and a part of Morocco did not obstruct his plans either, as Franco was an ally. In 1944, he was very careful not to grant independence to Algeria, following Marshal Pétain's forced exile in Sigmaringen, because such a decision would have triggered Arab uprisings in all the other colonies. That he probably regretted not doing so with hindsight is another matter! Even Winston Churchill was surprised that Hitler did not fully exploit the opportunity to support the Iraqi nationalists who had seized power in 1941. Impervious to the opinions of others, the Führer shunned the advice of generals who, like Rommel, had wanted to deal the British a fatal blow at the beginning of the war by taking control of the Suez Canal, the Persian Gulf and the oil wells[236].

"The Napoleon of Oil" finances Hitler

Hitler thought that Germany could expand at the expense of Russia, provided that Britain confined its action to the defence of its territories. Fuelled by anti-Communism, this policy was supported by certain

---

[236] Hitler's *Directive 32* planned for three armoured divisions to join up in Basra. 1. Rommel's *Afrika Corps* was to seize the port city of Tobruk, the Suez Canal and Cairo, and then advance to Iraq via Sinai and Palestine. 2. From Bulgaria, Field Marshal von Bock's Panzer formation was to cross the Bosphorus and then continue across Anatolia, in order to join the *Afrika Corps* in Aleppo. 3. After having captured the Caucasus and Baku, Field Marshal List's unit was to rapidly advance to Basra, via Iran and Iraq. However, there was a key point of contention between Hitler and some of his generals: *Directive 32* was to be implemented only *after* the successful completion of *Operation Barbarossa*, i.e. following the collapse of the Soviet Union...

prominent figures in London. Indeed, in its early days the Nazi party had been partially financed by Henri Deterding's *Royal Dutch-Shell*. Nicknamed the "Napoleon of Oil", Deterding, whose wife was a White Russian, saw in Hitler a means of regaining control of the Caucasian oilfields. On Deterding's behalf, Captain Vivian Standers, British spy and commercial agent for a machine gun manfacturer, liaised with Alfred Rosenberg[237], leader of the Nazi's foreign policy office.

While Franz von Papen[238] acted as an intermediary between the Nazi regime and the British business world, Rosenberg travelled to London to meet prominent pro-German figures, including Deterding. After having eliminated his left-wing opponents in the Nazi party during the *Night of the Long Knives* on 29 June 1934, the Führer moved closer to Prussian military and industrial circles. In 1935, Deterding initiated secret discussions to supply Germany with a year's supply of oil on

---

[237] *Le Crapouillot*, juillet 1933.

[238] Franz von Papen was appointed Chancellor of Germany in 1932. But he first came to fame in 1915 when, as Germany's military attaché in Washington, he was expelled from the U.S. From 1914, with the aid of naval attaché Karl Boy-Ed, von Papen ran a spy network and organised a number of exceptionally dangerous acts of sabotage, aimed at disrupting the American supply of weapons and munitions to the Allied powers. Under his orders, American ships carrying munitions would burst into flames at sea. He created a trade union which paid workers to organise strikes in weapons factories, when they weren't blown up by his team of saboteurs. British intelligence kept an eye on him, as American intelligence at the time was not very effective. According to Kurt von Schleicher – the Weimar Republic's last chancellor, assassinated in June 1934 by the *SS* – von Papen was so treacherous that he made even Judas Iscariot look a saint! It was von Papen who, believing that Hitler would be easy to manipulate, urged Paul von Hindenberg to appoint him chancellor...

credit. The affair led to such an outcry that *Shell's* board of directors pushed their chief to take retirement.

Deterding divorced, married his German secretary, and then left Britain to live in Germany. He called for European leaders to cooperate with Nazi Germany[239]. Though Hitler believed the Slavs to be an inferior race, the Tsarist émigrés, financed by *Shell*, supported the Nazis. General Yevgeny-Ludvig Karlovich Miller[240], one of the leaders of the *ROVS*, a group which united all White Russian military personnel in exile, declared he was ready to raise a hundred thousand troops to capture the Caucasus. When Deterding died six months after the war had been declared in 1939, Hitler had two German diplomats in Nazi uniform place a wreath on his grave.

Did German designs on the Caucasian oil-fields play a role in Rudolf Hess' decision to make a clandestine flight to Britain[241], only days before Hitler launched *Operation Barbarossa* against the Soviet Union? According to this hypothesis[242], Hitler had asked Hess to negotiate an armistice with the British in exchange for joint ownership of the Baku

---

[239] Yergin, Daniel, *Les hommes du pétrole*, Stock, Paris, 1991.

[240] In September 1937, General Yevgeny-Ludvig Karlovich Miller was kidnapped by the NKVD and then executed in Moscow on 11th May 1939. He was betrayed by his right-hand man, Nikolai Skoblin, a Soviet agent who, under Stalin's orders, had infiltrated the Nazi intelligence service. The White Russians, partly financed by Deterding, supported Hitler.

[241] Rudolph Hess, the Nazi regime's third key man after Goering, was born in Egypt (Alexandria) to an English mother.

[242] Pierre Fontaine, *Les secrets du pétrole*, Les sept couleurs, Paris, 1963.

oilfields[243].

Fritz Grobba and the Golden Square

In the Near East, Hitler reactivated the networks which had been built during the First World War by Baron von Oppenheim and the Kaiser's secret service. New faces appeared, such as Fritz Grobba, who had built his reputation in the 1941 Baghdad coup, led by officers from the *Golden Square*. An expert in oriental languages, he spent time in Palestine, where he worked as a dragoman, before joining the German foreign ministry's *Abteilung III*, the department responsible for Eastern affairs. As German ambassador to Iraq from 1932-39, he successfully completed his mission, the scope of which was expanded to include Saudi Arabia, where he had attempted to persuade King Ibn Saud to support Germany.

Faisal's successor to the Iraqi throne, King Ghazi, was notoriously pro-German. What's more, he had announced his plans to reclaim Kuwait for his kingdom. In April 1939, he died in a curious car accident... It was immediately claimed that his assassination was the work of Iraqi nationalists.

Nothing got past the British in Iraq. In a secret report written by *Air Staff Intelligence*[244] in June 1939, we learn that Iraqi trade with Germany

---

[243] Hitler totally abandoned his fanciful project of negotiating a separate peace deal with Britain, when Japan entered the war and Germany declared war against the U.S.

[244] *German Propaganda Activities*, Air Staff Intelligence, Baghdad – 17 June 1939.

doubled, as German products were sold well below their Berlin price, and that the III Reich's propaganda was increasingly effective. According to the report, moreover, teachers from Karl Hanshofer's[245] *Deutsche Akademie* in Munich tutored disadvantaged Iraqis so that they could then study at German universities.

The British secret services in Iraq gave particular attention to: the *Committee for the Defence of Palestine* and the Iraqi nationalist *Muthanna Club*; the pro-Palestinian Yunis al-Bahri, who came to fame as the presenter of Radio Berlin's Arab language service; and Dr. Amin Ruwayha, a Syrian- Palestinian deemed to be a dangerous anti-Zionist. Ruwayha later justified his pro-German stance. First of all, the Germans had not colonised a single Arab country: their hands were clean, so to speak. Secondly, they had declared war against the British and the French, enemies of the Arabs. Thirdly, they had never exploited or betrayed the Arab people. Fourthly, German was not a signatory to the secret *Sykes-Picot Agreement*. Finally – and this is the most surprising point - the Germans had lost Alsace-Lorraine, so they understood what it meant to be occupied by a foreign power[246].

In a similar vein, Rashid Ali al-Gaylani, the Iraqi prime minister, and the *Golden Square* colonels, hailed as national heroes for having

---

[245] Hanshofer was a German geopolitician who postulated that the survival of a state depends on its living space (*Lebensraum*). He was close to Rudolf Hess, one of his former students. He was imprisoned at Dachau for eight months, while his son, implicated in the plot to assassinate Hitler, was executed.

[246] Walid Amin Ruwayha, *Terrorism and Hostage-Taking in the Middle-East*, J.C.I., 1990. Ruwayha was exiled to Southern Rhodesia by the British, together with a number of other nationalists.

overthrown the pro-British regime in 1941, were not Nazis: they were Iraqi nationalists. Originally, they had planned to stage their coup on the 10 May. But they went ahead with their plans a month earlier when they learnt that the Ghurkhas[247] had disembarked in India and were soon to arrive in Basra. In any case, the conditions at the time appeared to be favourable for Rashid Ali to attempt a takeover by force. Since the Germans were occupying Greece and Crete, they would be able to support them, as the foreign intelligence service of the *SS* had seemed to promise. The British would not be able to send sufficient troop reinforcements, as the *Africa Korps* were gaining ground in the Libyan Desert. So Rashid Ali went ahead, and his troops surrounded the RAF base at Habbaniya. After having asked the British ambassador, Kinahan Cornwallis, to move all families living on the base to somewhere safe, he ordered his troops to begin the bombardment. British prisoners were taken, and Ali proposed to exchange them for the departure of the Ghurkhas.

Iraq's oilfields were placed under national control. The *Iraq Petroleum Company* was ordered to pay for their maintenance and to supply the Iraqi army with over four million litres of petrol, which was then diverted to the *Wehrmacht*. Rashid Ali and the *Golden Square* officers had thus honoured their deal concluded with Franz von Papen, the III Reich's ambassador to Constantinople: provide access to Iraqi oil in exchange for German military aid, so that they could liberate and then unify the Arab countries. The rest was now up to the Germans.

Despite the Iraqi bombardment of the RAF base at Habbaniya, the

---

[247] An elite regiment in the British Indian Army.

British stood their ground. They had made a small air-strip on the golf course, allowing them to have ammunition supplies flown in. Fritz Grobba, who represented the Führer in his dealings with Rashid Ali, finally arrived on 11 May. He was four days late and accompanied by a German contingent which fell well below Iraqi expectations. The Germans had suffered serious losses in Crete, Grobba claimed, hence the small number of troops available. A German colonel, who had made an assessment of Iraqi military needs, requested six *Messershimitt* squadrons. But they did not arrive. Nor did a large part of the weapons promised by General Dentz, Vichy's High Commissioner in Syria[248].

Like the Iraqis, Fritz Grobba was unaware that the German army was set to attack Stalin's Russia and that Hitler, who at this time was in favour of a separate peace with Britain, did not want to make any further commitments to the Iraqi cause. To make matters worse, Major Axel von Blomberg, dispatched to command the German troops in Iraq, had been killed on the flight to Baghdad. Mistaking his plane for a British bomber, an Iraqi, apparently, had shot at his aircraft. Having learnt that the British had captured Fallujah and would soon arrive in Baghdad, Fritz Grobba fled to Mossul on 30 May, and then moved on to Turkey[249]. Rashid Ali and the Mufti of Jerusalem sought refuge in Iran and then in Berlin.

Glubb Pasha and Operation Golden Carpet

John Bagot Glubb (also known as Glubb Pasha), an officer in the British

---

[248] Eppler, John, *Condor, l'espion de Rommel*, Robert Laffont, Paris, 1974.

[249] Mosley, Léonard, *La guerre du pétrole*, Presses de la Cité, Paris, 1973.

Army, is widely credited with regaining control of Baghdad. *Operation Golden Carpet* was led by Brigadier Joe Kingstone. Glubb Pasha's *Desert Patrol*, a unit comprised of Bedouin soldiers from the *Arab Legion*, cleared the way for Kingstone's troops (*Kingcol*).

Glubb Pasha, who had served as the commanding officer of *Desert Patrol* which guarded Transjordan's borders, had taken control of the *Arab Legion* in 1939. Nicknamed *Abu Hunaik*[250] ("the father with the little jaw") by his men, he transformed the *Arab Legion* into an elite Bedouin force, devoted to the Hashemite family - and British interests[251]. In 1941, he struggled to convince the Jordanians that the British were not losing the war. British-trained Arab troops rebelled or deserted. So there was a need to restore lost prestige, and the chance to recapture Baghdad provided the ideal opportunity.

Following a series of battles at Rutbah, not far from the border with Jordan, the priority was to secure the H3 pumping station of the Mosul – Haifa pipeline. Needless to say, Iraqi weaponry was no match for that of the British: *Kingcol* liberated RAF Habbaniya with ease. Random strafing by several *Messerschmitts* did little to help the Iraqis. On 31 May, the provisional government, established following the departure of Rashid Ali, accepted the terms of the armistice imposed by the British.

---

[250] Glubb Pasha was nicknamed *Abu Hunaik* because he had sustained an injury while fighting in France during the First World War and was left with a disfigured jaw.

[251] Transjordan was the only Arab country to have declared war against Germany in 1939. But Egypt, Syria, Lebanon, Saudi Arabia – countries under British and French control - declared war much later, in February 1945. Joining the war against Germany was a *sine qua non* for a seat at the UN.

Kinahan Cornwallis, who for the duration of the conflict had been forced to remain in the embassy with a number of other British nationals, notably Freya Stark, announced the return of Abdul Ilah, the reviled regent. Somerset de Chair, the intelligence agent attached to *Kingcol*, recounts in *The Golden Carpet*[252] that Iraqis spat at them as they passed by.

In 1946, King Abdullah I granted Jordanian nationality to Glubb Pasha, following his conversion to Islam. While the king held secret talks with Golda Meir and Moshe Sharett in 1948, the *Arab Legion* prevented the *Haganah*[253] from capturing Jerusalem. It was the only notable Arab victory of the first Arab-Israeli war, and was in fact down to Colonel Abdullah el-Tell. But Glubb Pasha and the king were not pleased by this exploit. They accused the colonel of insubordination and seeking to stage a coup. A hero for the Arabs, Abdullah el-Tell went into exile in Egypt, where he remained for twenty years.

In 1954, Saïd Ramadan, one of the leaders of the *Muslim Brotherhood*, was banished from Jerusalem by Glubb Pasha. But, worried by the rise of *Nassersim*, King Hussein was then forced to dismiss Glubb Pasha in 1956. When he returned to London, he was awareded a knighthood.

Palestine: the Stern Gang turns to Hitler

Arab nationalists, organised into armed groups by Izz ad-Din al-

---

[252] Somerset de Chair, *Le Tapis doré*, Tallandier, Paris, 1946.

[253] The *Haganah*, founded in June 1920, was the armed wing of the *Jewish Agency*. The Zionist left-wing formed the majority.

Qassam[254], were not the only ones to oppose the British occupation of Palestine. The British also faced resistance from Jewish settlers, who found that London was slow in keeping its promise to create a Jewish homeland. In the early days of the Second World War, the Zionist movement was divided as to which strategy to adopt vis-à-vis Britain and Germany. On the one hand, David Ben-Gurion (*Haganah*) and Vladimir Jabotinsky (*Irgun*)[255] advocated an alliance with the British. On the other hand, Abraham Stern (*Irgun*) looked to negotiate with the Germans, in the hope of reaching some form of formal agreement, similar to the Nazi-Soviet pact. In 1940, Stern split from the *Irgun* and formed his own armed unit, known as *Lehi* (Fighters for the Freedom of Israel) and entered into talks with both the Germans and the Italians. Naftali Lubenchik, Stern's representative, was sent to meet Werner von Hentig, the German foreign ministry's emissary to the *Italian Armistice Commission for Syria*, based in Beirut. The *Lehi* proposed to help the Germans capture Palestine in exchange for the creation of a Jewish state. Stern claimed that he could raise 40 000 soldiers, and clearly had

---

[254] Izz ad-Din al-Qassam (1882 – 1935) was a Syrian religious leader with close links to the *Muslim Brotherhood*. Sentenced to death for having led a revolt against French forces in Syria, he fled to Palestine, where he founded the *Black Hand*, an anti-British and anti-Zionist militia, independent from the Grand Mufti of Jerusalem's *fedayeen*. Pursued by the British police, he sought refuge in a cave not far from Ya'bad. Surrounded, he was killed in the ensuing shootout on 21 November 1935. The armed wing of *Hamas* bears his name.

[255] The *Irgun Zvai Leumi* (National Military Organisation) was founded in 1931 in response to growing dissension within the *Haganah*. Ze'ev Jabotinsky (1880-1940) was one of one of the group's leaders. Menachem Begin took over the leadership in 1943.

few qualms about becoming a Middle Eastern equivalent of Quisling[256].

Berlin, however, made no response to the proposition and the *Lehi* - or the *Stern Gang* as the British called them - continued their campaign of assassinations, kidnappings and bank robberies. Stern made a second attempt to convince the Germans, but the British had arrested his envoys in Syria. Following Stern's execution by the British in 1942, the *Lehi* was led by a troika, comprising the future Israeli Prime Minister Yitzhak Shamir, who was behind the assassination of Lord Moyne, Britain's Resident Minister of State in Cairo,[257] on 6 November 1944.

Arrested by the British in July 1946 for terrorism and collaboration with the Nazis, Shamir was sent to an internment camp in Eritrea. But he managed to escape, and then fled via Djibouti. He reached Jerusalem in September 1948, just in time to participate in the assassination of Count Folke Bernadotte, the UN Security Council official tasked with mediating the conflict.

Werner von Hentig, following the downfall of Hitler, continued his diplomatic career as an ambassador in Indonesia. He later became the Saudi royal family's adviser. In this capacity, he is said to have participated in the 1955 *Bandung Conference*, which ratified the *Non-*

---

[256] Vidkun Quisling, a Norwegian officer, came to power in April 1940, during the Nazi occupation. In 1945, he was executed for treason. Ever since, his name became synonymous with treachery. Indeed, the dictionary defines *quisling* as a national leader who collaborates with an enemy occupying his country.

[257] During a speech made on 9 June 1942 in the House of Lords, Lord Moyne declared that Jewish settlers in Palestine were not the true descendants of the ancient Hebrews and, therefore, had no legitimate claim to the Holy Land.

Alignment Movement.

Battle of Stalingrad, battle for oil

For the Nazis, the Caucasus was the birthplace of the Aryan race and defined the outer limit of Europe. Hitler's propaganda presented the *Wehrmacht* as the army which would liberate the Caucasians from Slavic tyranny. But the true objective was to seize control of the oilfields. Since German troops were ordered to behave in an exemplary fashion with the local population, in stark contrast to German- occupied East European countries where no such order was given, Hitler's soldiers were warmly welcomed, even by the Cossacks. The massacres carried out by Bolshevik forces following the defeat of the White Army were fresh in the minds of the Caucasians. What they did not know, however, was that they were to be governed by a *Gauleiter*[258], who was already studying the plans of his future palace in Tbilisi.

A confederation of *Wehrmacht* officers disagreed with the racial policies implemented in East Europe. In Ukraine, Gauleiter Erich Koch's extremism had been widely criticised, even by staunch supporters of Hitler. The officers were keen to ensure that the same errors were not repeated. According to them, the rigid application of Nazi ideological principles to occupied countries led to defeat, an opinion shared by Field Marshal Wilhelm von List, supreme commander of German forces in the Caucasus. The group of officers was led by Count Claus von

---

[258] Ostensibly, the *Gauleiter* governed the district under German rule. In reality, however, he also often led, behind the scenes, the puppet governments set up in the occupied countries.

Stauffenberg, who had attempted to assassinate Hitler on 20 July 1944, and Oskar von Niedermayer[259], the spy who had been sent on a mission to Afghanistan in 1915 by the Kaiser.

On 21 August 1942, German troops climbed to the summit of Mount Elbrus where, in a symbolic gesture, they planted the *Wehrmacht* flag. Disorganised and poorly equipped, the Soviet troops retreated. Hitler urgently needed to secure an oil supply for his army, since supplies from Romanian wells were insufficient. Seizing the oilfields at Maykop, Grozny and Baku was his last chance for victory. The objective seemed within his reach. He confided to Albert Speer his plan to push towards Iraq, Iran and even, evoking Napoleon, India[260]! Filmed by Goebbels' propaganda service, Hitler was presented with a birthday cake, representing the Caucasus and the Caspian: the Führer grabbed the slice marked Baku. The Germans reached Maykop, but failed to advance any further. As the weeks went by, their dream turned into nightmare. The Red Army counterattacked, blocking the advance of the *Wehrmacht*.

Aided by a thousand Communist agitators, the internal affairs commissar, Lavrentiy Pavlovich Beria[261], a Caucasian like Stalin,

---

[259] After Germany had capitulated on 9 May 1945, Oskar von Niedermayer was arrested by the Red Army and deported to Moscow, where he was sentenced to twenty-five years in prison. He died in Vladimir prison hospital on 25 September 1948.

[260] Eric Hoesli, *À la conquête du Caucase*, Éditions des Syrtes, Paris, 2006.

[261] Lavrentiy Pavlovich Beria, NKVD chief and former member of the Cheka, was Abkhazian. In 1931, he was appointed Secretary of the Communist Party in Georgia.

ruthlessly regained control. Entire ethnic groups, including the Chechens, were deported. Hitler refused to admit defeat, believing that he was a victim of a conspiracy hatched by his generals. So he dismissed Field Marshal von List and then attempted to command the troops himself. But Hitler, too, was forced to retreat. Maykop was liberated in January 1942, before the Germans even had the chance to exploit its oilfields and resupply their armed forces. On 13 February, it was a Communist flag which flew high above Mount Elbrus.

Although his general staff advised a withdrawal from Stalingrad to concentrate on the Caucasus, Hitler stuck to his plans, refusing to relinquish the Soviet city. Supplies to his army - and, hence the entire war - were hinging on this battle. When General Zhukov's troops encircled the Germans, the Führer ordered General von Paulus to hold his forces in position, even though there was still time to break out. Hitler ordered him to hold Stalingrad at all costs: victory or death. The Allied powers then proposed to help Stalin maintain the Caucasus. But Stalin refused, recalling that during the 1920s, both the British and the French had proceeded in the same way in an attempt to gain control of the oilfields. During the next three months, the Soviets regained control of Stalingrad, house by house. General von Paulus asked Hitler for permission to surrender. By way of reply, Hitler promoted him to the rank of field marshal! Hitler's message was clear: no Prussian field marshal had ever surrendered. Nonetheless, three days later, on 2 February, Field Marshal von Paulus and his men (94 000 troops, including 24 generals) capitulated[262]. The Battle of Stalingrad closed

---

[262] Field Marshal Friederich von Paulus was taken into custody by the Soviets, but he refused to cooperate with them at first. However, after having learned that his

Germany's road to Caucasian oil. Hitler had lost 850 000 soldiers....
and the war.

---

friends had been executed following a failed attempt to assassinate Hitler on 20
July 1944, he agreed to collaborate. In 1946, he appeared at the Nuremberg Trial
as a witness for the prosecution. He was finally released in 1953 and ended his
days in the German Democratic Republic.

Chapter XIII

GAAFAR JOHN EPPLER, THE *ABWEHR'S* SPY

During the 1930s, Admiral Canaris' *Abwehr*, the *Wehrmacht's* intelligence service, recruited some of its spies among Germans living abroad. In the Near East, "Eppler the Egyptian", born in Alexandria to a German mother and a Lebanese father in 1914, had the perfect profile. When Eppler's father died suddenly, Salah Gaafar[263], a prominent Egyptian magistrate, adopted him. Though not fascinated by Nazi ideology, Eppler dreamed of adventure and believed that supporting Hitler, whom he considered to be the greatest of all adventurers, would allow him to explore the world without ever getting bored. Moreover, like many Egyptian nationalists, Eppler believed that Germany's rise to power would provide Egypt with the means to push the British out of the country. An opinion shared by the founder of the *Muslim Brotherhood*, Hassan al-Banna, who had once told him that Muslims should take from Europe everything which might serve the Islamic cause and discard the rest even if, subsequently, this position would need to be revised, given that Germany, just like the British before them, would certainly not stand for the establishment of an independent Islamic state in the Near East. Eppler already had contacts with other nationalist groups and leaders,

---

[263] Salah Gaafar served as Supreme Court judge during the reign of both Kings Fouad and Farouk. He was later appointed minister of justice.

including Ahmed Hussein's *Green Shirts* (the Egyptian equivalent of the fascist *Black Shirts*), and a number of nationalist officers, notably Anwar el-Sadat. Consequently, when "Rohde", Germany's military attaché for Greece and Turkey, invited Eppler to join the *Abwehr*, he readily agreed.

Special missions in Iran and Afghanistan

Following a period of intense training in Germany, the *Abwehr* sent Eppler to the outer reaches of Iran, Turkey and the Soviet Union. He covered some 700 km on donkey-back, mapping routes and noting their condition *en route*. It was only much later that he understood the true purpose of his mission: Germany had planned to break through to the Euphrates and seize control of the oilfields in Mosul. Following Germany's failure to seize control of the Caucasus, however, this operation was abandoned.

The *Abwehr* then resumed its operations both in Iran – the new name for Persia, following the rise of Reza Shah - and in Afghanistan, continuing where Wilhelm II's agents (Wilhelm Wassmuss and Oskar Niedermayer) had left off. The Germans did not want to embarass the Iranian leader, Reza Shah, who was somewhat favourable to the Nazi regime. So Eppler discreetly made contact with Nasir Khan, chief of the *Qashqai*, and convinced him to support Germany, should this prove necessary in the future. Since the Islamic tribes of the Near East did not always appreciate being paid in coins adorned with a woman's head, albeit Queen Victoria's, he paid the tribal chief a significant sum of gold sovereigns, bearing the image of St. George.

During the Second World War, after the British forced the Shah to abdicate, the *Qashqai* more or less kept their promise. In 1943, aided by Otto Skorzeny's *SS* troops, the tribesmen attacked Allied convoys on the so-called *Lend-Lease Road*, constructed by the British and the Americans to transport weapons and supplies to the Soviet Union. But the tribesmen lacked commitment to the cause: the operation failed miserably. Though some of the German troops managed to flee to Turkey, the rest were captured or handed over to the British.

In 1939, Eppler trekked across Afghanistan in search of a tribal chief capable of capturing and holding Kabul. But his search proved fruitless. Though there was no shortage of tribal warriors, the country's chronic instability did not favour long-term plans. Having escaped death on a number of occasions, saved by luck and a loyal guide, he left Afghanistan with few regrets. Accordingly, Hitler abandoned his plans to invade British India – via this route, at any rate.

Romania, Iraq: a war for oil and a revolutionary putsch

With the declaration of the war, the supply of oil became one of the priorities for the III Reich. The *Brandenburgers*, the *Abwehr's* special operations unit, protected the factories producing synthetic fuel. In Romania, Eppler thwarted British intelligence plans to block the Danube by sinking barges loaded with cement. Under his orders, the *Brandenburgers* sunk the barges before they even had chance to leave the port. Had the British operation succeeded, German tankers would not have been able to access the oil fields.

In late 1939, Eppler wanted to create in Turkey a sleeper cell capable of rapidly seizing the Caucasus before the Red Army would have had chance to destroy the Baku oil wells and pipelines in response to a German attack. In the end, however, he ditched this plan, because the *Wehrmacht* would have taken too long to reach Azerbaijan, and Turkish cooperation was far from certain. In July 1940, while in Iraqi Kurdistan, Eppler refused the offer of an enormous salary to leave the *Abwehr* and join *Amt VI*[264], the foreign intelligence service of the *SS*, as he detested the division's chief, Walter Schellenberg.

A month later, in Baghdad, Eppler attended a meeting of a secret group, later known as the *Golden Square*, which would attempt to overthrow the Iraqi government in April 1941. The meeting was attended by Haj Amin al-Husseini, the Grand Mufti of Jerusalem, and Colonel Mahmud Salman, who represented the pro-independence Iraqi officers. The Grand Mufti, being more concerned by German financial support than anything else, appeared to Eppler to be neither serious nor reliable. The revolutionary committees he proposed to mobilise were figments of his imagination. What's more, the Holy War which he intended to declare against the British was fanciful. Eppler knew that Hassan al- Banna and the *Muslim Brotherhood* would quite naturally support an anti-British revolt in Iraq but that they would think twice if al-Hussseini were

---

[264] Section C13 of *Amt VI* was in charge of "Arab Affairs." Following the arrest of Admiral Wihlem Canaris, the Abwehr was abolished in 1944 and its remaining functions were transferred to *Ausland SD*, led by Walter Schellenberg. At the Nuremberg Trial, Schellenberg testified against his superiors. He was given a six-year prison sentence on 4 November 1949. Suffering from ill health, he was released after two years, and moved to Turin, where he died in 1952.

involved.

In January 1941, together with an officer from the OKW^{265}, Eppler made a sobering assessment of the Iraqi army, and organised another meeting with Mahmud Salman. With the nationalist Rashid Ali al-Gaylani in post as prime minister, the conspiracy entered its final phase. Salman remained realistic, because he knew that the British would defend Iraq – or, rather, its oilfields – to their last dying breath. He wanted to know how far the Germans were prepared to go. Eppler's reply was scarcely encouraging: everything would depend on the presence of the *Wehrmacht* on the ground.

When the revolt broke out, German military support was as limited as it was ineffectual. Eppler was forced to face the anger of disappointed Iraqi nationalists for whom the Nazis were *"paralytic dogs"*. Following the capture of Baghdad by Glubb Pasha's *Arab Legion*, Eppler helped Rashid Ali al- Gaylani make his way to Turkey, where he then had him flown to Berlin.

Upon his return to Berlin, Eppler was summoned by Hitler to act as an interpreter for his private audience with the Grand Mufti of Jerusalem. Hitler was curious to know where Eppler had learnt Arabic. Eppler explained that he was born in Alexandria, like Rudolf Hess, who had just parachuted into Britain in order to propose a peace deal. Though the German press condemned Hess, portraying him as a traitor, the *Führer* smiled when Eppler mentioned his name, as if the operation had

---

[265] The OKW - *Oberkommando der Wehrmacht* – was the German supreme command structure, led by Field Marshal Wilhelm Keitel.

been organised with his tacit approval. Though Hitler's attitude to the Grand Mufti was cordial, he appeared somewhat absent during the meeting. Eppler sensed that he was more concerned by the situation on the Eastern front than the fate of Arab nationalists in the Near East.

Condor, or Rommel's spy in Cairo

In early 1942, Eppler landed in Libya. Field Marshal Rommel, commander of the *Afrika Korps*, asked him to be his agent in Egypt. The only possible entry point into Egypt was in the extreme south, via the rocky plateaus of the Libyan Desert, a route which avoided the British *Long Range Desert Group*. This reconnaissance unit, created by Brigadier Ralph Bagnold and nicknamed the *Desert Scorpions*, patrolled zones reputed to be inaccessible.

Eppler was aided by the Austro-Hungarian count Laszlo Almasy[266] (nicknamed *Abu Ramla* - Father of the Sand - by the Bedouin) who had explored the Libyan Desert in 1933, and his radio operator, Peter Monkaster. Together they crossed the *Garet es-Saghar* (The Devil's

---

[266] Recruited by the *Abwehr* in 1940, Count Laszlo Almasy led an expedition in 1932 to locate the legendary Zerzura oasis and Cambyses' lost army (50 000 soldiers), said to have been wiped out by a sandstorm in 525 BC after having left the Siwah Oasis (Herodotus 3:26). The expedition team, among whom was Gilbert Clayton (former Arab Bureau chief), discovered the Cave of Swimmers, located in the Gilf Kebir plateau, proving that there had once been a river in the valley. After the war, Almasy was arrested and tried for treason by Hungary's communist regime, but was eventually acquitted. He moved to Cairo, where he was appointed director of the *Egyptian Desert Research Institute*. Loosely based on his life, the film *The English Patient* sparked much controversy in light of his Nazi past.

Garden), a vast expanse of granite rocks, and then the inhospitable *Gilf Kebir* (The Great Barrier), before reaching the Egyptian city of Asyut. When they finally arrived in Cairo in May, with a state-of-the-art radio transmitter and a large sum of forged pound notes in their baggage, they rented a houseboat on the Nile, which happened to be moored no more than a hundred metres away from that used by "Colonel Robertson", the local chief of British intelligence...

Much of the information communicated to Rommel came from Egypt's leading belly dancer Hekmet Fahmy, who lived on a houseboat close to Eppler's. Fahmy, like Eppler, was a nationalist and so readily agreed to help her friend. The careless pillow talk of British officers proved to be rich source of intelligence.

In July, Eppler's radio transmitter ceased to function. He no longer received confirmation that his messages had been received. So he asked Anwar el-Sadat, a signals officer in the Egyptian army at the time, to repair the transmitter. According to the future Egyptian president, the apparatus was ingeniously concealed: "*it would need a clever investigator to guess that inside this commonplace article of furniture there was a secret transmitter sending messages to the Wehrmacht.*"[267] But Saddat's efforts to repair the radio were in vain. It was only after the war that Eppler discovered the reason why: the German radio operators had been captured by the *Long Range Desert Group*. As a precaution, "Angelo", his chief in Berlin, immediately cut all communication. Rommel no longer had any information on

---

[267] Anwar el-Sadat, *Revolt on the Nile*, New York, 1957.

Montgomery's plans and, consequently, fell into the trap of El Alamein.

With the defeat of the *Afrika Korps*, Nazi Germany lost all possibility of ever gaining control of the Iraqi and Iranian oilfields. After having interrogated one of the German radio operators, British intelligence knew that agent *Condor* was transmitting from somewhere in Cairo. Eppler then committed a careless error. Disguised as a British officer, he managed to gain entry to the *Semiramis Hotel*, and ordered drinks at the bar, but he paid in pound notes rather than using the local currency. He then made the same mistake with "Yvette", a prostitute working for the *Jewish Agency*. He was arrested, along with Monkaster, and taken to an interrogation centre.

Cautious retreat

At first, Eppler refused to say anything to the British, despite their attempt to terrify him with a phoney trial which sentenced him to death. A few sessions of torture, however, loosened his tongue. But what he said was no longer of any interest. This time he really was sentenced to death. Luckily, his family successfully petitioned King Farouk, and his sentence was commuted to two years imprisonment. Immediately after his release in 1946, the KGB asked him to spy for the Soviet Union. He refused, believing, and no doubt with good reason, that one very rarely escapes death twice[268].

---

[268] *The Real Spy's Story Reads like Fiction and 40 Years later Inspires a Best-Seller*, Pamela Andriotakis, *People*, 15 December 1980

Chapter XIV

DAME FREYA STARK DABBLES IN ESPIONAGE

Even the British explorer Freya Stark, better known for her books recounting her adventures in Arabia and Persia[269] during the inter-war period, dabbled in espionage. Of an inquisitive nature, her extensive travels brought her into contact with sheikhs, diplomats, ministers and journalists. In 1940, she was recruited by the British Ministry of Information, created to counterattack German and Italian subversive activities in the Horn of Africa. Based in Aden, she put into practice the sort of propaganda techniques she had seen work so well in Mussolini's Italy.

Transferred to Baghdad in 1941, she worked with Kinahan Cornwallis, Britain's ambassador in Iraq, and became one of the central figures in the region, spearheading efforts to thwart the *Golden Square* revolt. Believing that German success was essentially due to Britain's deplorable image, she led a crusade for democracy. In Cairo, she created the *Ikhwan al Hurriya* (Brotherhood of Freedom) in a bid to unite pro-British Arabs, especially those engaged in the armed forces. According to her, the Brotherhood had a hundred thousand members

---

[269] *The Valleys of the Assassins*, which recounts her search for Hassan al-Sabbah's fortress, located in the Elburz Mountains, became a best-seller.

across Egypt[270], Palestine and Iraq, though others have tempered this claim, putting the figure at some forty thousand.

In 1943, Freya Stark spent six months in the United States, where she led a campaign to defend British policy in Palestine, as defined by the White Paper of 1939. In this way, she hoped to highlight some of the possible dangers of mass colonisation by Jewish settlers[271]. Terrorist attacks carried out by the *Irgun* and the *Stern Gang* had claimed many British lives[272]. Although her criticism of Zionism was philosophical and political in nature, and not in any way racist, she was accused of anti-Semitism. In Britain, Churchill was one of the main opponents of the White Paper, noting that the Arabs had done nothing for the Allied cause during the war, save for staging a revolt in Iraq[273]. When the war ended, Freya Stark went back to writing. In 1953, she was awarded a Cross of the British Empire and then, in 1972, was named a Dame of the British Empire.

---

[270] Betty Patchin Greene, *A Talk with Freya Stark*, Saudi Aramco World, September 1977.

[271] The British government's White Paper (*Palestine – Statement of Policy*, 17 May 1939) limited Jewish immigration into Palestine to 75 000 for 5 years and prohibited Zionist organisations from buying land in certain Palestinian regions.

[272] At the beginning of the Second World War, the *Irgun* suspended its assassination campaign, giving free rein to the *Stern Gang*. It resumed its campaign in February 1944. It is thought that over 300 British servicemen were killed between 1944 and 1948.

[273] Telegram from Prime Minister to Foreign Office, 12 January 1944, FO/371/40133.

Chapter XV

OIL: FRANCE TRAILS BEHIND THE BRITISH AND THE AMERICANS

U p until the First World War, France's lack of strategic vision and, worse still, its dependency on Anglo-Saxon oil companies (*Anglo-Persian Oil Company, Royal Dutch Shell, Standard Oil*) led the country to the brink of disaster. Ever since the Rothschilds had sold their Caucasian companies to *Royal Dutch Shell*, France was obliged to import the bulk of its oil from the United States. Refinery and distribution was in the hands of a powerful cartel, led by *Desmarais Frères* and the Deutsch de la Meurthe family[274]. Consequently, when the French parliament proposed to create a state monopoly for fuels, *Standard Oil*'s threat to stop supplying France was sufficient to veto the entire project[275].

For Germany, Britain and the United States, securing oil supplies was the number one priority. In France, however, few people of any influence were interested in finding oil in Mesopotamia. In 1913, prime

---

[274] In 1900, Henri Deutsch de la Meurthe, dubbed the "Oil King of Europe", presented one of the first petrol-driven cars at the *Exposition Universelle*, held in Paris.

[275] Faure, Edgar, « Le pétrole pendant la paix et pendant la guerre », *Nouvelle Revue Critique*, Paris, 1939.

minister Gaston Doumergue's interest in Mosul went no further than the construction of a French school there[276]. Marcel Sembat, one of the most prominent French socialist ministers, officially wished the Kaiser all the best for his voyage in the Near East, believing that the construction of the Berlin-Baghdad railway line would divert Germany's attention from international affairs of greater importance[277]. Georges Clemenceau dismissed the strategic significance of the Near East, describing it as a region of *"trifling importance"*! Though the radical Édouard Herriot[278] was more lucid - he was determined to thwart German colonial plans in Mesopotamia[279] - at no point did he ever think to mention oil...

In 1917, Henri Bérenger, an influential senator, was the only one to condemn France's lamentable energy policy. He was appointed chairman of the *General Committee for Oil*. But his appointment came too late. At the height of the war, France ran out of petrol! Clemenceau was then obliged to make an urgent appeal to U.S. President Wilson, begging him to make *Standard Oil* supply France. *"Petrol is as vital as blood in the coming battles"*, he wrote, stressing that without oil the Allies would lose the war. David Rockefeller, who had officially been on retirement since 1911, made a point of agreeing only at the very last minute. He savoured this vengeance because, with the *Sykes-Picot*

---

[276] André Nouschi, *Les origines de la CFP avant 1924*, in Claude Paillat, *Dossiers secrets de la France contemporaine* (tome II), Robert Laffont, Paris, 1992.

[277] Sembat, Marcel, *Faites un roi sinon faites la paix*, Eugène Figuière, Paris, 1913.

[278] Édouard Herriot served three times as French prime minister. He was president of the Radical Party and several times mayor of Lyon (1905-1942, 1942-1945, and 1945-1957).

[279] Aublé, Émile, *Bagdad*, Éditions et Librairies, Paris, 1917.

Agreement, the French and the British had excluded America - i.e. his company - from the Near East oil market. Although French oil consumption totalled 59 000 tonnes per month, *Standard Oil* agreed to supply a mere 29 000 tonnes in February 1918.

The solitary struggle of Bertrand Bareilles

At the end of the l9th century, the *Quai d'Orsay* ought to have vigorously defended French oil interests in the Ottoman Empire, if only to outwit Germany, which was occupying Alsace and Lorraine at the time. But the French ministry of foreign affairs proved to be criminally incompetent. Its representatives in Constantinople were, save for a few rare exceptions, either cretinous or corrupt. The most egregious example of what can only be described as treason was the contempt reserved for Bertrand Bareilles, preceptor to the son of Sultan Abdul Hamid II.

In September 1899, Bareilles was on the verge of securing a 45-year concession for an oil field, stretching from Mosul to Kirkuk[280]. But the French government failed to send him the letter necessary to secure the Sultan's *firman*. He contacted the French ambassador in Constantinople, Ernest Constans, and then the *Quai d'Orsay*, but to no avail. And yet, the matter was urgent. Exploration work really had to begin before the arrival of the Berlin-Baghdad railway in the vilayet of Mosul. Once the line was constructed, the Germans would have owned

---

[280] Bareilles, Roland, *Le crépuscule ottoman*, Privat, Paris, 2002. Roland Bareilles, grandson of Bertrand Bareilles, worked as a director for *Total* in Baghdad from 1950 to 1980.

land to a distance of 27km on either side of the railway, and Bareilles knew that the route had been carefully chosen by their geologists to pass through oil-rich zones.

Ernest Constans, who held the interior minister post several times between 1877 and 1892, was best known for his crackdown on the *Boulangist* movement[281]. As minister, he had compiled a number of files, containing compromising information on various key political figures. It is perhaps for this reason that it was so difficult to relieve him of his ambassadorial duties in Constantinople. Moreover, he took advantage of his embassy business contacts, notably with *Deutsche Bank*, to supplement his salary. During his entire mission, he sent not one briefing on the Sultan's policies to the *Quai d'Orsay*. In late 1900, Bareilles came to Paris after having been awarded the Order of Distinction, the highest order in the Ottoman Empire. But his voyage was in vain: not one of the diplomats he met had wanted to take the risk of offending Constans.

The banks, though interested in the concession, demanded that he cover part of the exploitation costs. As a French teacher at the most prestigious school in Constantinople, he earned a comfortable salary, but it was insufficient to borrow the sums needed to finance his venture.

---

[281] The rise of *Boulangisme*, a nationalist movement, was a threat to France's Third Republic. Among its demands, was the liberation of the Alsace Lorraine region, occupied by the Germans. The group was named after its leader, General Boulanger, former minister of war (7 January 1886 – 30 May 1887). According to the polemicist Léon Daudet, Ernest Constans was unscrupulous, utterly mediocre, universally despised, and considered to be something of second-rate policeman by the Republicans. (Roland Bareilles, *Le crépuscule ottoman*, Privat, Paris, 2002)

Greatly vexed, he returned to Turkey. Constans remained in post for over ten years! Bareilles had to wait for the arrival of his successor, Maurice Bompard, for a telegram regarding his drilling rights to be sent to Paris. But the letter, sent in October 1909 to the French finance ministry by the commercial attaché for the Levant, received no reply...

Bertrand Bareilles waited for years, during which time Germany increased its military and economic power and reinforced its influence in Turkey. Calouste Gulbenkian, a man of exceptional intelligence, worked in the shadows to promote German oil interests[282]. In 1907, he represented *Royal Dutch Shell* in Constantinople, a city he had been forced to flee in 1896 due to the massacre of the Armenians. Since he had contacts with the Ottoman Civil List ministers[283], all of whom were Armenian, he had a clear edge over Bareilles. What's more, his financial means were infinitely greater than those of his rival. Indeed, Gulbenkian not only came from a wealthy family but he was also backed by the Rothschilds. Nevertheless, the overthrow of Abdul Hamid II by the Young Turks favoured Bareilles.

Not only was his contract still valid, but also many of the officers had been his students. It was even said that he had inspired their ideals. But the clock was ticking. Turkey and the Near East had become a powder keg. Mesopotamian oil would be one of the key issues of the

---

[282] Throughout his life, Calouste Gulbenkian acted exclusively to further his own interests, his loyalty unscrupulously varying according to profit and loss. He supported the Sultan, but then backed the *Young Turks*. Likewise, he had supported the British against the French and then *vice versa*.

[283] The Ottoman Civil List managed the Sultan's assets which, since 1899, included the oil fields discovered in Mesopotamia.

forthcoming war. Gulbenkian, with great foresight, profitably acquired 5% of the shares in the *Turkish Petroleum Company* (TPC). When Archduke Franz Ferdinand was assassinated in Sarajevo, Turkey's grand vizier granted all relevant rights to the TPC for the oilfields in the vilayets of Mosul and Baghdad.

Not long afterwards, when Turkey was fighting the war alongside its German allies, Bareilles was forced to move to Paris. The various treaties signed after the war, coupled with the British withdrawal from Mosul, put paid to any remaining hopes he might have had of being able to profitably exploit his concession. He wrote several works on the Ottoman Empire[284]. In 1922, he penned a particularly prescient article for a local French newspaper, *La Dépêche du Midi*[285]. Since the Jewish community represented a mere eighth of the Palestinian population, he wrote, the creation of a Jewish homeland would anger Muslims and Christians. Bertrand Bareilles died in October 1933.

Calouste Gulbenkian and the spoils of war

In 1924, Raymond Poincaré, the French prime minister, created the *Compagnie française des pétroles* (CFP) to manage France's share of the "spoils of war" in Mesopotamia. But the 25% share in the *Iraq Petroleum Company* obtained by Ernest Mercier, the CFP's director, was called into question by the Americans and the British. Walter

---

[284] Bertrand Bareilles is the author of nine works on the Ottoman Empire, notably *Rapport secret sur le Congrès de Berlin adressé à la Sublime Porte*.

[285] « *Le problème sioniste* », Bertrand Bareilles, *La Dépêche du Midi,* Toulouse, 11 August1922.

Teagle, president of *Standard Oil*, sought to secure America's place in the race for Mesopotamian oil[286], invoking the so-called "open door policy". The Anglo- Saxons colluded to push the French out of the market. In 1928, Mercier took the matter to a tribunal. Gulbenkian, whose interests were also jeopardised, stepped into the breach. The British backed down, fearing that the details of their secret deals be made public. An agreement was reached. Gulbenkian kept his 5%, but France's share was shaved down to 23.75%.

In July 1928, a meeting in Ostend closed the door to the Americans. The *Turkish Petroleum Company* partners (*The Group of Five*)[287] agreed not to compete with each other for oil concessions in the former Ottoman Empire. Since there was some disagreement as to the precise geographical delimitation of this exclusion zone, Gulbenkinan drew its boundaries in red pen. Kuwait was excluded from this *Red Line Agreement*, as it had been a British protectorate since 1899.

---

[286] John Worthington, *Standard Oil's* chief geologist, claimed that the the Euphrates valley had immense oil potential.

[287] *The Group of Five* comprised: *Anglo-Persian Oil Company, Royal Dutch Shell, Compagnie Française des Pétroles (CFP), the Near East Development Corporation (NEDC) and Calouste Gulbenkian*. At its inception, the *NEDC* was controlled by five American companies but, in 1934, there were only two players left in this consortium, namely *Standard Oil of New Jersey* and *Standard Oil of New York (Socony)*. The NEDC had been created in such a way as to ensure that the American government did not appear to be defending uniquely the int erests of *Standard Oil*. Once the CFP left the *Group of Five*, the *Seven Sisters* cartel was formed. The name, an allusion to the seven daughters of Atlas, was first coined by the president of the Italian state oil company (*Ente Nazionale Idrocarburi*), Enric Mattei, who was killed in a mysterious plane crash in 1962.

André Maginot, decorated for his bravery during the First World War, wanted to create what he termed a "Latin Oil union". The idea was for France to import its oil from Venezula. This would have been to the detriment of the Anglo-Saxon oil companies, as they would have lost their captive markets. Gulbenkian proposed this arrangement, as he was at war with *Shell's* chief, Henri Deterding, because he had supported the Turks during the Greco-Turkish conflict. Unfortunately for France, its project for an oil union never came to fruition. Maginot, the minister for war, died of food poisoning in January 1932. He was said to have eaten a bad oyster…

Syria has no oil!

With Syria separated from Palestine, Jordan and the vilayet of Mosul, France had to settle for the pipeline which transported its share of oil, gained in the Iraqi war, towards Tripoli (Lebanon). Geologists from the *Iraqi Petroleum Company* (IPC) explored the north-east of the country, but the quantity of oil found was insufficient to justify the cost of its extraction. Plans for exploration were practically abandoned. But the Second World War changed the deal. According to Jacques Bergier, writer and former member of the *Bureau central de renseignement et d'action* (BCRA), De Gaulle's secret service, the British and the French were busy making plans to send their planes from Syria to bombard Baku[288], while the Germans were preparing to invade France. In Syria,

---

[288] Bergier, Jacques, « *La guerre secrète du pétrole* », *J'ai Lu*, Paris, 1968. The plan to attack Baku was exposed by the Germans. On 19 June 1940, a group of German troops had stumbled upon secret files from French supreme headquarters. The documents had been left on an abandoned train, close to Charité-sur-Loire.

the fierce clashes between Vichy forces, commanded by General Dentz, and Free French troops were partly explained by Germany's need to secure one of the key oil supply routes from Iraq. In 1945, the United States again attempted to push France out of the Near Eastern oil market, using France's collaboration with Nazi Germany as a pretext. But this argument did not stand up, because Washington had appointed Admiral Leahy as ambassador to Vichy!

The *Red Line Agreement* broke down in 1948, following the discovery of the Saudi oil eldorado. Since the Americans refused to share, Gulbenkian threatened to take the matter to an international tribunal, and made it clear that he would not be intimidated. The Americans were keen to avoid the details of their illicit agreements appearing in the press, so *Aramco* paid him 38 million tonnes of oil by way of compensation, making him one of the richest men in the world[289]. In 1956, the Syrian government granted concessions to independent operators from America and West Germany. They discovered oil at Karatchouk, Deir Ez-Zor and then at Hassake, in the north-east of the country. Today, Syria exports its oil and has, according to estimates, reserves totalling ten years!

Lady Espionnage of Palmyra

Much has been written about Marguerite d'Andurain, the Basque vicomtesse who acquired Palmyra's Zenobia hotel in 1927. The French

---

[289] Micael Gulbenkian, Calouste's grandson, was the chief executive of *Heritage Oil Corporation*, a Canadian company which has been operating in Kurdistan and Iraq since 2004.

secret services[290] suspected she was a British agent who was having an affair with Major Sinclair, chief of intelligence in Haifa. They were convinced she had infiltrated the Egyptian nationalist party *Wafd* on behalf of T.E. Lawrence and Gilbert Clayton. It was said that the information she had obtained from Saad Zaghloul, the leader of *Wafd*, enabled the British to find a weapons cache at his house, have him deported to Malta, and thwart a radical nationalist cell which had planned to block the Suez Canal.

Palmyra was once the ancient city of Tadmor, the first mention of which goes back to an Assyrian cuneiform tablet, dating from the nineteenth century BC. Later it was the capital of Zenobia, the warrior queen who, in 270, audaciously snatched some of Rome's eastern provinces and dominated a large part of the Near East. Then it was the mythical oasis where, in 1813, the flamboyant Lady Stanhope made a spectacular entrance on camel-back, accompanied by thirty Arab cavaliers. By 1934, however, Palmyra had become the principal point of surveillance for the pipeline which stretched from Kirkurk to Tripoli in Lebanon, via Haditha in Iraq. Accordingly, the city's airport had been extended, and a French Foreign Legion detachment was sent to support the *méharistes*[291] already in place. The Hotel Zenobia was the perfect place to observe passing foreigners, the movements of local tribal chiefs and

---

[290] The chief of the French intelligence service in the Near East (*Services de renseignement au Levant*) was Georges Catroux, future commander in chief of the *Free French* forces. In 1941, General de Gaulle appointed him High Commissioner to the Levant. In this post, he formally recognised the independence of Syria, following the defeat of Vichy's General Dentz and the brutal repression of the Damascus uprising.

[291] The French camel cavalry.

the activities of French forces.

A Syrian nationalist movement in Palmyra actively resisted French colonisation and the dismemberment of their country. But rather than acknowledging this, the Deuxième Bureau (French military intelligence) preferred to accuse the British secret services of sabotaging the pipeline. To counteract what it termed British pro-independence propaganda, the French formed a Bedouin unit, led by Müller[292], a méhariste captain, nicknamed the "French Lawrence". Capitain Müller summoned the Bedouin chiefs to a meeting at the Zenobia hotel. Subsequent to this meeting, there was much speculation as to the possible implication of the vicomtesse in the murder of three of the tribesmen, known to be irredentist, who had attended Müller's meeting[293].

Marguerite d'Andurain hit the headlines in 1933 when she divorced her husband and converted to Islam. In search of adventure, she planned to be the very first European woman to make the pilgrimage to Mecca. So she entered into a marriage of convenience with a Bedouin by the name of Soliman, a Saudi méhariste, whom she made swear before witnesses to never sleep with her. With her marriage to Soliman officialised, she became a citizen of the Kingdom of Hejaz and Najd[294]. Adopting the Islamic name of Zeinab, she set off with her new husband

---

[292] Captain Victor Müller, nicknamed the French Lawrence of Arabia by his colleagues (this was not a compliment in the French army!), was highly respected by the Bedouin. Indeed, he wrote a reference work on tribes in the Syrian Desert, entitled En Syrie avec les Bédouins.

[293] Kurt Singer, Omnibus pour l'espionnage, Marabout, Verviers, 1963.

[294] Saudi Arabia at this time was known as the "Kingdom of Hejaz and Najd".

to Jeddah. Notified of her arrival, however, the customs office at Hejaz informed her that, since she had only very recently converted to Islam, she was forbidden from entering the Holy City[295]. She was taken into custody in the deputy governor's harem, while her husband was free to continue his pilgrimage. Not long afterwards, however, she learned that her "passport husband"[296] had died.

According to witnesses, Soliman, shortly before his death, claimed he had been poisoned by the vicomtesse. She was immediately accused of murder and sent to prison. In accordance with Sharia law, she would have been sentenced to lapidation if she had been found guilty. There is little doubt that St John Philby, residing in Jeddah at the time, had access to her files. Did Philby advise Ibn Saud what he should do? Had the vicomtesse already met the Emir of Najd at the behest of Lawrence when she was living in Egypt[297]? We will never know. But the fact remains that she was not found guilty owing to a lack of evidence. She then returned to Syria, only to find herself accused of murdering one of her shepherds. She was acquitted, but the suspected murderer, known to be a former French secret service hit man, disappeared without a trace...

Double Agent

With a trail of mysterious deaths behind her in the Near East and the publication of Pierre Apestéguy's prize-winning adventure novel in

---

[295] *Ibid.*

[296] Marguerite d'Andurain, *Le mari passeport*, In Libro Veritas.

[297] Kurt Singer, *Omnibus pour l'espionnage*, Marabout, Verviers, 1963.

1939[298], the press were quick to portray the viscomtesse as a super spy, working for the *Deuxième Bureau*. Apestéguy, who had never once set foot in Palmyra, had evidently drawn inspiration from the vicometesse's police records to create his heroine Aurore de Lusignan. Portraying her in a positive light, he pitted her against Lawrence of Arabia! To get even with the French, who had driven Prince Faisal out of Damascus, Lawrence returns to Syria to organise a tribal revolt and destroy the pipeline belonging to the *Compagnie française des Pétroles!*[299]

In 1945, Marguerite d'Andurain was accused of having poisoned her nephew and godson, Raymond Clérisse. In his pocket, the police found a Paris metro ticket, on which had been written "*M's sweets taste odd.*" Arrested and imprisoned at *La Roquette*, the press had a field day. One newspaper, *L'Aurore*, carried the title: "*From Mauléon to Mecca, poisoner leaves 15 dead in her wake.*" According to *Le Parisien Libéré*, she was a double agent. *La Presse* portrayed her as a spy greater than Mata Hari. In one article, the author Pierre Apestéguy recalled how she always had the uncanny knack of playing a key role in the various battles for Middle Eastern oil.

Released in 1947, after the court ruled there was insufficient evidence for prosecution, she then teamed up with a band of Corsican smugglers to buy a yacht. According to some, she had planned to supply weapons to the Palestinians. Sensing she was in danger, she told her son that

---

[298] Pierre Apestéguy, *Le roi des sables,* Le Masque, Paris, 1939. The author was awarded the prestigious *Prix du roman d'aventures.*

[299] Lawrence ceased operations in the Near East in 1921.

they wanted her dead[300]. In 1948, her body was found floating in the Bay of Tangier. The police investigation rapidly led to the arrest of the guardian of her yacht, a so-called Renato Poncini, whose real name was Hans Abel, a German Jew and concentration camp survivor.

Since the viscountess had plans to smuggle weapons to the Arabs, it was believed that Hans Abel was an agent working for *Shai*, the intelligence service of the *Haganah*, the predecessor to Mossad. During the trial, he pleaded accidental death, claiming that she had fallen down the stairs on the yacht following an altercation. He had been furious that she planned to use the yacht to help Lucas, a former Gestapo agent imprisoned in Tangier escape, to South America. The court sentenced the assassin to twenty years, but he was released after ten years for *"good behaviour"*. It was later claimed that her killer was in fact a former Nazi[301]. Among the papers stolen from the viscomtesse there was, according to her son, an envelope full of documents marked "Philby".

In 1976, Jean Lacouture, a journalist for *Le Monde*, described her as being *"...the perfect example of an adventurer with noble aims and multiple means...regarded by the British as a highly active French agent, French military intelligence in Damascus regarded her as an agent who could only have gained by double-crossing."*[302]

---

[300] Jacques d'Andurain, *Drôle de mère* (tome I et II), In Libro Veritas, 2007.

[301] Kurt Singer, *Omnibus pour l'espionnage*, Marabout, Verviers, 1963.

[302] Marguerite d'Andurain was not only suspected of working as a spy for the British but also for the Germans and the Soviets. The Gaullist *Central Bureau of Intelligence and Operations (BCRA)*, based in Algiers, had assigned her to convince Vichy officials to switch sides.

The Bible, a treasure map for evangelical Christians...

Golda Meir liked to joke that Moses made a mistake when he left Egypt for the only place in the Near East with no oil! This was not an opinion shared by the British oil companies or the Rothschilds who, in the early twentieth century, had financed the first Jewish settlers.

Zvi Alexander, Israel's "Mr Oil", wrote an account of his forty year-long struggle to secure fuel supplies for the Jewish state[303]. A former member of the *Haganah*, Ben-Gurion's Zionist militia, he worked for the *Israel National Oil Company*, leading exploration efforts across the world, and coordinated various front organisations, created to circumvent the Arab embargo. He made his fortune from the exploitation of Egyptian oil in the Sinai Peninsula. This was in no small measure thanks to Jack Bitton, an Egyptian double agent who, according to some, was behind the arrest of Eli Cohen, a Mossad agent executed in Damascus in 1965.[304]

According to Alexander, Israel has no oil. But this is not the view of American evangelical Christians, who interpret Moses' blessing of Asher

---

[303] Alexander, Zvi, *Israel's Covert Efforts to Secure Oil Supplies*, Gefen Books, Jerusalem, 2004.

[304] In 1961, Eli Cohen, an Egyptian-born Jewish agent, had infiltrated the Arab community in Argentina by using the alias Kamel Amin Thaabe. He won the trust of Syrian embassy officials in Buenos Aires and then moved to Damascus, where he obtained access to the highest levels of government. He supplied Mossad with highly sensitive information.

(*"Most blessed of sons is Asher; let him bathe his feet in oil"*) as indicating the presence of an oilfield at the foot of Mount Carmel. In 1982, the evangelical Christian Harold Stephens swore that, two hours after having prayed with Menachem Begin, God appeared before him and told him of a seam of oil beneath the Dead Sea. Another evangelical, John Brown, claimed that God had ordered him to make the Israelis economically independent. With this in mind, he created *Zion Oil and Gaz Inc.*, convinced that he would discover an immense oil field before the return of the Messiah! In September 2007, Binyamin Ben-Eliezer, the minister for Israel's infrastructure, granted exploration licences to various companies, but so far they have not yet discovered oil[305].

However, abundant supplies of natural gas have been discovered offshore from the Gaza Strip[306]. British Gas had begun work to exploit the gas, but the group's efforts were cut short by Ariel Sharon, after Mossad's chief Meir Dagan declared that the Palestinians would use gas revenues to finance terrorism[307]. The fields, named *Gaza Marine 1* and *Gaza Marine 2*, granted to the Palestinians by the Oslo Accords, are said to have gas reserves ranging from 30 to 60 billion cubic metres. The Israeli Supreme Court contested Palestinian ownership of the offshore reserves, and the gas pipeline to Egypt was replaced by another one terminating in Israel (Ashkelon). The Palestinians suspect that Israel pumps gas from Gaza Marine by using the facilities located

---

[305] *La soif de pétrole irakien d'Israël*, par Gilles Munier, Afrique Asie, mars 2008.

[306] *Gaz à Gaza: la guerre pour l'indépendance économique*, par Amadeo Piegatore, Afrique Asie, mars 2008.

[307] *Does the Prospective Purchase of British Gas from Gaza's Coastal Waters Threaten Israel's National Security?* Lt.-Gen. Moshe Yaalon, *Jerusalem Center of Public Affairs*, 2007.

at the Med Yavne field. For a number of observers, Gaza's gas reserves would appear to be subject to the embargo and Israeli military operations[308].

The blood of the earth

France only really started to worry about its dependence on other countries to meet its energy needs following the Liberation, during the short period when General De Gaulle ruled the country. De Gaulle appointed Pierre Guillaumat[309], a former member of his intelligence service, the BCRA, to take charge of energy policy, and sought the help of Conrad Kilian, the geologist and explorer who had discovered the Saharan oilfields. But the project was postponed following his resignation. It was only when he returned to power and established ties with Iraq, following his meeting in February 1968 with the Iraqi president Abdul Rahman Arif, that France regained its influence in the Near East. Until the Gulf War, De Gaulle's successors had maintained close relations with Iraq, signing a number of agreements with the Ba'athist presidents, Ahmed Hassan al-Bakr and Saddam Hussein.

During the international embargo, *Elf* and *Total* secured contracts in Iraq and Iran. This upset the American government which had planned to tame the recalcitrant regimes in these countries. In 2002, Richard Lugar,

---

[308] The American company *Noble Energy* discovered a gas field close to Ashekelon, smaller than the one located in Gaza.

[309] His father, Louis Adolphe Guillaumat, was commander of the Allied Army of the Orient in 1917 and, during a short period in 1926, served in Aristide Briand's government as minister of war.

head of the US Senate's Foreign Relations Committee, informed the French government that it would have to contribute financially to the overthrow of Saddam Hussein if it wanted its share of Iraqi oil. Following the American occupation of Iraq in April 2003, *Total* teamed up with *Chevron*[310], America's second largest oil company. This cooperation, however, came to nothing: France was pushed out of the Iraqi market.

Following the First World War, Lord Curzon, former Viceroy of India and President of the Inter- Allied Petroleum Conference, declared that *"the Allied cause had floated to victory upon a wave of oil."* This still rings true today. But we should be careful not to confuse cause and effect. Oil is the cause of conflict. Indeed, Henry Bérenger, the senator responsible for the management of France's oil imports during the war, aptly remarked that *"the blood of the earth was the blood of victory."*

---

[310] In 2003, *Chevron* was condemned in the US for having illegally traded with Iraq during the international embargo. Condolezza Rice was a member of *Chevron's* board from 1991 to 2001. She resigned to join George W. Bush's team of advisers. *Chevron's* tanker, the Condolezza Rice, was immediately renamed following her departure!

Chapter XVI

THE MYSTERIOUS DEATH OF CONRAD KILIAN, AN UNWITTING SPY

Conrad Killian, French geologist and explorer, was the first to discover oil in the Sahara and the Fezzan. On the 29 April 1950, he was murdered in Grenoble. Who killed him? During a Parisian trade fair, a British Army major declared quite openly before stunned delegates that British intelligence had *"taken care of him"*. But should we take this declaration seriously? After having botched the investigation, the French police concluded that he had committed suicide even though, only days before his murder, a driver of a car had attempted to run him over while he was walking on the pavement. Why did the press claim that he had killed himself where his parents had been buried, whereas in fact his body had been found hanging from the window latch of a hotel room?

Murder disguised as suicide

Despite evidence to the contrary, the verdict of suicide was maintained. According to detectives, his slashed wrists together with the blood splattered walls of his hotel room proved that he had attempted to kill himself, first with a kitchen knife and then with a broken bottle of eau de cologne, both of which were found in the hotel room. Having not managed to bleed to death, he then hanged himself!

The staging of this scene, however, was far from convincing. Rather than cutting his wrists with a broken bottle, Kilian could have used the cut-throat razor, found in his wash bag. The police failed to note that it is impossible for a man of five foot ten inches to hang himself from a window catch only three feet from the floor. Moreover, Kilian's eyes were closed, whereas those of somebody who has been hanged remain open.

Friends of the geologist were convinced that his killers tortured him in an attempt to have him reveal his secrets, and then disguised his death – clumsily - as a suicide. Indeed, a few days before his death, he had told one of his friends not to believe any verdict of suicide, should he be found dead one day. Others believe that Kilian, known for his courage, had fought with his killers, triggering perhaps a heart attack. But General Paul Grossin, who later became the chief of the *SDECE* (France's foreign intelligence service), was adamant: Kilian had been murdered.

In fact, prior to his murder, he had already survived a number of attempts on his life. In 1943, while in the Algerian mountain region of Hoggar, his guide attempted to kill him by serving him tea, poisoned with a Tuareg poison known as *borbor*, a concoction of toxic desert plants which is mixed, according to legend, with human brains! Only days prior to this, he had chanced upon a gang illegally mining wolframite – a source of tungsten - on behalf of a British company in Nigeria. Outraged, he reported them to the Governor General of Algeria. A few days later, the mine was duly closed. But Kilian's guide was captured, tortured and then killed (he was shot twice in the head). His new guide, who served him the poisoned tea, had no doubt been paid by the British. Close to death, Kilian was transported on camel-back to Tamanrasset and then to Algiers where, after spending several months in a critical condition, he made a miraculous recovery, though for the rest of his life he would suffer the after-effects of the poison, including severe bouts of nervous depression which gave him the appearance of a lunatic.

Desert crazy

Kilian[311] discovered the Sahara and the Tuareg tribe at the age of 24. This was in 1922, when he participated in a Swiss expedition which had set off in search of the legendary emeralds of the Garamantes, a nomadic Berber tribe said to be the ancient inhabitants of Fezzan. Having left the group following an argument with one of its members, he took a guide and continued his exploration, collecting fossils on the way.

Kilian was bewitched by the desert's beauty and the majesty of its inhabitants. No sooner had he come back home than he was eager to return to Algeria and Libya, an Italian colony at the time[312]. When his

---

[311] Conrad Kilian was the son of Wilfrid Killian, a renowned professor of geology at the University of Grenoble. His great uncle was Georges Cuvier, widely regarded as the "father of palaeontology".

[312] Libya was formed from three Ottoman provinces: Cyrenaica; Tripolitania and Fezzan. It was granted to Italy for having fought alongside the Allies during the First World War. Omar Al-Mukhtar, leader of the *Senussi* armed resistance movement, fought to the death against the Italian occupying forces. At the same time, the chief

father died, he used part of his inheritance to finance an expedition to the Western Sahara. Although engaged, he asked his fiancée to postpone their marriage until his return. He spent three years roaming the sands. During his voyage, he made friends with the Sheikh of Ghat, a Fezzan oasis which no foreigner had yet dare explore. In these lands, Europeans were treated with suspicion, with good reason considering the colonial ambitions of the great powers. They were considered enemies and killed on the spot.

While exploring a series of cave paintings in the Hoggar mountain range, he found an emerald, which had been polished and shaped into a jewel. Encouraged by this, he continued his exploration and discovered in the area a series of chariot tracks, made by the Garmantes some 4000 years ago. Kilian's research displeased the British company *Pearson*[313], which at the time was prospecting for oil in the Algerian Sahara, and aroused suspicion among certain politicians

---

of the *Senussi*, Sayyid Idris, sought refuge in Cairo. Backed by the British, he declared himself emir of Cyrenaica in 1949. On 27 December 1951, Idris was made king, following the declaration of independence of the Kingdom of Libya on 24 December. He was overthrown by a group of army officers led by Colonel Gaddafi on 1 September 1969.

[313] Samuel Pearson founded the *Pearson* enterprise in 1844. The company branched into the oil market under the leadership of his grandson, Weetman Pearson, later known as Viscount Cowdray. In 1909, he created the *Mexican Eagle Petroleum Corporation* (*MEAPC*) to manage his investments in Mexican oilfields. In 1919, *Shell* bought *MEAPC*, in a deal negotiated shortly before the Armistice by Calouste Gulbenkian. Today *Pearson* is a multinational publishing company. It held 21% of the *RTL* media group until 2001, when it sold its share to *Bertelsmann*. Its London headquarters are located in the building originally constructed for the oil companies *Shell-Mex* and *BP Ltd*.

in France, even though his expedition had been approved by the French authorities.

Profoundly patriotic and pugnacious, he was not a man given to compromise. Upon his return to France in 1929, he succumbed to depression and misogyny when he learnt that his fiancée, having received no news from him since his departure, had married. He then returned to the Sorbonne University to complete his thesis. Convinced of the importance of his work, however, he refused "*to beg for his doctorate*", believing that his discoveries alone were sufficient to warrant this academic distinction.

Kilian sent his mission report to various French ministries and asked President Gaston Doumergue to have the Saharan borders rectified in such a way that the oil-rich Fezzan would be located in the French part of the region. But the various government ministers he contacted were not interested in his discoveries. It was as if, following the 1920 *San Remo Conference*, it had been agreed somewhere that everything relating to oil was strictly a British domain.

In January 1935, Kilian vociferously opposed the French prime minister, Pierre Laval, who had entered into negotiations with Benito Mussolini to redefine the Libyan border in the Sahara. France gave away the Aouzou Strip together with the areas Kilian had explored in the Fezzan region. Mussolini was not even remotely grateful for this gift because, in his view, these territories were merely worthless stretches of sand! But what are we to make of Pierre Laval, who refused to answer Kilian's letters?

242 | P a g e

Espionage in the Ténéré

The story of his first voyage and the articles he published in the magazine *L'Illustration* meant that Kilian came to be widely considered as an expert on southern Algeria. So it was no surprise that, in 1935, the explorer Roger Frison-Roche turned to him for information on the Hoggar cave paintings and the mythical *Garet el Djenoun* (Mountain of Genies)[314] which towers to a staggering 3375 metres. As his third expedition was financed by the French ministry of defence, he was ordered to respect the new Libyan border. He successfully completed his mission and, using his first aid kit, even performed an emergency caesarean birth in the middle of the desert to save a mother and her baby! Following his advice, a *méhariste* detachment was created in I-n-Ezzane, close to Djanet. On one of the desert routes, he found that the water well had been deliberately blocked to stop him from continuing his journey, proof that his enemies still loomed large. When he returned to Paris, he found his flat had been burgled. The thieves failed to find his files, concealed in the secret compartment of his Louis XIII cabinet, and his maps, which he had given to a friend for safekeeping. On his maps, he had marked all the areas where oil was likely to be located. Sure enough, several years later, oil was found at these very same locations.

The French Baku

As a lieutenant in the French artillery regiment during the Second World

---

[314] Roger Frison-Roche, *L'Appel du Hoggar,* Flammarion, Paris, 1936.

War, Kilian led a valiant defence of Vauban's fort at *Le Quesnoy*, and took command of the Oise valley. Short of ammunition, following a series German assaults and intensive bombing raids, he surrendered with the honours of war, meaning that, though taken prisoner of war, he was permitted to keep his weapons, a privilege seldom granted by victors. In 1942, he was released, along with a group of veterans from the First World War[315]. He then joined the geological laboratory at the University of Algiers. His appointment came at pivotal moment. The war was not yet over, and the Americans were preparing to land in North Africa. Among the troops, there were teams of prospectors who had studied Kilian's work. Both *Shell* and *Aramco* offered him a fortune for his knowledge, but, being patriotic, he refused to compromise. Events during his 1943 mission, when he was poisoned and his desert guide murdered, confirmed that the war for oil had been declared. This war for black gold, however, was essentially between the Americans and the British, owing to France's singular lack of interest for oil.

Very few in government were curious to learn what Kilian had discovered, with the notable exceptions of Marshal Leclerc and General De Gaulle who, for reasons of national security, once had him and his precious documents brought home from Algiers on a naval destroyer. In 1946, De Gaulle had planned to meet him, but stepped down only days before their meeting was scheduled. Kilian had explained to government officials at the *Quai d'Orsay* that millions of barrels were

---

[315] Although Conrad Kilian was declared unfit for military service in 1916, he used his contacts to enter the ranks of the French army. Sent to the front, he participated in the summer offensive of 1918, and was awarded the *Croix de Guerre*, the French military cross. He reached the rank of second-lieutenant.

concealed beneath the sand. Though he rigorously supported his assertions with solid evidence, they dismissed him as a crackpot!

Kilian placed his last hopes in Marshal Leclerc. The French 2nd Armoured Division's capture of Kufra drew public attention to the Fezzan region. Kilian, appointed representative for the prestigious French research institute *CNRS*, met him at the ministry of defence in August 1947. With Italy now out of the game, he proposed the annexation of Fezzan, describing it as patch of sand floating on a sea of oil[316]. Given that Fezzan was land-locked, he suggested the government hand over Kufra to the British, who controlled the eastern coastal region of Cyrenaica, in exchange for a corridor leading to the port of Brega, on the Gulf of Sirte[317]. For political and humanitarian reasons, Kilian suggested that the oil revenue then be shared between the neighbouring countries of the Sahara. Leclerc agreed and gave the order to send the French navy to Brega. But the order was never executed because six months later, on 28 November 1947, Leclerc was killed in a bizarre plane accident[318] while flying over the very areas identified by Kilian...[319]

---

[316] Euloge Boissonnade, *Conrad Killian*, France-Empire, Paris, 1982.

[317] A certain proportion of Libyan oil is today shipped from Brega, a port with its own refinery.

[318] To this day, the presence of an unknown passenger in the plane remains unexplained. The peculiar type of burns observed on the bodies was not accounted for, either. According to a witness, the remains of the aircraft and the area close to the accident were covered with a beige coloured mousse, which evaporated to the touch. The origin of this substance remains a mystery.

[319] Claude Muller, *Les mystères du Dauphiné*, Éditions De Borée, 2001.

Sensing his life was in danger, Kilian sent his reports in a wax sealed envelope to the *Académie des Sciences* in Paris for safekeeping in case he, too, should have a strange accident. And sure enough, a year later, this is precisely what happened when, one night, the driver of a car with no lights mounted the pavement and attempted to run him over. Meanwhile, the bouts of depression, the after-effects of the poisoned tea he drank in 1943, were becoming increasingly frequent and began to alter his personality.

Unanswered questions

Why did Robert Schuman[320], a minister who had somehow managed to become a permanent fixture of France's Fourth Republic, refuse to meet Kilian? Why did he choose to ignore Kilian's reports, whereas the Soviets considered the Fezzan region to be the French equivalent of Baku? Why did the French government refuse to accept Canada's offer to finance 49% of the exploration and exploitation costs and, what's more, to wipe off France's war debt, which had been estimated at 50 billion francs?

It was believed that British intelligence had leaned on Schuman. In June 1940, the future "father of Europe" had served as Marshal Pétain's Assistant Secretary of State for Refugees. As a member of the French

---

[320] Robert Schuman served as minister in the various governments of the Fourth Republic from 1946 to 1953. Notably, he was appointed foreign affairs minister on nine separate occasions. In March 1948, he signed the North Atlantic Treaty which took France into NATO. He was elected president of the first European parliament in 1958 and was henceforth dubbed the "father of Europe".

parliament, he voted in favour of Pétain being granted plenary powers. Following the liberation of France, the high court which directed the series of trials known as the *épuration légale*, dismissed the charges brought against him because there was evidence that he had resisted the German occupying power. Indeed, Schuman had been arrested by the Gestapo for refusing to collaborate, and was sent to prison in Germany. Some criticise him, however, for living a little too discreetly in the Free Zone, where he had sought refuge after his escape in 1942.

Not all the civil servants and politicians in the Fourth Republic had cut their links made during the war with Britain's *Secret Intelligence Service*. It should always be born in mind that the Anglo-Saxon oil lobby is never too far from British intelligence. This explains why Conrad Kilian's reports were ignored and why the police investigation into his murder was hastily concluded.

In 1957, the envelope Kilian had deposited at the *Académie des Sciences* for safekeeping was finally opened. The documents contained therein confirmed that Kilian had accurately located the Algerian oil fields at Fezzan, Ejeleh and Hassi Messaoud before their official "discovery".

Chapter XVII

KERMIT ROOSEVELT, AJAX AND THE ECONOMIC HIT-MEN

After having nationalised the Iranian oil industry on 1 May 1951, Mohammad Mossadegh was not surprised to discover that Churchill was plotting to overthrow him. Immediately taking action, he closed the British embassy and had the personnel of the *Anglo-Iranian Oil Company* deported. Britain imposed an embargo and threatened to seize Iranian tankers transporting what it regarded to be "red oil", and asked President Truman to support a military operation to capture the oilfields in Arabistan. Truman, coming to the end of his mandate, rejected the British proposal having, it would seem, nothing but contempt for old British colonial ways.

The hand of Moscow

American policy on Iran changed completely with the election of Dwight Eisenhower in November 1952. Britain immediately dispatched Christopher Montague Woodhouse[321] to Washington to convince the

---

[321] Baron Christopher Montague Woodhouse was the Director General of the *Royal Institute of International Affairs* (1955-1959) and a Conservative Member of Parliament.

CIA and the State Department to intervene in Iran. This was a period in history when it took more than oil to drag the Americans into an armed conflict. So *"C"* - Sir John Sinclair, British secret service chief from 1953 to 1956 - advised him to play on American fears of a Communist conspiracy. This strategy paid off. Indeed, the British project was a godsend for the Dulles brothers, rising stars in the new administration. Both John Foster (Secretary of State) and Allen (Director of Central Intelligence) saw the hand of Moscow practically everywhere. Allen, who had written reports on psychological and covert wars as well as guerrilla warfare and sabotage, saw the British proposition as an opportunity to put theory into practice.

Woodhouse explained to them that Iran bordered the Soviet Union, had a pro-Soviet communist party (*Tudeh Party*) and was led by a nationalist prime minister with anti-Western tendencies. There was a serious risk of "another Korea" happening in the Near East. The Dulles were convinced. When Eisenhower took office the following January, Allen Dulles told London that he was ready to overthrow Mossadegh. He suggested that the coup, which had been planned by the archaeologist and spy Donald Wilber[322], be led by Kermit Roosevelt, the grandson of Theodore Roosevelt. The operation already had its code name: *TP-Ajax*[323].

Being of a pragmatic nature, his brother, John Foster Dulles, already saw the advantages to be gained from the coup, which would enable

---

[322] Donald Wilber, a former member of the Office of Strategic Services (OSS), gave his account of the coup which overthrew Dr Mossadegh in *Regime Change in Iran: Overthrow of Premier Mossadegh of Iran, November 1952 – August 1953.*

[323] Named *Operation Boot* by Britain's *Secret Intelligence Service*.

the Americans to occupy what was until then considered to be British hunting ground[324]. Dulles knew where he stood with Reza Shah, whom he had first met in 1947 while in Iran. When the Shah came to Washington, he had organised a dinner in his honour in November 1949, inviting members of the highly influential and secretive *Council of Foreign Relations* (CFR).

The (very) quite American

Kermit Roosevelt Jr., 37 years old, managed the CIA's Near East and Africa division. He grew up with the adventures of his father, who had fought in the British Mesopotamian campaign as an honorary captain in General Maude's expeditionary forces[325]. During the Second World War[326], he joined the Office of Strategic Services (OSS), the CIA's predecessor, and carried out intelligence missions in Italy and Egypt. According to Kim Philby, who was in regular contact with Roosevelt in Beirut, he was the epitome of the courteous and quiet American, and was the very last person one would have suspected of carrying out dirty tricks[327]. When his activities came to light, admirers described him as a

---

[324] Nathan Miller, *Spying for America*, Dell Publishing, New York, 1990.

[325] Kermit's father, Captain Kermit Roosevelt M.C., had served as an officer in the British *Machine Gun Corps*, formed in October 1915. His experience of the conflict in Mesopotamia is recounted in *War in the Garden of Eden*, published in 1919.

[326] America's foreign intelligence service cast a very wide net. Among the 24 000 personal files declassified in 2008, we find the names of Ernest Hemingway, Arthur Meier Schlesigner Jr. (assistant to President John F. Kennedy) and even the gangster Charles "Lucky" Luciano.

[327] Stephen Kinzer, *All the Shah's Men: An American Coup and the Roots of Middle East Terror*, Wiley, Hoboken, 2003.

gentleman spy, quietly confident.

In June 1953, Kermit Roosevelt landed in Beirut. Rather than flying to Tehran, he chose to drive in order to avoid airport security, tighter than the routine border controls in northern Iraq. He moved into a villa, which he rented under the name of James Lockridge, or just *Jim* to his friends. It was here that he orchestrated a no-expenses-spared campaign which attacked Mossadegh on all fronts.

The Shah: Suspicion and Indecision

Operation Ajax was planned to be carried out in successive stages. First of all, the "free press" began to spread various rumours about the Iranian prime minister. To prepare public opinion for the next stage of the plan, Roosevelt had the press print the story that the Shah had relieved Mossadegh of his prime ministerial duties and had appointed Fazlollah Zahedi as his replacement.

In August, the pressure was increased. Demonstrators brandishing portraits of the Shah blocked roads, while the "free press" became increasingly vehement, accusing Mossadegh of being a communist. At the same time, there were stories claiming that he was secretly working for the British and that he was of Jewish ancestry. According to Richard Cottam, who wrote most of the articles in his Washington office, eighty percent of Iranian newspapers were financed by the CIA[328].

Only one problem remained, but it was a big one: they had yet to

---

[328] *Ibid.*

convince the Shah to support the operation. The monarch, aged 32 at the time, procrastinated. He was very cautious and lacked courage, according to the doctored CIA report[329]. Moreover, he had absolutely no faith in Westerners. Roosevelt decided to compel him to sign the decree replacing Mossadegh with Zahedi. To this end, *Jim* called upon General Herbert Schwarzkopf[330], who, from 1942 to 1948, had commanded and restructured the notoriously pro-German *Imperial Iranian Gendarmerie*. Schwarzkopf arrived in Teheran with two enormous bags, filled with millions of dollars with which he planned to pay conspirators and buy government officials. He was received by the Shah, who told him he had not yet decided. The Shah was not certain that the army would support him and feared being overthrown. But he was clearly shaken. Following the meeting, Shwarzkopf deemed it was time for Kermit Roosevelt to emerge from the shadows and explain to the Shah what was about to happen.

Prudent, Roosevelt decided to proceed by stages. First of all, he asked Assadollah Rashidian, an agent in whom the British had complete confidence[331], to meet the Shah and explain to him that the British and the Americans were preparing a coup to overthrow Mossadegh and that, moreover, he had no choice but to support this operation. During his meeting with Rashidian, the monarch nodded his head in vague

---

[329] James Risen, "Secrets of History: the CIA in Iran", *New York Times*, 16 April 2000. The original report is said to have been destroyed...

[330] Father of General Norman Schwarzkopf, who commanded Coalition Forces during the first American invasion of Iraq in 1991.

[331] The Rashidian brothers, who came from an influential family with connections to the Iranian aristocracy, managed Britain's Secret Intelligence Service contacts in Iran.

agreement. Roosevelt then instructed his agent in the Shah's royal court, "Rosenkrantz", to step in. Rosenkrantz told the Shah that an American official, working on behalf of Eisenhower and Churchill, urgently wished to meet him. The Shah agreed and had one his drivers pick him up at his villa.

"Good evening, Mr Roosevelt..."

Kermit Roosevelt already knew the Shah. Six years previously, he had met him for the publication of a book on the history of oil. The monarch recognised him immediately: *"Good evening Mr Roosevelt. I cannot say that I expected to see you, but this is a pleasure."* Kermit assured him that he spoke on behalf of the British and American secret services. This was to be confirmed the following evening by the time announcement used by BBC radio to close one of its broadcasts. Instead of saying, as usual, *"It is now midnight..."* the broadcaster would state *"It is now* exactly *midnight..."* He politely warned the Shah that if he refused to support the operation, another coup would be quickly organised, implying that he would be the next to be overthrown. Somewhat defiantly, the Shah said he preferred to hear the coded radio broadcast before their next meeting.

Roosevelt then decided to reveal the details of *Operation Ajax*. As the operation advanced, it became increasingly risky to hold meetings at his villa, so Roosevelt drove around Tehran in a fake taxi. After much hesitation, the Shah finally promised to sign the decrees, after which he planned to seek refuge at his Caspian holiday home in Ramsar. But he panicked and fled with his wife, Soraya, before signing the documents.

This was the first setback. Roosevelt dispatched to the Caspian an agent, a colonel in the Iranian Imperial Guard, to obtain the Shah's signature. On August 12, the agent returned with the documents, duly signed.

With everything in place for the big event, Kermit Roosevelt moved to his new command post, the American embassy. A popular American song at the time, taken from a Broadway musical, was chosen as the anthem for Operation Ajax: *Luck be a Lady Tonight.*

Fiasco

There was another setback. The coup, scheduled for Friday 15 August, was delayed to respect the Muslim weekend. It was explained to Roosevelt that Friday was sacred for the Iranians, even for those who conspired with the Americans...

On the day, nothing went as planned. Mossadegh escaped arrest. On the radio, he condemned the conspiracy, and accused the Shah of being a stooge. Reza Shah hopped on board his twin-engine Beechcraft and flew to find refuge in Baghdad, which was ruled by a pro-British monarchy at the time. Roosevelt was devastated. What had gone wrong?

Some claim that a communist cell had obtained details of the coup. A reward was offered for the arrest of General Zahedi. In the streets, supporters of Mossadegh and *The Tudeh Party* declared victory. Kermit informed Washington that the coup had failed. John Waller[332], chief of the CIA's Iran office, advised him to leave the country if he sensed his life was in danger[333], but Kermit chose to stay.

Black propaganda

Kermit Roosevelt was not a man to admit defeat. He knew he had to move quickly in order to surprise his opponents, who would not expect the conspirators to make a second coup attempt so soon. The following evening, he met General Zahedi, hidden away in an inconspicuous suburb in Teheran. Zahedi confirmed he would give the operation his full support. The *firman* signed by the Shah would be used to give a veneer of legitimacy to the second coup attempt. Copies were sent to the press, foreign journalists, military officers, and were distributed liberally among the population.

The next day, Kermit ordered his supporters to abandon all scruples and use whatever means necessary. Agitators, claiming to be Mossadegh supporters, carried out various atrocities. A doctored version of the failed coup was issued to the newspapers. The "free press" claimed that the prime minister had attempted to dethrone the Shah, but that this attempted putsch had been stopped by patriotic officers.

---

[332] In 1976, John Waller was appointed Inspector General of the CIA, a post he held until his retirement in 1980. He has written a number of works on the history of espionage.

[333] Stephen Kinzer, *All the Shah's Men: An American Coup and the Roots of Middle East Terror*, Wiley, Hoboken, 2003.

General McClure, the American military attaché to Teheran, toured the army bases, promising promotion and fortune for those who would help overthrow Mossadegh. Meanwhile, Roosevelt's superiors in Washington grew increasingly anxious and asked Roosevelt to leave Iran, but Roosevelt stuck to his plan. He summoned two US-trained Iranian agents and ordered them to organise violent "communist" demonstrations. The mosques had to be targeted, he told them. The idea was then for the patriots to crush this communist uprising and restore law and order in the name of the Shah. Fearing for their lives, the agents refused. Furious, he gave them no choice. If they did what he asked, he would pay them 50 000 dollars. If not, he would kill them on the spot! Needless to say, they chose the cash. Tensions in Iran mounted, as the assassination of a religious leader was said to be the work of *Tudeh*. Thousands of people, led by CIA-paid agitators, soon took to the streets, sweeping along in their wake honest demonstrators as well as looters. The Shah's statue was knocked down.

Iran was on the verge of bloody anarchy. Mossadegh failed to see exactly what was happening. For him, the right to protest was sacred, and so he stopped the police from intervening! To confuse matters further, Kermit Roosevelt, never one to miss a trick, asked the American ambassador Loy Henderson to contact the prime minister and propose that the US help Iran in its fight against subversion. During his meeting with Henderson, Mossadegh was shocked to learn that the US supported the Shah, who had fled the country. The ambassador had the nerve to retort that the Prophet Muhammad had once fled Mecca for Medina and that, ever since, his prestige has never ceased to grow. He then condemned the violent reprisals carried out by his supporters, hardly in keeping with the legendary Iranian hospitality, he claimed.

The next day Mossadegh made two fatal errors. First of all, he stopped his supporters from demonstrating and had their weapons confiscated. Secondly, and inexplicably, he asked General Mohammad Daftary, a close associate of Zahedi, to restore order in Teheran. Meanwhile, at the US embassy, Kermit Roosevelt continued his campaign of subversion.

In preparation for the big day, he secured the help of Abol-Ghasem Kashani, an influential nationalist cleric and fierce opponent of Mossadegh. In exchange for 10 000 dollars, he became an ardent defender of the Shah and promised that a public call for jihad against communism would be made in Qom, the holy city of Iran.

The Star-Spangled Banner

The mass demonstration scheduled for August 19 was the highlight of Operation Ajax. Thousands of Iranians, among whom were there were a great many Bedouin tribesmen who had come at the behest of their chiefs, took to the streets. Members of sports clubs, circus artists and thugs armed with iron bars, all flanked by CIA-paid undercover troops, were followed by a frenzied crowd chanting *"Zindabad Shah! ... Zindabad Shah!"* (Long live the Shah!). Pro-government units were quickly overwhelmed. Attempts by the communist *Tudeh Party* to regain control of the situation failed. The moment had arrived for General Zahedi to come out of hiding. Standing on top of a tank in front of Radio Tehran's studios, he was cheered by a rapturous crowd, convinced he was the saviour of the nation. This moment of glory was something of a revenge for the man who had been kidnapped by Fitzroy Maclean's

SAS in 1942 and then sent to a British prison camp in Palestine for having colluded with Nazi Germany. Terrified or moved at the idea of broadcasting Zahedi's speech, the radio station's technician chose the wrong national anthem: he played *The Star-Spangled Banner!* But the coup was not yet complete, as the conspirators had still to arrest the ousted prime minister and await the return of the Shah, who at that very moment was dining at Rome's *Excelsior Hotel*.

In the end, Mohammad Mossadegh, suffering from illness, turned himself in. He telephoned Zahedi, and arranged a meeting with him at the Officers' Club. The Shah, having left Rome, arrived in Baghdad, where he hopped into his *Beechcraft* to make the flight back to Iran. Mossadegh was sentenced to death. After hearing the verdict, he thanked the court for his glorious entry into history! His sentence was then commuted to three years imprisonment. But his foreign affairs minister, Hossein Fatemi, was less fortunate. Following a secret tribunal, he was executed. General Zahedi was confirmed in his functions as the new Iranian prime minister. The US paid him a million dollar bonus[334] and allocated Iran five million dollars worth of subsidies.

Reza Shah thanked Kermit Roosevelt, to whom he was hugely indebted. Having acquired a taste for this type of relatively bloodless form of operation, Allen Dulles asked him to overthrow the government of Guatemala. Believing that what he had achieved in Iran could not be exported elsewhere, Roosevelt refused the proposition. He resigned from the CIA when, in 1958, Dulles directed him to cooperate with British intelligence in an operation to oust the Egyptian president Gamal

---

[334] *Ibid.*

Abdel Nasser[335], with whom he had always maintained good relations. Roosevelt then joined *Gulf Oil* as "Government Relations Director" and, in 1960, was appointed the company's vice-president. In 1979, he published *Countercoup*, his personal account of Operation Ajax[336].

Eisenhower had always denied that the US had participated in the Iranian coup. In 2000, after secret documents had been leaked to the *New York Times*, Secretary of State Madeleine Albright admitted that the US had "*played a significant role*" in the coup which overthrew Mossadegh.

Kermit Roosevelt, father of the "economic hitmen"?

Iran agreed to pay 70 million dollars to the *Anglo-Persian Company* by way of compensation for having nationalised its oilfields. A consortium, managed by *Standard Oil of New Jersey*, was then created. Members of this group included *Anglo-Iranian, Royal Dutch Shell,* and the *Compagnie françaises des pétroles*. The Americans and the British each took 40% of the shares. Their partners, including the French, shared the remaining 20%.

John Perkins, the author of *Confessions of an Economic Hitman*[337], was recruited in the late 60s by America's *National Security Agency*

---

[335] Nathan Miller, *Spying for America*, Dell Publishing, New York, 1990.

[336] Kermit Roosevelt, *Countercoup: The Struggle for the Control of Iran,* McGraw-Hill, New York, 1980.

[337] John Perkins, *Confessions of an Economic Hitman*, Berrett-Koehler Publ Inc.

(NSA)[338]. Perkins believes that Kermit Roosevelt was the very first "economic hitman". Following the success of *Operation Ajax*, the American administration considered that it was more profitable to overthrow regimes in a bloodless coup rather than by means of military intervention. The only risk in the case of the Iranian coup was that Kermit Roosevelt was a CIA agent meaning that, had he been arrested and exposed, American diplomatic credibility would have been severely tainted. To avoid this risk, it was decided to recruit new agents and place them in private companies operating abroad, such as *Halliburton* or *Bechtel*. Thus, should one of the agents be exposed, there would be no direct proof linking their activities to the American government. According to Perkins, these agents want the world to obey the United States, the leader of the global empire[339]. His book became a best-seller.

In an interview for *Democracy Now!*, an independent news channel[340], Perkins explained how, on one occasion, he had convinced the Saudis to invest their petrodollars in American public funds and had them agree to use the interest earned to finance public works in Saudi Arabia. Needless to say, the works were carried out by American companies.

---

[338] The *National Security Agency* (NSA) specialises in Signals Intelligence (SIGINT), collecting and analysing global electronic communications.

[339] John Perkins, *Confessions of an Economic Hitman*, Berrett-Koehler Publ Inc.

[340] *Democracy Now!* is an American internet news programme which is also broadcast by 1,400 radio and television stations across the world. In 2008, Amy Goodman, one of its co-founders, was awarded the *Right Livelihood Award* (dubbed the "Alternative Nobel Prize") by the Swedish Parliament. She was arrested while she reported on an anti-war demonstration outside of the 2008 Republican Convention, which nominated John McCain as presidential candidate.

In exchange, Washington ensured that the Saud family remained in power.

According to Perkins, America had made the same sort of proposal to Iraq, but Saddam Hussein refused. When the economic hitmen do not succeed the first time, they implement Plan B. The CIA agents – or "jackals", as Perkins calls them – intervened in Iraq but to no avail. Saddam was neither overthrown nor assassinated. What happened next was predictable. The GIs were sent to Iraq, writes Perkins, *"to kill or be killed"*. They are still there today...

Epilogue

PRIVATE ESPIONAGE: AN IMMINENT DANGER

Spies in the James Bond league are a luxury only Hollywood can afford. We are no longer in the age when Ian Fleming was trained at *Camp X* to be parachuted behind German lines. Globalisation means that governments are forced to privatise their secret services. The intelligence market is so lucrative that a multitude of private military companies, such as *Blackwater*[341], have piled in to grab their share. Aside from their clients and intelligence operatives coming to the end of their career, nobody views this deregulation as being beneficial. It is, rather, an open door to all forms of abuse.

The highly mediatised intrusions of *Kroll*, an economic intelligence agency, give some idea of the risks countries now take if they dare criticise the United States. In March 1991, at the behest of Kuwait, Jules Kroll, appearing on America's CBS channel, condemned the French media conglomerate *Hachette* for its links to Saddam Hussein's Iraq, which held 8% of its capital. This revelation was calculated to embarrass the *Quai d'Orsay* and thwart the French defence manufacturers *Matra*,

---

[341] *Blackwater* was one of the largest American private military companies. A group of *Blackwater* contractors were convicted for their role in the 2007 Nisour Square massacre in Baghdad. The company is now known as *Academi*.

a rival to the American companies in the Middle Eastern market. *Kroll* mounted a fresh attack in the "frigates to Taiwan" scandal, carrying out an investigation into the activities of Roland Dumas[342], President Mitterand's foreign affairs minister, at the very moment when he was holding secret negotiations with Palestinian and Arab leaders. Who – or which country- benefited from the findings of this inquiry?

In 1993, Charles Pasqua, interior minister at the time, demanded that the United States recall its CIA agents who had infiltrated the Balladur government in a bid to obtain details of France's strategy in the GATT negotiations. But if Pasqua had been dealing with a private economic intelligence consultancy, he would probably not have dared order France's *Directorate of Territorial Security* (DST) - which, in the end, dropped all proceedings against *Kroll* - to arrest its employees for espionage. Between "allies", this sort of thing is not considered good form.

"Big Brother is watching you"

In the US, bounty hunters and private detective agencies, such as the legendary *Pinkerton*, have been competing with FBI for some time now. Likewise, it has become standard practice for the intelligence services to resort to private contractors in order to widen the scope of their action. But the private sector's involvement in espionage is now on an unprecedented scale.

Admiral Michael McConnell, who was appointed director of US National

---

[342] Roland Dumas, *L'Épreuve, les preuves,* Michel Lafon, Paris, 2003.

Intelligence by George W Bush, revealed that 70% of the budget (some 60 million dollars) falls into the hands of private companies. This is considered to be perfectly normal. Before his appointment at the head of US intelligence, McConnell was the senior vice president of *Booz-Allen-Hamilton*, a management consultancy with close ties to the Pentagon. McConnel was involved in the highly controversial *Total Information Awareness* project, which was viewed by the American media as an attempt to create a Big Brother society. Using the pretext of the prevention of terrorism, *Booz-Allen-Hamilton* proposed a system in which all databases would be integrated to create a central pool of data, the idea being to track "deviants". In response to pressure from defenders of civil liberties, the US Senate refused to finance the project.

According to *The Nation*, over half of the personnel controlling CIA human resources are under private contract. The volume of intelligence activities carried out by private contractors is so large that it is now practically impossible to distinguish information provided by bona fide government officials from that supplied by private agents. Consequently, the intelligence services of multinational enterprises, such as *Lockheed Martin* or *Raytheon*, are able to use the *President's Daily Brief* to influence White House decisions for their benefit.

Pathway to a privatised intelligence service

The two Gulf Wars exposed the weakness of the CIA, especially when it came to gathering intelligence on the ground. Though capable of tapping all telecommunications in the world using its ECHELON programme, and despite having a sophisticated satellite image system, the US failed to secure reliable information on what was really happening in Iraq.

The US was blind and relied on contradictory stories from various sources, meaning that it was easily manipulated by agents representing the oil companies, the defence industry, or the Israel lobby. This is the view of the former chief of CIA operations in Iraqi Kurdistan during the 1990s[343], Robert Baer, who inspired the character Bob Barnes, played by George Clooney in the Hollywood film *Syriana*.

Having abandoned human intelligence (HUMINT) for signals intelligence *(*SIGINT*)*, the CIA has been reduced to bribing members of humanitarian organisations, journalists and business executives. And the results? At the very best, this policy has improved the planning of minor military operations and has enabled US intelligence to obtain photos in areas invisible to spy planes, drones and satellites. A well-known news photographer, arrested under a bridge in Baghdad, narrowly escaped death thanks to his French passport.

Regardless of whether the decline of the CIA has been provoked or not, it has undeniably paved the way for the privatisation of the intelligence services. But the commercialisation of armed conflict is not limited to operations on the battlefield, as demonstrated by events in Iraq. In March 2004, four *Blackwater* "contractors" (mercenaries) were ambushed in Fallujah and killed. Their bodies were burned by a furious crowd and then hanged from a bridge over the Euphrates. Abu Ghraib

---

[343] Robert Baer, *La chute de la CIA*, E. Lattès, 2002.

prison was staffed by agents from Fort Huachuca[344] where private companies, such as *CACI*[345] and *Titan*[346], teach the "art" of how to destroy a prisoner's personality. According to the testimony of one Iraqi woman who had been tortured, however, what happened at Abu Ghraib is nothing compared to the atrocities committed in the secret prisons.[347]

Mystery Train

For private companies, the line between military action and intelligence is very fine, if not inexistent. According to one of the directors working for *Aegis Defence Services*, intelligence in Iraq is a matter of *"understanding the water in which we swim"*, a matter of life or death. This company, created by Tim Spicer, a former lieutenant-colonel in the British Army, ran *Project Matrix*, a programme which provided the US army with intelligence on insurgent activity in urban areas. As part of the programme, the company ran vaccination programmes and financed the construction of football clubs to win "hearts and minds". Patients and football enthusiasts trusted the staff, and so they talked freely. As a result, the company obtained priceless information, enabling US army troops to locate terrorist cells hidden in Iraqi suburbs. But the true moment of fame for *Aegis* came in 2005, when a video surfaced on the internet. In the short film, we see gung-ho "contractors" shooting

---

[344] Fort Huachuca is the US Army's main intelligence training centre.

[345] *Caci International* is a private military company, established in 1962. A group of its employees were implicated in the 2004 Abu Ghraib prison scandal.

[346] *Idem.*

[347] Interview with the author in Damascus, 2004.

randomly at Iraqi motorists, to the tune of Elvis Presley's *Mystery Train!*

In February 2007, *Blackwater* chief Erik Prince took the plunge and launched his own private intelligence company, *Total Intelligence Solutions* (TIS). Joseph Cofer Black, former director of the CIA's *Counter Terrorist Centre*, was the chairman of TIS. Black is best known for the American programme of "extraordinary renditions", i.e. the extrajudicial transfer of suspected Islamic terrorists to Guantanamo or other countries liable to pay little attention to the methods used to make them talk.

Black was joined by Robert Richer, the CIA's former deputy director of operations. Richer is said to be friends with King Abdullah II of Jordan and Enrique Prado, a former CIA paramilitary officer specialising in Latin America operations. Craig Johnson, former member of the *Defense Intelligence Agency*, was also employed by TIS.

Private consultancies claim to respect the law. They are said to use only *Open-source intelligence* (OSINT), that is to say publically available information. Nevertheless, in contrast to directors of government intellience agencies, Cofer Black and his like are not democratically accountable - not yet, at any rate.

A threat to civil liberties

Following the election of George H W Bush, CIA chief[348] during the

---

[348] George H. W. Bush was director of the CIA from 1976 to 1977.

Reagan administration and founder of *Zapata Petroleum Company*[349], the protection of American vital interests has come to be defined in terms of the planet's hydrocarbon reserves and, concomitantly, the security of their supply. Consequently, the control of pipeline countries has substituted foreign policy. Georgia's attack of South Ossetia in August 2008 was aimed at securing the Baku-Tbilisi-Ceyhan (BTC) pipeline, which was to be connected to Israel's *Tipline* in Ashkelon.

In Central Asia and Eastern Europe, the James Bonds of today are agents of influence who work for so-called philanthropic organisations, such as the *Open Society Foundations*, founded by multi-billionaire sepculator George Soros, the man who financed the "coloured revolutions" in Georgia and Ukraine.

Since Western public opinion is opposed to the idea of soldiers risking their lives for geopolitical reasons or for oil, it is highly likely that a growing number of American and European operations will be carried out by private military contractors. This is already the case in Iran, where "contractors" supply weapons to the *Kurdistan Free Life Party* (PJAK), a front organisation for the PKK, and the *People's Resistance Movement of Iran* (*Jundallah*), once criticised for its links with Bin Laden. Private agents are also attempting to revive the Khuzestan Arab separatist movement, widely condemned when it was supported by Saddam Hussein.

---

[349] The *Zapata Petroleum Company* was created in 1953 by George H W Bush and his business partners. A year later he created the subsidiary, *Zapata Off-Shore Company*. Some of the company files happened to be destroyed after Bush was appointed US Vice-President in 1981...

In contrast to government agencies, private military companies are motivated purely by profit. It is highly likely, then, that they will resort to provoking incidents in order to grab a larger share of the military and intelligence market. In the future, they will no doubt be contracted to protect European borders, as is already the case in America, where Mexicans with enough money to bribe officials can cross the border with ease. And, soon, if we are not careful, they will be contracted to break strikes, police our troubled suburbs, and spy on those defined as being political or sexual deviants, according to their clients' arbitrary criteria. In 1961, President Eisenhower, in his farewell address to the nation[350], presciently alluded to the danger that one day the military-industrial complex would restrict our individual freedoms. This danger, it would seem, is now imminent.

---

[350] In his farewell address, made on 17 January 1961, Eisenhower warned: *"In the councils of government, we must guard against the acquisition of unwarranted influence, whether sought or unsought, by the military-industrial complex. The potential for the disastrous rise of misplaced power exists and will persist. We must never let the weight of this combination endanger our liberties or democratic processes. We should take nothing for granted."*

Bibliography

AURIANT, *La vie du Chevalier Théodore de Lascaris ou l'imposteur malgré lui*, Gallimard, Paris, 1940.

BAGOT, John (Glubb Pasha), *War in the Desert*, Hodder and Stoughton, London 1960.

BAREILLES, Roland, *Le crépuscule ottoman*, Éditions Privat, Toulouse, 2002.

BENOIST-MÉCHIN, Jacques, *Ibn Séoud ou la naissance d'un royaume*, Albin Michel, Paris, 1955.

BODY, Marcel, *Les groupes communistes français de Russie, 1918-1921*, Éditions Allia, Paris, 1988.

BOISSONNADE, Euloge, *Conrad Kilian*, France-Empire, Paris, 1982.

BOUKROUH, Nour-Eddine, *Islam sans islamisme*, Samar, Alger, 2006.

BROWN, Anthony Gave, *Philby, père et fils, la trahison dans le sang*, Pygmalion, Paris, 1987.

CHERADAME, André, *Le plan pangermaniste démasqué*, Plon, Paris, 1916.

CHERFILS, Christian, *Bonaparte et l'islam*, Alcazar Publishing Ltd, Studley, 2005.

DE CHAIR, Somerset, *Le Tapis doré*, Tallandier, Paris, 1946.

DESTREMEAU, Christian et Moncelon, Jean, *Louis Massignon, le « cheikh admirable »*, Le Capucin, Paris, 2005.

DIVER, Maud, *Le défenseur d'Herat*, Payot, Paris, 1936.

DOUGHTY, Charles, *Voyages dans l'Arabie déserte*, Karthala, Paris, 2002

DUMAS, Alexandre, *Chamil et la résistance tchétchène contre les Russes*, Nautilus, Paris, 2001.

EPPLER, John, *Condor, l'espion de Rommel*, Robert Laffont, Paris, 1974.

ESSAD, Bey, *L'épopée du pétrole*, Payot, Paris, 1934.

FALK, André, *Visa pour l'Arabie*, Gallimard, Paris, 1958.

FONTAINE, Pierre, *La mort étrange de Conrad Kilian*, Les Sept Couleurs, Paris, 1959.

FREETH, Zahra, *Explorers of Arabia from the Renaissance to the End of the Victorian Era*, Allen & Urwin, London, 1978.

FRANCK, Gerold, *Le groupe Stern attaque*, Robert Laffont, Paris, 1963.

GALLOIS, Pierre, *Le sang du pétrole*, L'Age d'Homme, Paris, 1996.

HAJJAR, Joseph, *Napoléon II et ses visées orientales*, Éditions Tlass, Damas, 1988.

HOESLI, Eric, *À la conquête du Caucase*, Éditions des Syrtes, Paris, 2006.

HOPKIRK, Peter, *On Secret Service East of Contantinople*, Oxford University Press, 1995. *Like Hidden Fire, The Plot to bring down the British Empire*, Kodansha Globe, 1997. *Setting the East Ablaze*, Kodanqsha International, New York, 1984.

KERYELL, Jacques (sous la direction de), *Louis Massignon et ses contemporains*, Karthala, Paris, 1997.

KINZER, Stephen, *All the Shah's Men: An American Coup and the Roots of Middle East Terror*, Wiley, Hoboken, 2003.

KNIGHTLEY, Phillip et Simpson Colin, *Les vies secrètes de Lawrence d'Arabie*, Robert Laffont, Paris, 1970.

KOSTINER, Joseph, *The Making of Saudi Arabia*, Oxford University Press, 1993.

LARTEGUY, Jean, *Tout l'or du diable*, Presses de la Cité, Paris, 1974.

LAURENS, Henry, *Le Chevalier de Lascaris et les origines du Grand Jeu*, Les Cahiers de l'Orient, no. 7, 1987.

LAWRENCE, T. E., *Les Sept piliers de la sagesse*, Payot, Paris, 1936.

LIAS, Godfrey, *Légionnaires de Glubb-Pacha*, Hachette, Paris, 1959

LOCKHART, Bruce, *Memoirs of a British Agent*, Putnam, London, 1932.

LOCKHART, Robin, *L'As de l'espionnage*, Fayard, Paris, 1971.

LONGGRIGG, Stephen, *Iraq: 1900 to 1950*, Oxford University Press, 1953.

LYON, Wallace, *Kurds, Arabs and Britons*, Tauris Publishers, London, 2002

MACLEAN, Fitzroy, *Diplomate et franc-tireur*, Gallimard, Paris, 1952.

MASSE, Danielle, *Burckhardt, le Bédouin de Pétra*, Plein Sud, Toulon, 1996.

MASSIGNON, Louis, *Parole donnée*, Julliard, Paris, 1962.

McKale, Donald, *War by Revolution*, The Kent State University, Press, Ohio, 1998.

MONTEIL, Vincent-Mansour, *Lawrence d'Arabie, le lévrier fatal*, Hachette, Paris, 1987.

MONROE, Elizabeth, *Philby of Arabia*, Faber and Faber, London, 1973.

MUNIER, Gilles, *Guide de l'Irak*, Jean Picollec Editeur, Paris, 2000.

PAGE, Bruce, Knightley, Philip et Leich, David, *Philby: l'Intelligence Service aux mains d'un agent soviétique*, Robert Laffont, 1968.

PALGRAVE, William Gifford, *Palgrave d'Arabie*, Éditions France-Empire, Paris, 1992.

PERKINS, John, *Confessions of an Economic Hitman*, Berrett-Koehler Publ. Inc, 2004

PHILBY, St John, *Arabian Jubilee*, Robert Hale Ltd, London, 1952. *Sa'udi Arabia*, Ernest Benn, London, 1955.

REDISSI, Hamadi, *Le pacte du Nadjd*, Le Seuil, Paris, 2007.

ROSSI, Pierre, *L'Irak des révoltes*, Le Seuil, Paris, 1962.

SAID, Edward, *L'Orientalisme: L'Orient créé par l'Occident*, Paris, Le Seuil, 1997.

SAINT PROT, Charles, *Histoire de l'Irak*, Ellipses, Paris, 1999.

SINGER, Kurt, *Omnibus pour l'espionnage*, Marabout, Verviers, 1963.

SULEIMAN, Moussa, *Songe et mensonge de Lawrence*, Sindbad, Paris, 1973.

SOANE, Ely Banister, *To Mesopotamia and Kurdistan in Disguise*, John Murray, London 1912.

SPENCE, Richard, *Trust No One, The Secret World of Sidney Reilly*, Feral House, Los Angeles, 2002.

SPENCER, Samuel, *Decision for War, 1917: the Laconia Sinking and the Zimmermann Telegram*, R. R. Smith, 1953.

SPILLMANN, Georges, *Napoléon et l'islam*, Perrin, Paris, 1969.

SYKES, Christopher, *Wassmuss, le Lawrence allemand*, Payot, Paris, 1936.

TIDRIK, Kathryn, *Heart Beguiling Araby: The English Romance with Arabia*, Tauris, London, 1981.

TROELLER, Gary, *The Birth of Saudi Arabia*, Frank Cass, London, 1976.

VERNIER, Bernard, *L'Irak d'aujourd'hui*, Armand Colin, Paris, 1963.

WALLACH, Janet, *La reine du désert*, Bayard Éditions, Paris, 1997.

WINSTONE, H. V. F., *Captain Shakespear*, Quarter Books Limited, London, 1978. *Gertrude Bell*, Constable, London, 1978.

YERGIN, Daniel, Les hommes du pétrole, Stock, Paris, 1991.

ZISCHKA, Anton, *La guerre secrète pour le pétrole*, Payot, Paris, 1934.

Index

Other publications

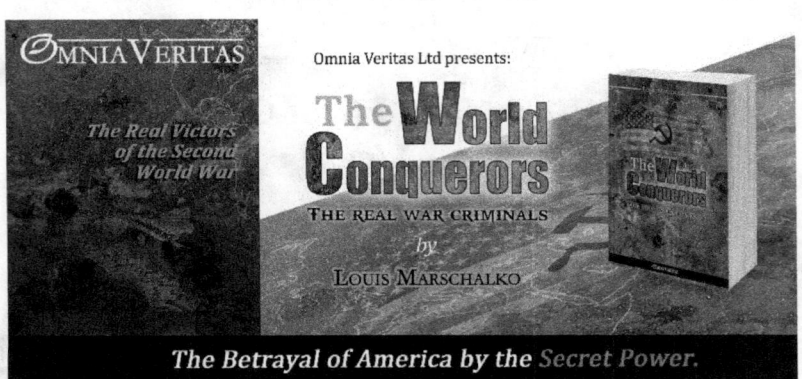

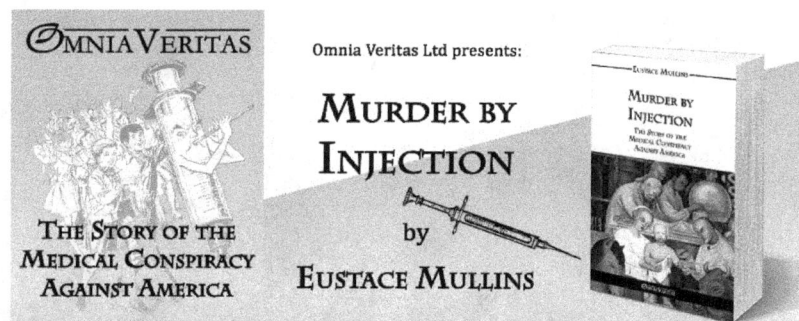

Omnia Veritas Ltd presents:

MURDER BY INJECTION

by

EUSTACE MULLINS

THE STORY OF THE MEDICAL CONSPIRACY AGAINST AMERICA

The cynicism and malice of these conspirators is something beyond the imagination of most Americans.

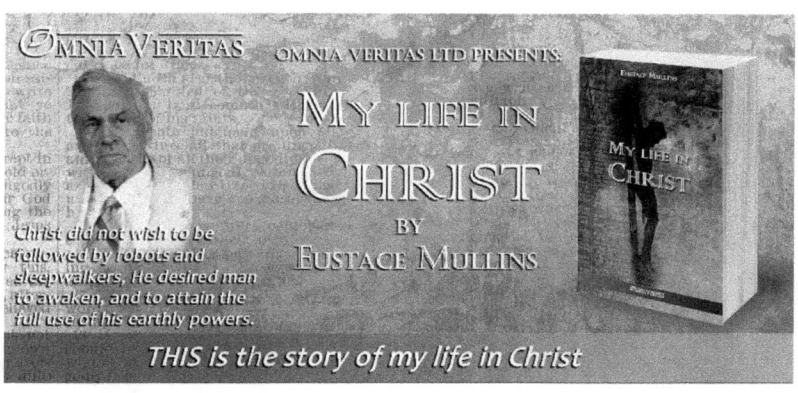

OMNIA VERITAS LTD PRESENTS:

MY LIFE IN CHRIST

BY

EUSTACE MULLINS

Christ did not wish to be followed by robots and sleepwalkers, He desired man to awaken, and to attain the full use of his earthly powers.

THIS is the story of my life in Christ

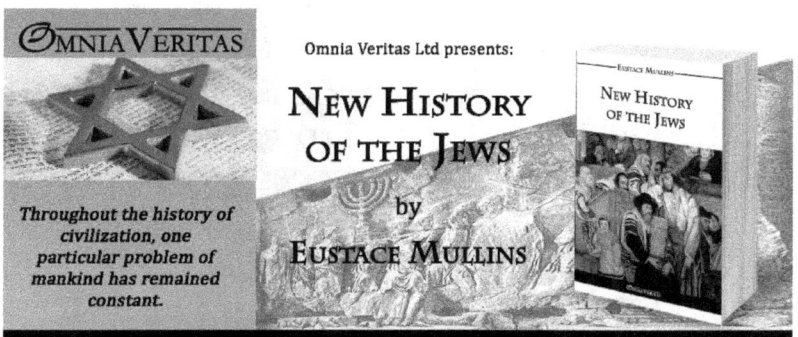

Omnia Veritas Ltd presents:

NEW HISTORY OF THE JEWS

by

EUSTACE MULLINS

Throughout the history of civilization, one particular problem of mankind has remained constant.

Only one people has irritated its host nations in every part of the civilized world

Omnia Veritas Ltd presents:

THE CURSE OF CANAAN
A demonology of history
by
EUSTACE MULLINS

Liberalism, more popularly known as secular humanism, can be traced in an unbroken line all the way back to the Biblical "Curse of Canaan."

Humanism is the logical result of the demonology of history

Omnia Veritas Ltd presents:

THE RAPE OF JUSTICE
by
EUSTACE MULLINS

AMERICA'S TRIBUNALS EXPOSED

American should know just what is going on in our courts

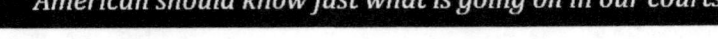

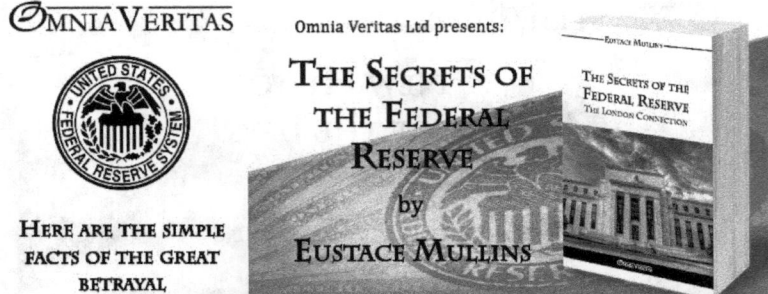

Omnia Veritas Ltd presents:

THE SECRETS OF THE FEDERAL RESERVE
by
EUSTACE MULLINS

HERE ARE THE SIMPLE FACTS OF THE GREAT BETRAYAL

Will we continue to be enslaved by the Babylonian debt money system?

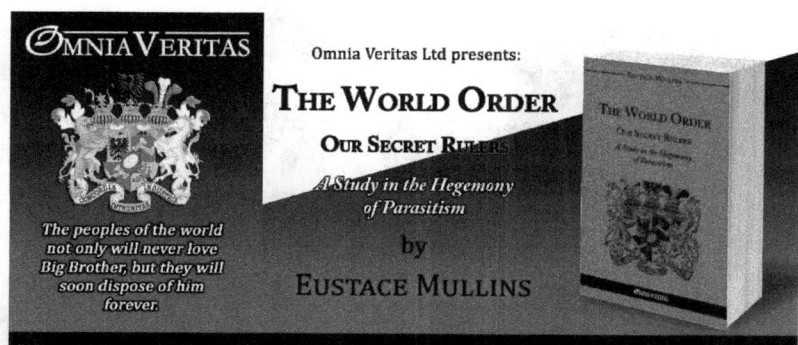

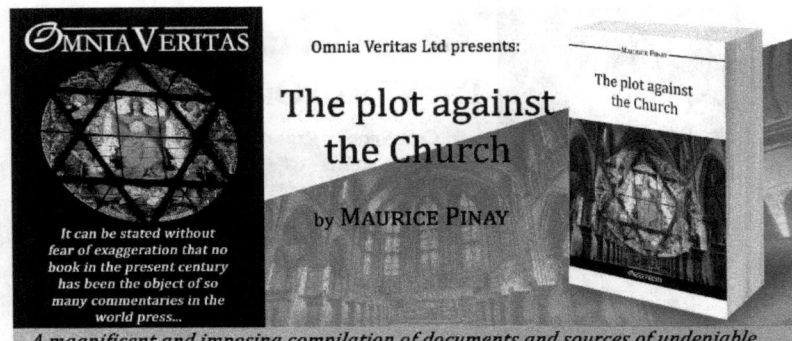

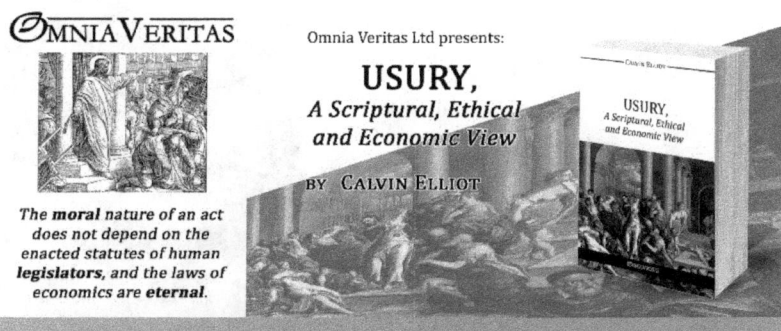
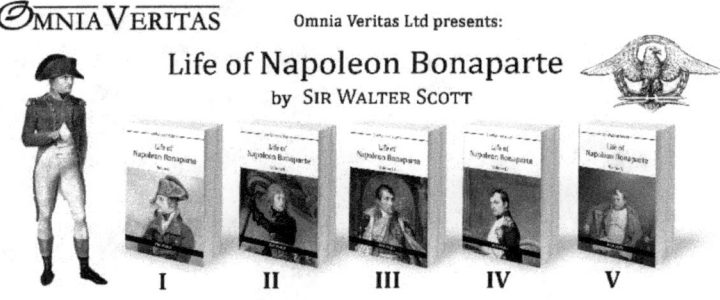